SURVEILLANCE, PRIVACY AND TRANSATLANTIC RELATIONS

Recent revelations, by Edward Snowden and others, of the vast network of government spying enabled by modern technology have raised major concerns both in the European Union and the United States on how to protect privacy in the face of increasing governmental surveillance.

This book brings together some of the leading experts in the fields of constitutional law, criminal law and human rights from the US and the EU to examine the protection of privacy in the digital era, as well as the challenges that counter-terrorism cooperation between governments pose to human rights. It examines the state of privacy protections on both sides of the Atlantic, the best mechanisms for preserving privacy, and whether the EU and the US should develop joint transnational mechanisms to protect privacy on a reciprocal basis.

As technology enables governments to know more and more about their citizens, and about the citizens of other nations, this volume offers critical perspectives on how best to respond to one of the most challenging developments of the twenty-first century.

Volume 1 in Hart Studies in Security and Justice

Hart Studies in Security and Justice
Series editor: Liora Lazarus

The interplay between security and justice has always featured prominently in legal scholarship, but it has taken on a particular urgency since the new Millennium. The new scholarly questions that arise are theoretical, doctrinal and empirical, cutting across a range of traditional sub-disciplines within the legal academy. They address some of the most pressing legal issues of our time, such as the legal status of the 'the war on terror', the nature of states of exception, targeted killing, preventive pre-trial detention, mass surveillance and the numerous other threats that security poses to human rights, the rule of law and liberal democracy.

The purpose of this series is to engage with security and justice scholarship broadly conceived, and to promote a sophisticated and complex understanding of the important challenges it faces. The series is inclusive, promoting new and established scholars from a range of disciplines. It covers doctrinal, empirical, historical and theoretical work, as well as studies which focus on domestic, comparative and international dimensions of emerging security and justice fields. The series also strives to promote the most inclusive range of politics and methodologies, scrutinizing received wisdom and established paradigmatic approaches, and promoting an intellectual dialogue between its authors and the wider field of law as a whole.

Surveillance, Privacy and Transatlantic Relations

Edited by
David D Cole, Federico Fabbrini and
Stephen Schulhofer

·HART·
OXFORD · LONDON · NEW YORK · NEW DELHI · SYDNEY

HART PUBLISHING
Bloomsbury Publishing Plc
Kemp House, Chawley Park, Cumnor Hill, Oxford, OX2 9PH, UK

HART PUBLISHING, the Hart/Stag logo, BLOOMSBURY and the Diana logo are
trademarks of Bloomsbury Publishing Plc
First published in Great Britain 2017

First published in hardback, 2017
Paperback edition, 2019

A catalogue record for this book is available from the British Library.

Library of Congress Cataloging-in-Publication Data

Names: Cole, David, 1958- | Fabbrini, Federico, 1985- editor. | Schulhofer, Stephen J., editor.

Title: Surveillance, privacy, and transatlantic relations / edited by David D. Cole, Federico Fabbrini,
and Stephen Schulhofer.

Description: Oxford [UK] ; Portland, Oregon : Hart Publishing, 2017. | Series: Hart studies in security and
justice ; v. 1 | Includes bibliographical references and index.

Identifiers: LCCN 2016045782 (print) | LCCN 2016046047 (ebook) | ISBN 9781509905416
(hardback) | ISBN 9781509905423 (Epub)

Subjects: LCSH: Privacy, Right of—United States. | Privacy, Right of—European Union
countries. | Electronic surveillance—Law and legislation—United States. | Electronic surveillance—Law and
legislation—European Union countries.

Classification: LCC K3263 .S87 2017 (print) | LCC K3263 (ebook) | DDC 323.44/88094—dc23

LC record available at https://lccn.loc.gov/2016045782

ISBN: HB: 978-1-50990-541-6
PB: 978-1-50993-004-3
ePDF: 978-1-50990-543-0
ePub: 978-1-50990-542-3

Typeset by Compuscript Ltd, Shannon

To find out more about our authors and books visit www.hartpublishing.co.uk. Here you will find
extracts, author information, details of forthcoming events and the option to sign up for our
newsletters.

CONTENTS

Part IV: Perspective of NGOs and Oversight Authorities

Part V: Transatlantic Perspective

LIST OF CONTRIBUTORS

David Bilchitz is Professor of Fundamental Rights and Constitutional Law at the University of Johannesburg; Director of the South African Institute for Advanced Constitutional, Public, Human Rights and International Law, University of Johannesburg; and Secretary General of the International Association of Constitutional Law.

Hilde Bos-Ollermann is Secretary to the Review Committee on the Intelligence and Security Services of the Netherlands.

David Cole is Hon. George J. Mitchell Professor in Law and Public Policy, Georgetown Law Center and National Legal Director of the American Civil Liberties Union.

Federico Fabbrini is Full Professor of Law at the School of Law & Government, Dublin City University.

Jonathan Hafetz is Professor of Law at Seton Hall Law School, Newark, NJ.

Peter Hustinx is the former Data Protection Supervisor of the European Union.

Gabriele Marino Noberasco is MPhil Researcher in Law at the University of Exeter.

Tuomas Ojanen is Professor of Constitutional Law at the University of Helsinki.

Byliana Petkova is Postdoctoral Fellow, New York University and Visiting Fellow, Yale Information Society Project.

Marc Rotenberg is Director of the Electronic Privacy Information Centre, Washington D.C.

Stephen Schulhofer is Robert McKay Professor of Law at New York University Law School.

Christopher Slobogin is Milton Underwood Professor of Law at Vanderbilt University Law School, Nashville, TN.

Arianna Vedaschi is Professor of Constitutional Law at Bocconi University, Milan.

1

Introduction: Privacy and Surveillance in Transatlantic Perspective

DAVID COLE, FEDERICO FABBRINI AND STEPHEN SCHULHOFER

Since the early stages of the project of European integration, the United States (US) has been considered the paradigmatic comparative model for studying the European Union's (EU) own multilayered regime for the protection of fundamental rights. In the 1980s, the US federal system—with its well-established overlapping federal and state sources of human rights protections—was taken as a point of reference to explain the emergence in Europe of a human rights architecture extending beyond the member states, and to predict the possible federalising dynamics that a supranational human rights regime might produce in the EU.[1] More recent studies have confirmed that the European system for the protection of fundamental rights has experienced challenges and transformations analogous to those of the US federal system.[2]

The comparison between the EU and US rights protection systems remains fertile terrain for scholarly engagement, but attention has increasingly shifted to whether and how the EU and the US systems interact. In particular, as a result of technological developments and globalisation, the protection of fundamental rights within both the EU and the US has increasingly been the object of concern for institutions and actors on the opposite side of the Atlantic.[3] The analysis of the means by which the EU and the US protect fundamental rights at home has evolved from an academic interest into an urgent policy focus; and questions

---

[1] See J Frowein, S Schulhofer and M Shapiro, 'The Protection of Fundamental Rights as a Vehicle of Integration', in M Cappelletti, M Seccombe and JHH Weiler (eds), *Integration Through Law: Europe and the American Federal Experience. Vol1, Book 3* (Berlin, de Gruyter 1986) 231.

[2] See F Fabbrini, *Fundamental Rights in Europe: Challenges and Transformations in Comparative Perspective* (Oxford, Oxford University Press, 2014).

[3] See D Cole, 'English Lessons: A Comparative Analysis of UK and US Responses to Terrorism' (2009) *Current Legal Problems* 137.

about the relationships between human rights protection within the EU and the US are now of central importance to the conduct of transatlantic relations.[4]

This book focuses specifically on the transatlantic challenges posed by the protection of the right to privacy from government surveillance and corporate intrusion. The past decade has witnessed exponential growth in the technological capacity to gather personal information through electronic surveillance and the collection and mining of information stored in digital form. Threats to privacy resulting from growing capabilities are compounded by increasing private-sector and governmental incentives to exploit these capabilities. The counter-terrorism and national-security missions stimulate an all-but-insatiable appetite for intelligence, and ordinary law enforcement has a mounting need for information in an environment of intensifying transnational criminal conduct, itself facilitated by the internet.[5] Simultaneously, the increasing dominance of internet-driven business platforms generates commercial imperatives for private-sector firms to maximise the gathering, storage and analysis of the personal transactional records of their customers, which are now a crucial revenue source for many successful businesses.

Privacy represents a central tenet in the constitutional systems of both the US and the EU. The idea of a common law right to privacy emerged in American scholarly work of the late nineteenth century,[6] but the US constitutional right of privacy is founded upon the Fourth Amendment of the US Constitution itself, which dates to 1789 and prohibits unreasonable searches.[7] The 50 US states all have their own privacy protections in state constitutions, legislation and judicial interpretations.[8] In post-war Europe, privacy rights have expanded through the case law of national and European courts,[9] and have been codified in EU law: currently, the EU Charter of Fundamental Rights[10] and the Data Protection Directive[11]—soon

---

[4] See E Fahey and D Curtin (eds), *A Transatlantic Community of Law: Legal Perspectives on the Relationship Between the EU and US Legal Orders* (Cambridge, Cambridge University Press, 2014).
[5] See B Schneier, *Data and Goliath: The Hidden Battles to Capture Your Data and Control Your World* (W.W. Norton, 2015).
[6] See S Warren and L Brandeis, 'The Right to Privacy' (1890) 4 *Harvard Law Review* 193 (discussing already the possibility to recognise a right to privacy in the US).
[7] See *Katz v United States*, 389 US 347 (1967) (holding that the Fourth Amendment protects a person's reasonable expectation of privacy).
[8] See R Krotoszynski Jr , *Privacy Revisited: A Global Perspective on the Right to be Left Alone* (Oxford, Oxford University Press, 2016).
[9] See Const. Ct. Germany BVerfGE 27, 1 (6), judgment of 16 July 1969, *Mikrozensusurteil* (on the right to privacy in the field of statistics); Const. Ct. Germany BVerfGE 65, 1, judgment of 15 December 1983; *Volkszählungsurteil* (on the right to informational self-determination in matters related to the census); Const. Ct. Italy, judgment of 26 March 1990, n. 139/1990 (stating that the Italian Constitution protects a right to privacy); Cons. Const. France, judgment of 18 January 1995, n° 94-352 DC (stating that the right to privacy is implied in the constitutional sources of law through which the court reviews legislation).
[10] EU Charter of Fundamental Rights OJ 2012 C 326/395 Arts 7–8.
[11] Directive 95/46/EC OJ 1995 L 281/31.

to be replaced by a Data Protection Regulation[12]—provide the framework for privacy protection.[13] While it has become commonplace to note that US notions of privacy are built on ideas of individual liberty, whereas European views of privacy are premised on dignity, both sides of the Atlantic regard privacy as an indispensable feature of a constitutional democracy based on the rule of law.[14]

Nevertheless, following Edward Snowden's disclosures in 2013 of a secret, massive programme of surveillance by the US National Security Agency (NSA), possible differences in the European and American conceptions of privacy have prominently emerged.[15] In particular, several EU countries and institutions have raised grave concerns that the US privacy protections failed to meet European standards—not only because US law grants only limited protection against invasion of privacy by private actors, but also because US law imposed insufficient limits on government authorities pursuing national security, especially when it comes to the privacy interests of non-US citizens. In 2014, the European Parliament (EP) took video testimony from Edward Snowden's, condemned the wide-ranging and intrusive scope of NSA surveillance of Europeans, and called for a revision of transatlantic relations.[16] And in 2015, in a lawsuit filed by Max Schrems, an Austrian privacy activist, pointing to Snowden's revelations, the European Court of Justice (ECJ) identified the inadequacy of US legal protections for data transferred to US corporations as a basis for invalidating a 2000 European Commission decision that had allowed private companies to transfer data from the EU to the US pursuant to the Safe Harbour agreement.[17]

Yet the transatlantic divide on privacy and surveillance may be less dramatic than is conventionally asserted, and the EU and the US may be converging in at least some respects.[18] The Snowden revelations triggered a sharp debate within the US, prompted US corporations to become much more vocal defenders of their customers' privacy, and led to the adoption of important privacy-enhancing reforms of national security surveillance powers by Congress[19] and the President.[20] At the same time, following tragic terrorist attacks in Paris, Brussels, and elsewhere in

---

[12] Regulation (EU) 2016/679 OJ 2016 L 119/1.

[13] See L Bygrave, *Data Privacy Law: An International Perspective* (Oxford, Oxford University Press, 2014).

[14] See J Whitman, 'The Two Western Culture of Privacy: Dignity Versus Liberty' (2004) 113 *Yale Law Journal* 1151.

[15] See D Cole, 'Can Privacy Be Saved?', *The New York Review of Books*, 6 March 2014.

[16] European Parliament resolution of 12 March 2014 on the US NSA surveillance programme, surveillance bodies in various Member States and their impact on EU citizens' fundamental rights and on transatlantic co-operation in Justice and Home Affairs, P7_TA(2014)0230, §10.

[17] Case C-362/14 *Schrems*: ECLI:EU:C:2015:650.

[18] See F Bignami and G Resta, 'Transatlantic Privacy Regulation: Conflict and Cooperation' (2015) 78 *Law & Contemporary Problems* 231.

[19] See USA Freedom Act 2015, Public Law 114-23.

[20] See Presidential Policy Directive 28 (PPD-28) on Signal Intelligence Activities, 17 January 2014.

Europe public authorities in several EU Member States have assumed broader surveillance powers vis-à-vis their citizens than US authorities have with respect to US citizens.[21] And in the wake of the ECJ's invalidation of the Safe Harbour agreement for transatlantic sharing of data, executive officials in the EU and the US have sought to smooth their differences by approving in February 2016 a new data sharing agreement—the EU–US Privacy Shield[22]—securing the transatlantic free movement of personal data, on the presumption that (after a series of reforms) the EU and the US systems of privacy protections can be rendered compatible.

The state of transatlantic relations remains characterised by reciprocal concerns about how to balance the protection of fundamental rights with counter-terrorism imperatives. The recent US government effort to compel the technology company Apple to devise backdoor software to unlock the iPhone used by the perpetrator of the San Bernardino terror attack raised concerns not only in the US but also in Europe, where some have interpreted this move as the latest evidence of transatlantic privacy clash.[23] Is there really a fundamental divide between the EU and the US on matters of privacy and surveillance? Can Europeans count on their privacy being protected from US foreign intelligence programmes? And, vice versa, can Americans in turn trust that European security services will not infringe on their privacy rights? What are the interrelations between private data collection and government surveillance on each side of the Atlantic? What is the best way to ensure that privacy remains protected both in the EU and the US, notwithstanding growing security concerns and the challenges posed by rapidly developing technology?

This book addresses these questions. By offering the perspectives of privacy scholars and practitioners from Europe, the US and elsewhere, it seeks to improve understanding on both sides of the Atlantic on issues of surveillance, privacy and transatlantic relations, all of which are of crucial importance for human rights, national security and Euro-American unity. The book consists of essays originally presented in March 2015 at a conference sponsored by the Research Group on 'Constitutional Responses to Terrorism' of the International Association of Constitutional Law and hosted by Anne Wayembergh and Céline Cocq at the Institut d'Etudes Européen of the Université Libre de Bruxelles. The book is structured in five sections.

Part I explores issues of privacy and surveillance in the EU and the US from an internal perspective. The contributions of this part offer an in-depth account of the basic privacy rules existing in each legal system, with the aim of introducing readers on each side of the Atlantic to the specificities of the other system's laws.

---

[21] See, eg, Loi du 24 juillet 2015 relative au renseignement, JORF no 171, July 26, 2015 (French law expanding surveillance powers) and Investigatory Powers Bill 143, 2015–16 (British draft law expanding surveillance powers).

[22] Commission Communication, 'Transatlantic Data Flows: Restoring Trust through Strong Safeguards', 29 February 2016, COM(2016)117 final.

[23] See M Valsania, 'FBI batte Apple: sbloccato iPhone del terrorista', *Il Sole 24 Ore*, 30 March 2016.

Tuomas Ojanen outlines the normative basis for the protection of privacy and personal data in the EU constitutional system and reviews the latest case law of the ECJ. After analysing the provisions of the EU Charter of Fundamental Rights and data protection legislation, Ojanen argues that the ECJ has recently promoted what he views as an uncompromising vision of privacy, even in the context of national security. In particular, Ojanen notes that in cases such as *Digital Rights Ireland*,[24] and *Schrems*,[25] the ECJ has suggested that the right to privacy may include an essential core of protection, which cannot be balanced against competing individual rights and public interests, and discusses the implications that such an absolutist position poses for legislation and executive action within the EU.

Christopher Slobogin offers a corresponding picture of the premises of constitutional privacy protection in the US. Slobogin first explains that as a matter of US constitutional law, privacy is protected only against governmental action, and those protections attach only when government officials infringe 'a reasonable expectation of privacy' or interfere in a significant way with an individual's 'possessory interest' in tangible property. Courts in the US have generally construed these doctrinal prerequisites strictly, with the result that until recently, movements in public spaces and personal information surrendered to a third party, such as an internet service provider, have received no constitutional protection. Employing a transatlantic comparative approach, Slobogin argues that American courts should look to European models for regulating pervasive public surveillance (which he labels 'panvasive' surveillance), by requiring that such surveillance systems be authorised by representative legislative bodies, with effective mechanisms of oversight. At the same time, Slobogin proposes that the US rule denying constitutional protection to personal information shared with a third party should be modified to require antecedent judicial approval, based on objective indications of suspicion, where government officials seek access to such data in connection with targeted investigations of particular individuals.

Part II moves the conversation on privacy and surveillance beyond the domestic sphere by exploring in more detail comparative dimensions of US and EU human rights and national security law. The contributions of this part examine in comparative perspective the similarities and differences within the EU and US federal privacy regimes and understandings. Bilyana Petkova emphasises the important role that federalism plays in both regimes for the protection of individual rights. She examines the multilayered systems for protecting privacy that have emerged in the US as a result of intersecting and overlapping requirements of state and national laws and the overlapping enforcement jurisdiction of state and national officials. Petkova sees great value in this federal approach, and explores the extent to which it has the potential to emerge in Europe as well.

---

[24] Joined Cases C-293/12 & C-594/12, *Digital Rights Ireland*, ECLI:EU:C:2014:238.
[25] *Schrems* (n 17 above).

Arianna Vedaschi and Gabriele Marino Noberasco take up a different comparative dimension of EU–US privacy and surveillance law, namely the controversy over the sharing of passenger name recognition (PNR) data between Europe and the US. For years, Europeans have questioned the legality under EU privacy protections of a requirement imposed by the US government that air carriers disclose personal data about passengers travelling on flights bound to the US. Although the use of PNR data as a way to prevent terrorism has increasingly taken hold also in the EU, and has been recently codified in legislation,[26] Vedaschi and Marino argue that the sharing of PNR data constitutes an infringement on privacy rights at odds with the constitutional standards proclaimed by the ECJ. By discussing the case law of the ECJ—including a pending EP challenge against a PNR agreement between the EU and Canada[27]—Vedaschi and Marino point to a possible divergence in understanding of privacy in the EU and the US, and offer this case study as an illustration of the differences that persist between the two legal regimes.

Part III addresses the role private corporations play in either defending or threatening privacy. In the digital age, national borders are far less significant than they once were, especially with respect to computer data, and private companies are often the holders of massive troves of information about their customers' private lives. As a result, any effort to protect privacy in the digital age must examine not just state actors, but the private sector as well, and the interrelations between multinational corporations and states. Jonathan Hafetz examines how financial pressures and public sentiment are forcing technology companies to be more active in protecting the privacy interests of their clients and customers. He describes some of the mechanisms that companies have used to enhance consumer privacy protection. At the same time, Hafetz draws attention to significant variation in these private sector solutions. Hafetz then assesses these developments through the lens of the Corporate Social Responsibility movement and notes reasons for both optimism and pessimism. Technology companies will face increasing public insistence that they protect the privacy of their clientele. But powerful incentives built into their own business models, including their reliance on user data as a source of revenue, will limit their willingness to accede to privacy-protective demands.

David Bilchitz starts with the proposition that if privacy is to be protected in the digital age it must be enforceable not only against state actors but against private corporations as well. He explores the potential normative and legal arguments for implying, from the fundamental right to privacy, an obligation on private companies to safeguard the privacy of their customers, and argues that without such an obligation, privacy rights may be rendered meaningless in the digital age, given

---

[26] See Directive (EU) 2016/681, OJ 2016 L 119/132.
[27] See European Parliament Resolution of 25 November 2014 on seeking an opinion from the ECJ on the compatibility with the Treaties of the Agreement between Canada and the EU on the transfer and processing of Passenger Name Record data, P8_TA(2014)0058.

the wealth of personal data we share with private corporations every minute of the day. Bilchitz draws on the case law of South African courts—which, despite their common law background, are heavily influenced by European doctrines of proportionality and human rights protection—as an example of how constitutional rights may imply limitations on private as well as state actors in this realm.

Part IV introduces the privacy perspectives, respectively, of national surveillance oversight bodies and non-governmental organisations (NGOs), actors directly involved in policing and promoting privacy compliance. Hilde Bos-Ollermann draws on her experience as the Secretary of the Review Committee for the Intelligence and Security Services of the Netherlands to stress the need for adequate governmental institutional oversight. Given the inevitable secrecy surrounding a great deal of surveillance, official oversight institutions with access to secret information and programmes can play a very important part in checking abuses. Bos-Ollermann maintains that some forms of surveillance are necessary, but insists that certain minimum safeguards are required for such surveillance to be acceptable: in particular, foreseeability, specific limits on purpose and use, and robust oversight. She then draws on her own experience to detail the challenges and opportunities that oversight of such surveillance presents.

Marc Rotenberg, the executive director of the Electronic Privacy Information Coalition (EPIC), a US privacy NGO, discusses the role of civil society in challenging government programmes that threaten privacy. He describes the work of EPIC, both at home and abroad, and focuses in particular on the tactic of filing amicus, or 'friend-of-the-court' briefs, in cases raising privacy questions. In addition, he describes EPIC's pursuit of the disclosure of secret information through freedom of information laws. Rotenberg stresses that EPIC operates both domestically and globally, and that precisely because of the cross-border issues raised by security and surveillance alike, organisations seeking to address privacy in the globalised world today must similarly work across borders.

Part V brings to bear many of the insights derived from the previous chapters, with a view toward discussing possible ways forward in transatlantic relations and privacy protection. This final section continues and develops a dialogue between its editors. In prior work, we have presented alternative views on how best to address one of the central challenges to preserving privacy in the transatlantic context: namely, the fact that domestic legal regimes impose little or no restrictions on their governments conducting surveillance of foreign nationals outside their borders.[28] The three of us are in accord in recognising the urgent need

---

[28] See D Cole and F Fabbrini, 'Bridging the Transatlantic Divide? The United States, the European Union and the Protection of Privacy Across Borders' (2016) 14 *International Journal of Constitutional Law* 220 and S Schulhofer, 'An International Right to Privacy? Be Careful What You Wish For' (2016) 14 *International Journal of Constitutional Law* 238.

to reinvigorate privacy safeguards in order to adapt to the challenges of the digital age. But we differ on the most effective means to achieve this end. David Cole and Federico Fabbrini favor a formal compact to specify the terms of transatlantic cooperation in the protection of cross-border privacy. Stephen Schulhofer criticises this internationalist approach and suggests that safeguards developed at the domestic level are more likely to offer a privacy-protective solution in the face of twenty-first-century challenges.

The last part of the book expands upon this earlier debate by developing further the value and limitations of domestic versus transatlantic means of extending cross-border privacy protections to EU and US citizens. Stephen Schulhofer predicts that solutions achieved through multilateral negotiation will give disproportionate influence to executive and national-security authorities on both sides of the Atlantic, while giving short shrift to privacy advocates, and therefore will result in agreements that likely will do more harm than good from the standpoint of assuring effective protection of privacy. He worries that transnational agreements will 'revert to the mean', and risk exerting downward pressure on privacy protections in whatever country has protections more robust than those settled upon in the agreement. And he contends that safeguards realised through institutions and advocacy on the domestic front are more likely to provide a check on excessive government over-reach, even as to the rights of non-citizens.

David Cole and Federico Fabbrini, by contrast, question the sufficiency of purely domestic solutions to problems of privacy that are transnational in scope. They believe it is unlikely that domestic institutions and laws will extend protections to foreign nationals abroad without some sort of reciprocal benefit from foreign nations for a country's own nationals. And as long as that is the case, the only protection one nation's citizens are likely to receive from spying by another nation will be through bilateral or multilateral agreements. In their view, security officials are just as likely to be involved in the formulation of domestic as transnational limits on surveillance for national security purposes. And previous international human rights agreements have not led to a reversion to the mean, but have lifted rights protections in many parts of the globe.

In addition, Cole and Fabbrini argue that the dichotomy between domestic and transatlantic avenues to privacy protection may be too artificial. They point to the recent *Schrems* judgment of the ECJ, and the resulting transatlantic agreement, the EU–US Privacy Shield, as an illustration of how domestic and transatlantic avenues can be mutually reinforcing. There, a domestic EU decision prompted a transatlantic negotiation that has improved privacy protections for EU nationals when their data is transferred to the US. Such domestic-transatlantic interplay seems inevitable in the modern era, when data flows across borders freely and commerce depends on it continuing to do so, and when citizens are increasingly insistent on preserving the privacy of their personal data. While there are undoubtedly risks in any transatlantic negotiation, Cole and Fabbrini contend that an accord between the EU and the US may be the only way to ensure that domestic privacy protections are not circumvented by national security agencies evading domestic limits by cooperating across borders.

The book concludes, fittingly, with an essay by Peter Hustinx, who served as the first EU Data Protection Supervisor (EDPS) from 2004 to 2014. The EDPS was created by an EU regulation to ensure compliance with the EU data protection law by the EU institutions, the Member States and private actors.[29] It has been, and is, one of the most vocal players in pressing for privacy safeguards in transatlantic relations. In his contribution, Hustinx brings to bear the experience he acquired in a decade as the EDPS to reconsider many of the issues discussed in the book, and to propose some options for moving forward. For Hustinx, privacy represents a fundamental right that requires more protection than ever in a rapidly changing technological world. Restrictions on privacy, he maintains, should be limited to what is strictly necessary to further legitimate government interests, according to the principle of proportionality. And Hustinx stresses that thinking about the protection of privacy in transnational terms is increasingly necessary, especially in the context of EU–US relations.

In conclusion, while the struggle against global terrorism poses challenges that cut across state borders,[30] so too does the struggle to preserve and protect privacy. Both goals are central concerns for the EU and the US. How best to protect privacy and to reconcile it with the need for legitimate government surveillance has always been, and will remain, a matter on which reasonable people disagree. What is beyond dispute, however, is that their thoughtful navigation in the digital era will increasingly require the engagement of public and private actors on both sides of the Atlantic, informed by a deep understanding of each other's norms and systems, and of their interconnections. Our hope is that the various perspectives embraced in this book contribute to the transatlantic understanding that is essential if we are to address in a meaningful way one of the most pressing problems of our time.

---

[29] Regulation 45/2001/EC, OJ 2001 L 8/1.
[30] See F Fabbrini and V Jackson (eds), *Constitutionalism Across Borders in the Struggle Against Terrorism* (Cheltenham, Edward Elgar Publishing, 2016).

Part I

Domestic Perspective

2

Rights-based Review of Electronic Surveillance after *Digital Rights Ireland* and *Schrems* in the European Union

TUOMAS OJANEN[*]

I. Introduction

With its landmark judgments in the cases of *Digital Rights Ireland*[1] and *Schrems*,[2] the Court of Justice of the European Union (CJEU) has become trailblazer, at least in Europe, if not globally, in defining how electronic surveillance should be assessed in light of fundamental rights. The significance of these two distinct, yet inter-related judgments is greatly intensified by their direct link with the contemporary debate over the balance between privacy and security in the counter-terrorism context after the revelations by former CIA contractor Edward Snowden, as well as by recent terrorist attacks in November 2015 in Paris. After all, the Paris attacks have widely been regarded as a kind of 'wake-up call' for more surveillance in Europe and the United States. Even in Finland, probably worldwide regarded as a model country of rights' protection alongside the other Nordic countries, the President of the Republic urged the raising of the level of electronic surveillance by the Finnish intelligence to 'meet the European standards' immediately after the Paris terror attacks.[3] Currently, constitutional and legislative reforms are under

[*] This article is the product of the project 'Laws of Surveillance and Security', funded by the Academy Finland, and draws much on fundamental rights assessments and other research done within the Surveille project (Surveillance: Ethical Issues, Legal Limitations, and Efficieny). I was Part-time Professor within the Surveille project at the Law Department of the European University Institute between 1.2.2012-30.6.2015. https://surveille.eui.eu/ (7.12.2015).
[1] Joined cases C-293/12, C-594/12 *Digital Rights Ireland and Seitlinger and Others* (EU: C: 2014:238).
[2] Case C-362/14 *Maximillian Schrems v Data Protection Commissioner* judgment 6 October 2015 (not yet reported).
[3] YLE/news, Finland mulls constitution changes, web surveillance powers for intelligence police, news 15.11.2015, available at: www.yle.fi/uutiset/finland_mulls_constitution_changes_web_surveillance_powers_for_intelligence_police/8456920 (7.12.2015).

consideration to facilitate more effective civilian and military intelligence operation in Finland.[4]

This chapter will address the judgments of *Digital Rights Ireland* and *Schrems*
in the light of the following kinds of questions: How to assess surveillance for
its intrusion into fundamental rights? What rights are affected and what is their
weight, as well as the intensity of the interference through surveillance? Do privacy
and data protection rights contain an inviolable 'essence' that is absolute in the
sense that no limitations or balancing against competing interests are allowed?
What institutional implications do these two judgments by the CJEU have on the
assessment of surveillance in light of fundamental rights?

It is submitted in this chapter that *Digital Rights Ireland* and *Schrems* combine
to illustrate a set of parameters for rights-based review that should be taken into
account by the legislators, courts and other authorities both in Europe at the EU
and the Member States level in a number of situations, particularly when drafting
and reviewing legislation on surveillance or when deciding about the authorisation
of using a particular surveillance technology. It is also argued that the judgments
suggest the necessity of such a pluralistic form of review where both the legislature
and the judiciary are entrusted with a shared duty to ensure compliance with fundamental rights, and even so that a positive obligation is primarily imposed on the
legislature concerned, to provide the legislative framework required.

This chapter, therefore, will focus specifically on the approach by the EU legal
order to the protection of privacy in the context of surveillance, in light of the
recent judgments of the CJEU, and it will not examine the implications of these
rulings on transatlantic relations. There is a multifarious discussion on these issues
elsewhere,[5] and other chapters of this book will focus on this specifically.

---

[4] Juha Lavapuro, 'Finnish Government and the Desire to Constitutionalize Mass Surveillance:
Toward Permanent State of Emergency?' (2015) *Verfassungsblog*, available at: http://verfassungsblog.
de/en/author/juha-lavapuro/ (7 December 2015).

[5] See Franziska Boehm and Mark D Cole, 'Data retention after the Judgment of the Court of Justice
of the European Union', Munster/Luxembourg, 30 June 2014; Federico Fabbrini, 'Human Rights in
the Digital Age: The European Court of Justice Ruling in the Data Retention Case and its Lessons for
Privacy and Surveillance in the US'; Guild, Elspeth and Carrera, Sergio, 'The Political and Judicial Life
of Metadata: Digital Rights Ireland and the Trail of the Data Retention Directive', 2014. CEPS Paper in
Liberty and Security No 65, May 2014 [Policy Paper]; Oral Linskey, 'The Data Retention Directive is
incompatible with the rights to privacy and data protection and is invalid in its entirety: Digital Rights
Ireland'. Joined Cases C-293 and 594/12, *Digital Rights Ireland Ltd and Seitlinger and others*, Judgment
of the Court of Justice (Grand Chamber) 8 April 2014, *CML Rev* 2014, v 51, n 6. Xavier Tracol, 'Legislative genesis and judicial death of a directive: The European Court of Justice invalidated the data
retention directive (2006/24/EC) thereby creating a sustained period of legal uncertainty about the
validity of national laws which enacted it' *Computer Law and Security Review*, Dec 2014, Vol 30 Issue 6,
pp736–746 and Tuomas Ojanen, 'Privacy Is More Than Just a Seven-Letter Word: The Court of Justice
of the European Union Sets Constitutional Limits on Mass Surveillance', Court of Justice of the European Union, Decision of 8 April 2014 in Joined Cases C-293/12 and C-594/12, *Digital Rights Ireland
and Seitlinger and Others. European Constitutional Law Review*, 10: 528–41, 2014. See, eg, Verfassugs-
blog for debate about the implications of *Schrems* on not only fundamental rights protection and the
rights-security interface but also for the US and European business community.

This chapter is structured as follows. Section II will outline the CJEU's judgments in *Digital Rights Ireland* and *Schrems*, and will situate them in the wider context of the EU system for the protection of fundamental rights. Section III, which is the fulcrum of this chapter, will analyse in detail the parameters of rights-based review of surveillance suggested by the CJEU's judgments. Section IV will provide a brief reflection of the implications of these two judgments on institutional arrangements for the review of legislative measures of surveillance in light of fundamental rights by the legislature and the judiciary. Section V will briefly conclude.

II. Summary of *Digital Rights Ireland* and *Schrems* and Their Wider Context Within the EU's System for the Protection of Fundamental Rights

In *Digital Rights Ireland*, delivered on 8 April 2014, the CJEU essentially ruled that the EU Data Retention Directive[6] was invalid ex tunc because the EU legislature had 'exceeded the limits imposed by compliance with the principle of proportionality' in the light of Articles 7, 8 and 52(1) of the Charter of Fundamental Rights of the European Union (EUCFR).[7] According to the CJEU, the Directive failed to lay down 'clear and precise rules governing the extent of the interference with the fundamental rights enshrined in Articles 7 and 8 of the Charter', as well as entailed 'a wide-ranging and particularly serious interference with those fundamental rights in the legal order of the EU, without such an interference being precisely circumscribed by provisions to ensure that it is actually limited to what is strictly necessary'.[8] As the CJEU did not limit the temporal effects of its judgment, the finding of the invalidity takes effect from the date on which the directive had entered into force, ie on 15 March 2006.

In *Schrems*, delivered on 6 October 2015, the CJEU decided to invalidate the European Commission's US Safe Harbour decision,[9] essentially underlying that 'legislation is not limited to what is strictly necessary where it authorises, on a generalised basis, storage of all the personal data of all the persons whose data is

---

[6] Directive 2006/24/EC of the European Parliament and of the Council of 15 March 2006 on the retention of data generated or processed in connection with the provision of publicly available electronic communications services or of public communications networks and amending Directive 2002/58/EC.

[7] Joined cases C-293/12, C-594/12 *Digital Rights Ireland and Seitlinger and Others*, at paragraph 69.

[8] Joined cases C-293/12, C-594/12 *Digital Rights Ireland and Seitlinger and Others*, at paragraph 65.

[9] Commission Decision 2000/520/EC of 26 July 2000 pursuant to Directive 95/46/EC of the European Parliament and of the Council on the adequacy of the protection provided by the safe harbour privacy principles and related frequently asked questions issued by the US Department of Commerce ([2000] OJ L215/7).

transferred from the EU to the United States without any differentiation, limitation or exception being made in the light of the objective pursued and without an objective criterion being laid down for determining the limits of access of the public authorities to the data and of its subsequent use'. Moreover, the CJEU emphasised that legislation permitting 'the public authorities to have access on a generalised basis to the content of electronic communications must be regarded as compromising the essence of the fundamental right to respect for private life… [under the EUCFR]'.[10]

The *Digital Rights Ireland* and *Schrems* judgments are two distinct rulings in two different cases. Yet, they are closely inter-related and must be read in tandem. Both judgments are also by the Grand Chamber of the CJEU, an enlarged composition of 15 judges reserved for high-profile cases. Therefore, these two judgments should be viewed as precedents, defining the status of privacy and data protection rights in the EU legal order when we are dealing with electronic surveillance, particularly indiscriminate blanket access to personal data. However, as will be discussed in detail later, there are also certain important aspects where these two judgments differ from each other and where particularly the *Schrems* judgment brings added value, to the extent that it can be even seen as making history of European law.

Aside from setting out the EU law approach with regard to the manner in which electronic mass surveillance should be approached in light of privacy and data protection rights, the *Digital Rights Ireland* and *Schrems* judgments amount to a vindication of privacy as a fundamental (and human) right. The erosion of privacy in the fight against terrorism and in respect of increasing surveillance has been a matter of great concern in recent years but the judgments demonstrate that privacy must indeed be taken seriously while countering terrorism and serious crime.[11]

However, it should be added that *Digital Rights Ireland* and *Schrems* have *not* rendered privacy 'a super-fundamental right that reigns supreme above all other rights'.[12] The statement by the CJEU that 'legislation permitting the public authorities to have access on a generalised basis to the content of electronic communications must be regarded as compromising the essence of the fundamental right to respect for private life' does not elevate privacy to a supreme fundamental right. This is because the idea of the existence of an inviolable essence of fundamental rights, including privacy, is explicitly affirmed by Article 52(1) of the EUCFR, setting

---

[10] Case C-362/14 *Maximillian Schrems v Data Protection Commissioner* at paragraph 94.

[11] See, eg, Martin Scheinin, 'Report by the Special Rapporteur on the Promotion and Protection Human Rights and Fundamental Freedoms while Countering Terrorism', A/HRC/13/37, para 17 (28 December 2009).

[12] According to Daniel Sarmiento, privacy has become a' super-fundamental right' after *Schrems*. See Daniel Sarmiento, 'What Schrems, Delvigne and Celaj tell us about the state of fundamental rights in the EU' (2015) *Verfassungsblog*. Available at: http://verfassungsblog.de/what-schrems-delvigne-and-celaj-tell-us-about-the-state-of-fundamental-rights-in-the-eu/#.ViEfSc47RRk (7.12.2015).

out the permissible limitations to fundamental rights guaranteed by the Charter. Indeed, Article 52(1) neatly illustrates the European thinking that every fundamental right—and not just absolute or non-derogable rights like the prohibition against torture, but also those that permit limitations or restrictions—should be understood to include an inviolable essential core that allows no balancing or limitations. The major contribution by the *Schrems* judgment is 'only' that the CJEU de facto confirms this European way of thinking about fundamental rights by applying the 'essence test'. This is even more so, and represents a major step forward in the history of European law, because the CJEU's counterpart in Strasbourg, the European Court of Human Rights, is yet to affirm the same view under the privacy provision of Article 8 of the European Human Rights Convention (the ECHR).[13]

The two judgments are also undoubtedly one of the most significant judgments ever given by the CJEU on fundamental rights within the EU legal order in general, particularly insofar as judicial review of the compatibility of EU legislation with fundamental rights is concerned. Previously, the Court has often been criticised for not reviewing EU measures as strictly as national laws[14] but with a string of other judgments in such cases as *Test-Achats*,[15] and *Volker und Markus Schecke and Eifert*,[16] the judgments in *Digital Rights Ireland* and *Schrems* indicate both the ability and willingness of the CJEU to embark on a rigorous and systematic rights-based review of EU legislative measures for their compliance with the EUCFR. In fact, it is now even plausible to argue that the tendency by the CJEU is towards applying a higher standard of scrutiny to measures by the EU institutions than by the Member States.[17]

Finally, the judgments in *Digital Rights Ireland* and *Schrems* feature as a continuation of such constitutional dynamics that have significantly strengthened the status of fundamental rights within the EU legal order in recent years, as well as transformed the CJEU into a supranational constitutional court that is rapidly becoming a forerunner of rights protection in several areas, including counter-terrorism.[18] In particular, the entry into force of the Lisbon Treaty in December 2009, rendering the EU Charter of Fundamental Rights a legal binding rights catalogue with the same legal value as the founding treaties of the EU, has produced important constitutional dynamics in the use of the CFR by the CJEU. After all, while the other EU institutions started taking the Charter into account in their

---

[13] Martin Scheinin, 'The Essence of Privacy, and Varying Degrees of Intrusion', (2016) *Verfassungsblog* available at: http://verfassungsblog.de/en/the-essence-of-privacy-and-varying-degrees-of-intrusion/(7.12.2015).

[14] See, eg, J Coppel and O'Neill, 'The European Court of Justice: Taking Rights Seriously?' (1992) 19 *CML Rev* 669.

[15] C-236/09 *Association Belge des Consommateurs Test-Achats and Others* U:C: 2011:100.

[16] Cases C-92/09 and C-93/09 *Volker und Markus Schecke and Eifert* EU: C: 2010: 662.

[17] See, eg, Sarmiento, 'Schrems, Delvigne and Celaj' (2015).

[18] Other judgments by the CJEU showing its commitment to the protection of fundamental rights in the area of counter-terrorism include, above all, Joined Cases C-402/05 P and C-415/05 P, *Kadi and Al Barakaat* [2008] ECR I-6351 and Joined Cases C-584/10 P, C-593/10 P and C-595/10 P *Council, Commission and United Kingdom v. Kadi*, judgment of 18 July 2013, nyr.

practices in the 2000s, the CJEU took notice of the Charter against a backdrop of judicial self-restraint.[19] However, today the Charter has really become a point of reference for the CJEU.[20]

III. The Parameters of Rights-based Review of Surveillance

A. Denial of Trade-off Between Privacy and Security *in abstracto*

Since 9/11, much of the political and public discourse on surveillance and fundamental rights has been about an abstract trade-off between rights versus security in terms of 'striking a new balance between liberty and security'.[21] The outcome of this way of thinking has usually been that 'respecting civil liberties has often real costs in the form of reduced security'.[22] Despite counterclaims by strong political actors, including by President Obama and the European Parliament, the 'new balancing approach' has resulted in the erosion of the right to privacy for the sake of 'better' security'.[23]

However, one of the major lessons from *Digital Rights Ireland* and *Schrems* is that a trade-off between privacy and security in abstracto should be rejected. Instead, there should be a systematic and rigorous case-by-case assessment of surveillance in accordance with the permissible limitations test in which the system for the protection of fundamental rights provides the framework for balancing, by way of applying the test of permissible limitations and the requirement of proportionality in that process *in concreto*, save occasions on which the essence of a fundamental right is triggered by surveillance.[24]

---

[19] Prior to the Lisbon Treaty, there were a few cases in which the Court did take judicial notice of the Charter as the acquis of fundamental rights recognised in the EU legal order in the 2000s. See, eg, the first reference by the CJEU to the Charter in Case C-540/03 *Parliament v the Commission and the Council*, para 38.

[20] Federico Fabbrini, 'The EU Charter of Fundamental Rights and the Right to Data Privacy: the ECJ as a Human Rights Court' in S de Vries (ed), *Five Years Legally Binding Charter of Fundamental Rights* (Oxford, Hart Publishing, 2015) pp 261–86.

[21] Richard A Posner, *Not a Suicide Pact: The Constitution in a Time of National Emergency* (Oxford, Oxford University Press, 2006). See also W Kip Viscusi and Richard J Zeckhauser, 'Recollection Bias and the Combat of Terrorism' (2005) 34 *Journal of Legal Studies* 27.

[22] Eric Posner and Adrian Vermeulen, *Terror in the balance: Security, Liberty and the Courts* (Oxford, Oxford University Press, 2007) 32.

[23] For critical analysis of a range of constructions by governments to justify their unilateral exceptions to human rights in the name of countering terrorism, see Martin Scheinin and Mathias Vermeulen, 'Unilateral Exceptions to International Law: Systematic Legal Analysis and Critique of Doctrines that Seek to Deny or Reduce the Applicability of Human Rights Norms in the Fight against Terrorism', EUI Working Papers Law No 2010/08, especially at 49–50.

[24] Martin Scheinin and Tom Sorell, 'Surveille Deliverable D4.10, Synthesis report from WP4, merging the ethics and law analysis and discussing their outcomes', (2015) at 8–9, available at: https://surveille.eui.eu/wp-content/uploads/2015/04/D4.10-Synthesis-report-from-WP4.pdf.

B. Privacy and Data Protection as a Proxy for Reviewing Fundamental Rights Intrusions by Surveillance

Surveillance may affect a range of fundamental rights, either directly or indirectly through a 'chilling effect' originating in an interference with privacy or data protection rights affecting the enjoyment or exercise of other fundamental rights. Aside from privacy and data protection rights, surveillance can constitute an interference with such classic civil and political rights as freedom of movement, freedom of association and assembly, freedom of expression and the right not to be discriminated against.[25]

However, the judgments by the CJEU in *Digital Rights Ireland* and *Schrems* strongly suggest that, among various rights potentially impacted by surveillance, the right to privacy and the right to the protection of personal data are not only the most immediately affected rights. They also provide a proxy for assessing fundamental rights intrusions by surveillance.[26] In *Digital Rights Ireland*, for instance, the CJEU concluded that the obligation on providers of publicly available electronic communications services or of public communications networks to retain the traffic and location data for the purpose of making them accessible, if necessary, to the competent national authorities raised 'questions relating to respect for private life and communications under Article 7 of the Charter, the protection of personal data under Article 8 of the Charter and respect for freedom of expression under Article 11 of the Charter'. However, the CJEU's subsequent reasoning only revolved around the right to privacy and the protection of personal data because the directive 'directly and specifically affects private life' and because the retention of data 'constitutes the processing of personal data' and, therefore, 'necessarily has to satisfy the data protection requirements arising from that article'.[27]

While indicating that privacy and data protection rights offer a useful proxy for assessing the overall fundamental rights impact of surveillance, *Digital Rights Ireland* and *Schrems* also show that the right to privacy is the primary right for fundamental rights assessment although the right to the protection of personal data may bring added value. Indeed, both judgments are probably a disappointment for all those who have argued in recent years that there is a fundamental distinction between privacy rights and the right to data protection and specifically, that Article 8 of the EUCFR enshrines the protection of personal data as a truly autonomous right.[28]

---

[25] Scheinin and Sorell, 'Surveille Deliverable D4.10' at 7–8.
[26] This was one of the major findings of fundamental rights assessments within the Surveille project. See Scheinin and Sorell (n 24) 4.
[27] Joined cases C-293/12, C-594/12 *Digital Rights Ireland and Seitlinger and Others* at paragraphs 28 and 29.
[28] For the relationship between the two CFREU provisions, see, eg, Maria Tzanou, 'The Added Value of Data Protection as a Fundamental Right in the EU Legal Order in the Context of Law Enforcement' (2012, PhD thesis at the European University Institute). See also Opinion of Advocate General Cruz Villalón, delivered on 12.12.2013, at paragraphs 55–67, analysing 'the combination of the right to privacy and the right to protection of personal data'.

While the CJEU takes judicial notice of personal data in many paragraphs in both rulings, the judgments overall reflect the distinction between privacy and data protection only to a limited degree. In both cases, the essence of the CJEU's reasoning starts from the premise that Articles 7 and 8 of the CFREU are closely linked so that the protection of personal data is 'especially important for the right to respect for private life enshrined in Article 7 of the Charter'.[29]

However, the CJEU's judgments also indicate that the right to privacy cannot exhaust the spectrum of fundamental rights assessment of surveillance and that the right to the protection of personal data is capable of bringing added value. Therefore, data protection needs to be addressed separately from other attributes within the 'family' of privacy rights so as not to miss certain types of fundamental rights impacted by surveillance.[30]

C. Permissible Limitations Test as the Framework of Review

i. General Remarks on the Permissible Test Under Article 52(1) of the EUCFR and Its Application by the CJEU

Most fundamental rights—and human rights for that matter—fail to be absolute. Hence, these rights usually permit restrictions or limitations that serve a legitimate aim, are prescribed by the law in a precise and foreseeable manner, and are both necessary and proportionate in nature. Several domestic constitutions or international human rights treaties contain more or less detailed provisions that provide for conditions for limiting rights protected by them. A reference can here be made to limitations clauses in Articles 8–11 of the ECHR and Article 52(1) of the EUCFR.

What is common to fundamental rights affected by surveillance is that these rights are not absolute but indeed permit limitations. Hence, the key question revolving around rights-based review of surveillance relates to the permissibility of limitations to fundamental rights, ie the permissible limitations test: does a fundamental right intrusion by surveillance serve a legitimate aim, is provided by the law in a precise and foreseeable manner, and is necessary and proportionate, including respect the inviolable essence of fundamental rights?

In this regard, the message by *Digital Rights Ireland* and *Schrems* is plain and unequivocal. While limitations are permissible within the system for the protection of fundamental rights under the EUCFR and allow due attention to the legitimate interest of public security in the fight against terrorism, surveillance constitutes an interference with privacy and data protection rights and, accordingly, should be reviewed systematically for its permissibility through a rigorous

---

[29] Joined cases C-293/12, C-594/12 *Digital Rights Ireland and Seitlinger and Others*, at paragraph 53.
[30] Again, this was also one of the main findings of fundamental rights assessments within the Surveille project. See Scheinin and Sorell (n 24) at 4.

step-by-step analysis under the permissible limitations test clause of Article 52(1) of the EUCFR which largely, if not exclusively, codifies well established case law by the CJEU.[31]

Article 52(1) of the EUCFR formulates the permissible limitations test as follows:

> 'Any limitation on the exercise of the rights and freedoms laid down by the Charter must be provided for by law, respect their essence and, subject to the principle of proportionality, limitations may be made to those rights and freedoms only if they are necessary and genuinely meet objectives of general interest recognised by the Union or the need to protect the rights and freedoms of others.'

On a closer analysis, the permissible limitations test under Article 52(1) of the EUCFR comprises the following distinct, yet inter-related conditions for the determination whether an interference with fundamental rights is justified:

(i)   Any limitations must be provided by the law.
(ii)   The essence of a fundamental right is not subject to limitations.
(iii)   Limitations must have a legitimate aim in that it corresponds with the objectives of general interest recognised by the EU or the need to protect the rights and freedoms of others.
(iv)   Limitations ought to be necessary for genuinely reaching the legitimate aim.
(v)   Limitations must conform to the principle of proportionality.

Once read in conjunction with Article 52(3) of the EUCFR, affirming the status of the ECHR as the 'minimum standard of protection,' the permissible limitations test also includes the condition that any restrictions must be consistent with the European Convention on Human Rights.

In addition, given that several provisions of the EUCFR are also based on the rights guaranteed in instruments adopted in the field of human rights within the United Nations, the International Labour Organisation and the Council of Europe, there is a strong case for the interpretive principle of the EUCFR, including the permissible limitations test clause under Article 52(1), that these provisions must be interpreted by taking into account those instruments, including the interpretation given to them by their monitoring bodies.[32]

Each condition (i)–(vi) listed above has an autonomous function to fulfil. As these conditions are also cumulative, failure to meet one of these conditions

---

[31] It is well-established in the case law of the CJEU that 'restrictions may be imposed on the exercise of those rights, in particular in the context of a common organisation of a market, provided that those restrictions in fact correspond to objectives of general interest pursued by the Community and do not constitute, with regard to the aim pursued, disproportionate and unreasonable interference undermining the very substance of those rights'. See, eg, C-292/97 *Karlsson and Others* [2000] ECR I-2737 at paragraph 18.

[32] See EU Network of Independent Experts on Fundamental Rights, Commentary of the Charter of Fundamental Rights of the European Union, 17–18.

is sufficient to trigger a violation of fundamental rights protected by the EUCFR. Given all these characteristics, the permissible limitations test under Article 52(1) of the EUCFR also generates both substantive as well as doctrinal coherence between the Charter and the ECHR and other human rights treaties, notably the International Covenant on Civil and Political Rights (the ICCPR),[33] as well as the domestic systems for the protection of fundamental rights.[34] However, Article 52(1) of the EUCFR also brings added value, particularly insofar as it makes explicit the 'essence test' although this condition, as such, originates in well-established case law by the CJEU.[35]

The CJEU's application of the test of permissible limitations in *Digital Rights Ireland* and *Schrems* contains many similarities with each other, yet also differs in some essential respects. In particular, *Digital Rights Ireland* provides a neat example of the application of the permissible limitations test under Article 52(1) of the Charter after the CJEU had identified the affected fundamental rights and the interference with those rights from the Data Retention Directive. The reasoning of the CJEU progresses systematically through various conditions although the bulk of the reasoning goes to the proportionality of the interference whereas other conditions attracted less judicial attention. The emphasis on proportionality in *Digital Rights Ireland* is explained by the fact that the CJEU quite bluntly rejected the claim by some parties that the retention of extensive metadata by the directive would violate the essence of privacy because the directive 'does not permit the acquisition of knowledge of the content of the electronic communications as such.'[36] Similarly, it was 'apparent' for the CJEU in light of its previous case law that the material objective of the Data Retention Directive, namely 'the fight against international terrorism in order to maintain international peace and security', as well as 'the fight against serious crime in order to ensure public security' constituted an objective of general interest within the meaning of Article 52(1) of the Charter. In addition, the CJEU noted that the Directive served to protect the rights and freedoms of others as 'Article 6 of the Charter lays down the right of any person not only to liberty, but also to security.'[37]

In *Digital Rights Ireland*, the CJEU did not address separately the requirement that any limitations must be 'provided for by law' although the Advocate General's

---

[33] For the permissible limitations test under the ICCPR, see Martin Scheinin, 'The right to privacy. Report of the Special Rapporteur on the promotion and protection of human rights and fundamental freedoms while countering terrorism', (A/HRC/13/37, December 2009) para 17.

[34] For instance, the permissible limitations test under Finnish constitutional law includes seven distinct yet inter-related and cumulative conditions that largely, if not exclusively, are parallel with Article 52(1) of the Charter.

[35] The emphasis by the CJEU on the idea of the inviolable 'essence' can be traced as far back as the classic *Nold* case in the early 1970s: 'Within the Community legal order it likewise seems legitimate that these rights should, if necessary, be subject to certain limits justified by the overall objectives pursued by the Community, on condition that the substance of these rights is left untouched.' Case C-4/73 *Nold v Commission* (1974) ECR 491 at para 14.

[36] Joined cases C-293/12, C-594/12 *Digital Rights Ireland and Seitlinger and Others* at para 39.

[37] Joined cases C-293/12, C-594/12 *Digital Rights Ireland and Seitlinger and Others* at para 42.

Opinion in the case included a lengthy discussion of this requirement.[38] However, several passages of the CJEU's reasoning effectively paraphrased such essential features of this requirement that the 'provided for by law' condition does not only require that the restriction should have some basis in legislation but also refers to the quality of the law in question. In essence, the quality of the law entails it to be accessible to the individual concerned and protect that individual from arbitrariness through, inter alia, precision and foreseeability. Accordingly, any measure giving, for example, law enforcement authorities power to interfere with fundamental rights, should contain explicit, detailed provisions which are sufficiently clear, sufficiently foreseeable and meet the required degree of certainty with respect to their application.[39]

In *Schrems*, in turn, the CJEU's reasoning did not address in detail distinct conditions of the permissible limitations test, simply because of the following two reasons: On the one hand, a considerable proportion of the judgment goes to the judicial analysis of the question whether the Commission's Safe Harbour decision prevents the supervisory authorities of the Member States from being able to examine the claim that the law and practices in force in the US do not ensure an 'adequate level of protection' within the meaning of the Data Protection Directive, essentially prohibiting the transfer of personal data to a third country which does not ensure an adequate level of protection.[40]

On the other hand, the outcome of *Schrems*—that Commission's Safe Harbour Decision 2000/52 is invalid—originated in the finding by the CJEU that 'legislation permitting the public authorities to have access on a generalised basis to the content of electronic communication' triggered the application of the essence test under Article 52(1) of the Charter. After finding the violation of the essence of privacy, there was no longer a need for the CJEU to review further the fulfillment of the other conditions for permissible limitations under Article 52(1), simply because that finding sufficed to determine the outcome of the case. Hence, the right to privacy was able to function in the same way in *Schrems* as such 'absolute' and non-derogable rights as, for example, the prohibition against torture can always do: If some specific conduct can be defined as torture, then its absolute prohibition cannot be outweighed by any competing interest, no matter what its weight.

Below, some further lessons from *Digital Rights Ireland* and *Schrems* for rights-based review of surveillance are delineated more carefully.

---

[38] Opinion of Advocate General Cruz Villalón, delivered on 12 December 2013 at paras 108–132.

[39] According to the European Court of Human Rights, this condition 'not only requires that the impugned measure should have some basis in domestic law, but also refers to the quality of the law in question, requiring that it should be accessible to the person concerned and foreseeable as to its effects', *Rotaru v Romania* judgment of 4 May 2000 (Application No 28341/95), § 52. For the requirements of foreseeability and precision, see, eg, *Malone v the United Kingdom* judgment of 2 August 1984, Series A no 82, p 32, § 67 and *Rotaru v Romania* judgment of 4 May 2000 (Application No 28341/95), § 57.

[40] Directive 95/46/EC of the European Parliament and of the Council of 24 October 1995 on the protection of individuals with regard to the processing of personal data and on the free movement of such data ([1995] OJ L 281/31).

ii. The Distinction Between Content and Metadata

In *Digital Rights Ireland*, the court quite bluntly rejected the argument raised by some of the parties that the Data Retention Directive entails the violation of the essence of the fundamental rights to privacy and data protection. Even if the retention of extensive metadata by the directive does constitute a particularly serious interference with those rights, the CJEU nonetheless concluded that the directive 'does not permit the acquisition of knowledge of the content of the electronic communications as such'.[41]

Thus, the CJEU's reasoning suggests that the interference by data retention came close to the essence of privacy but did not cross that border. Hence, the final outcome was based on the application of a proportionality test in *Digital Rights Ireland* as already noted above. By contrast, as the CJEU did identify the intrusion by the Safe Harbour decision as falling under the essence of privacy in *Schrems*, there was no need for a proportionality assessment under Article 52 (1)–(2) of the Charter.

The Court's reliance on the distinction between 'content' and 'metadata' can certainly be criticised as being orthodox and even obsolete. After all, the distinction between the content of the electronic communications and such metadata as traffic data and location data is rapidly fading away in a modern network environment. A lot of information, including sensitive information, about an individual can easily be revealed by monitoring the use of communications services through traffic data collection, storage and processing. Hence, the processing of metadata cannot any longer be invariably seen as falling within such 'peripheral areas' of privacy where limitations would be permissible more easily than in the context of the content of electronic communications. Indeed, the more systematic and wider the collection, retention and analysis of metadata becomes, the closer it can be seen as moving towards the core area of privacy and data protection with the outcome that at least the most massive, systematic forms of collection and analysis of metadata can be regarded as constituting an intrusion into the inviolable core of privacy.[42]

Actually, a benevolent reading of the CJEU's judgment in *Digital Rights Ireland* suggests that the distinction between content and metadata is one of degree, not of kind, for the CJEU, too. A reference can here made by those observations by the Court in the *Digital Rights Ireland* judgment where the Court underscored that the interference by data retention with privacy and data protection rights should be regarded as being 'wide-ranging' and 'particularly serious'.[43] The CJEU also noted that the retained location and traffic data taken as a whole, 'may allow very precise conclusions to be drawn concerning the private lives of the persons whose data

---

[41] Joined cases C-293/12, C-594/12 *Digital Rights Ireland and Seitlinger and Others* at para 39.
[42] See Statement by Martin Scheinin, LIBE Committee Inquiry on Electronic Mass Surveillance of EU Citizens, Hearing, European Parliament, 14 October 2013 p 4.
[43] Joined cases C-293/12, C-594/12 *Digital Rights Ireland and Seitlinger and Others* at para 37.

has been retained, such as the habits of everyday life, permanent or temporary places of residence, daily or other movements, the activities carried out, the social relationships of those persons and the social environments frequented by them'.[44] Finally, echoing the concern originally formulated by the German Constitutional Court, the Court even emphasised that the fact that 'data are retained and subsequently used without the subscriber or registered user being informed is likely to generate in the minds of the persons concerned the feeling that their private lives are the subject of constant surveillance'.[45]

iii. Essence of Privacy: The Capacity of Privacy to Function as a Rule Allowing No Limitations or Balancing

As already noted, the most remarkable addition by *Schrems* is that the CJEU de facto applied the essence test under Article 52(1) of the Charter.

The importance of this finding by the CJEU cannot be overplayed. The confirmation by the Court of a violation of the essence of privacy confirms that non-absolute fundamental rights, such as privacy rights, cannot only be categorised as principles allowing for weighing and balancing in the context of surveillance.[46] In addition, there truly are occasions on which privacy rights must be treated as *rules* that apply in an all-or-nothing fashion and are capable of determining the outcome of the case with no room for balancing, no matter how weighty or pressing the legitimate aim, or any other legal arguments made.[47]

It also deserves emphasis that *mere access is an intrusion* into the essence of privacy when it provides for indiscriminate access to 'content'. As Martin Scheinin has noted, this finding pulls the rug from under surveillance advocates' claims that 'mere access does not amount to processing, and therefore mere access to the flow of communications does not amount to an intrusion until the automated selectors and algorithms have made their job and the human eye starts to "process" a much more narrow set of data'.[48]

Of course, as the essential question is now the scope of application of a rule, the identification of the essence of privacy is a matter of moment-to-moment interpretation. However, the need for interpretation should not lose sight of the fact that the essence of fundamental rights, including privacy rights, bears the characteristics of a rule and, accordingly, is not subject to any further balancing. Article

---

[44] Joined cases C-293/12, C-594/12 *Digital Rights Ireland and Seitlinger and Others* at paragraph 37.

[45] Joined cases C-293/12, C-594/12 *Digital Rights Ireland and Seitlinger and Others* at paragraph 37.

[46] In *Schrems*, the CJEU also confirmed the violation of the essence of the right to effective judicial protection under Article 47 of the EUCFR. See Case C-362/14 *Maximillian Schrems v Data Protection Commissioner* at paragraph 95.

[47] Scheinin (n 24).

[48] Scheinin (n 24). Scheinin took the view that paragraph 94 of *Schrems* is formulated in a way that 'gives a generic answer concerning the contours of the right to privacy under Article 7 of the Charter'. Hence, the ruling can also be interpreted as prohibiting 'access through the upstream method of capturing the data flow in a fibre-optic cable is to be regarded as compromising the essence of privacy and therefore as prohibited under the Charter, without a need even to engage in a proportionality analysis.'

52(1) of the EUCFR also clearly displays that the essential content of fundamental rights must always be respected within its scope of application.

Aside from the content of electronic communications, it seems plausible to assert in light of the case law by European courts that the essence of privacy rights include the prohibition of indiscriminate or blanket mass surveillance and biometric data.[49] However, it is still unclear whether the right to the protection of personal data under Article 8 of the EUCFR, would be capable of including an inviolable essence within the meaning of Article 52(1) of the EUCFR as a distinct fundamental right and, if yes, what could constitute such an essence. Even if the processing of sensitive data has been formulated as a prohibition, it allows for derogations and leaves room for the pull of balancing against a number of compelling interests.

iv. Standard and Intensity of Review of Surveillance

Although *Schrems* displays that some elements of privacy are capable of assuming the character of a rule applying in an all-or-nothing fashion and determining the outcome of the case with no need or even possibility to address other considerations under the permissible limitations test, *Digital Rights Ireland* indicates that privacy and data protection rights usually feature as principles that can be subject to a process of balancing. Indeed, *Schrems* cannot conceal the fact that the proportionality test often—but not always!—emerges as essential and unavoidable feature from the maze of rights-based review of legislation.[50]

The *Digital Rights Ireland* judgment also displays some important further aspects that should be taken into account in assessing fundamental rights intrusion by surveillance practices by way of applying the permissible limitations test, including the proportionality test as one—and often decisive—phase in the overall assessment process.

As already noted, the CJEU underscored in *Digital Rights Ireland* that the interference with the rights to privacy and the protection of personal data should be regarded as being 'wide-ranging' and 'particularly serious'. The seriousness of the intrusion, in turn, had significant implications for the standard and intensity of review of data retention within the framework of the proportionality test. To begin with, the CJEU emphasised the importance of assessing the scope of the EU legislature's discretion in light of a number of factors, such as the area concerned, the nature of the right at issue guaranteed by the Charter, the nature and seriousness of the interference and the object pursued by the interference. In view of the important role played by the protection of personal data in the light of the fundamental right to respect for private life and the extent and seriousness of the interference with that right caused by the directive, the Court concluded that

---

[49] See *S and Marper v The United Kingdom* 30562/04 and 30566/04, judgment of 4 November 2008.
[50] See Robert Alexy, *A Theory of Constitutional Rights* (Oxford, Oxford University Press, 2002) 74.

the EU legislature's discretion was 'reduced'. The outcome of this finding was that the standard of review of that discretion by the legislature 'should be strict.'[51] From these premises, the CJEU then embarked on a very rigorous assessment of the Data Retention Directive in light of the proportionality test, ending up concluding that several aspects of the directive failed.

In conclusion, therefore, it warrants emphasis that the depth of the intrusion by surveillance into privacy and data protection rights, as well as the weight of privacy and data protection rights in the context of electronic surveillance, affect the intensity of review and, accordingly, direct and shape the concrete application of the proportionality test.

IV. Institutional Implications: Towards More Pluralistic Forms of Review?

Digital Rights Ireland and *Schrems* cannot be understood as total knockouts by the CJEU to mandatory data retention and transatlantic transfers of data between Europe and the United States. To be sure, the undertone of the *Digital Rights Ireland* judgment seems to be that some form of mandatory data retention in order to combat serious crime and terrorism might be compatible with fundamental rights although the judgment clearly displays that electronic mass surveillance based on vaguely defined provisions violates the right to respect for private life and the protection of personal data under the Charter. *Schrems* is even clearer in this regard, for the CJEU has certainly not prohibited transnational data flows between Europe and the US. After all, the Data Protection Directive allows such a transfer, and provides that the European Commission may find that a third country ensures an adequate level of protection by reason of its domestic law or its international commitments. The point is 'only' that the third country in question should be capable of ensuring an adequate level of protection of the personal data transferred.[52]

From this point of view, both *Digital Rights Ireland* and *Schrems* can be understood as instances of a constitutional dialogue between the CJEU and the EU legislature in which the CJEU does not only invalidate a legal measure but also indicates how the legislator could enact valid legislation accomplishing the main objective of the invalidated law. It falls beyond the scope of this chapter to ponder the question of how to regulate data retention or transatlantic data flow in compliance with the EUCFR. Instead, it suffices to say that both judgments seem

---

[51] Joined cases C-293/12, C-594/12 *Digital Rights Ireland and Seitlinger and Others* at paragraph 48.

[52] Directive 95/46/EC of the European Parliament and of the Council of 24 October 1995 on the protection of individuals with regard to the processing of personal data and on the free movement of such data ([1995] OJ L 281/31).

to delineate quite clearly such points that should be taken into account by the EU legislature (or national legislatures acting within the scope of application of EU law) when curtailing legislative framework on data retention or transatlantic data flow to what is 'strictly necessary'. These points can largely, if not exclusively, be inferred from those flaws identified by the CJEU that combined to trigger the invalidity of the Data Retention Directive and the Commission's Safe Harbour Decision.

It is beyond the powers of the courts, including the CJEU, to ensure that laws are drafted according to the requirements of fundamental rights. Especially on occasions on which legislative measures themselves constitute intrusions into fundamental rights—as, for example, legislative measures on surveillance do—the legislature has a positive obligation to provide for essential guarantees, clearly and precisely laid down by the law, to prevent the interference from going beyond what is strictly necessary. As courts, including the CJEU, fail to have competence to provide such a legislative framework required, judicial review may even emerge as a secondary mode of securing compliance of such serious interferences with fundamental rights.

It is, therefore, submitted that constitutional development in the EU should be increasingly towards ex ante review of legislative proposals for their compliance with fundamental rights. This development should eventually result into a system of review paradigm that is institutionally pluralist and predominantly rights-based outcome as the legislature ex ante and the judiciary ex post would be entrusted with a shared duty to protect fundamental rights. If ex ante review mechanisms of draft legislation for its compliance with fundamental rights are improved within the EU, this could also reduce the risk of entrusting with the judiciary, instead of the legislature, the power to make ultimate decisions about the law of the land, including the laws of surveillance and security.

Of course, all this would require in reality that proposals for legislative or other measures on surveillance to be adopted by the EU legislature or by its counterparts in the Member States would systematically be reviewed for their compatibility with fundamental rights. However, the multi-faceted problem of improving the compliance of EU legislative proposals, not to speak of domestic legislation falling within the scope of application of EU law, with the EUCFR, falls beyond the scope of this chapter. Thus, it is here generally only noted that the legislative processes of the EU have been improved for the purpose of securing that the legislative acts or other measures would be in conformity with fundamental rights since the proclamation of the EU Charter of Fundamental Rights in 2000.[53] While these developments illustrate the shift of a constitutional culture within the EU towards improving compliance of EU legislative proposals with the requirements of the EU Charter of Fundamental Rights, *Digital Rights Ireland* and *Schrems* also

---

[53] See, eg, EU Network of Independent Experts on Fundamental Rights, Commentary of the Charter of Fundamental Rights of the European Union, 2006 at 15.

combine to show that securing the compliance of EU acts with fundamental rights still requires hard graft.

V. Conclusion

Digital Rights Ireland and *Schrems* are landmark rulings that illustrate the ECJ's development of a structured test with distinct phases and elements to assess fundamental rights intrusions by surveillance. The major lessons from the judgments are that, first, surveillance should be assessed for its compatibility with fundamental rights through a step-by-step process of the permissible limitations test under Article 52(1) of the EUCFR. The second lesson is that the right to privacy and the right to the protection of personal data can be relied upon as a proxy for fundamental rights assessments. The third lesson is that some intrusions by surveillance into privacy or other fundamental rights may even violate the essence of those rights and should therefore be rejected, without a need for a proportionality assessment in comparison to the security benefit obtained. In addition, the CJEU's rulings in *Digital Rights Ireland* and *Schrems* combine to show that the distinction between 'content' and 'metadata' cannot any longer be treated as the most decisive factor for the assessment of fundamental rights intrusions by surveillance although the CJEU can still be criticised in this regard for being a bit too conventional.

Finally, one can emerge from the maze of *Digital Rights Ireland* and *Schrems* with an institutional message: not only the courts but also the legislator(s) should take seriously the duty to protect fundamental rights. In practice, this requires that ex ante review of legislative measures before their enactment should still significantly be improved within the EU although first steps have already been taken in the right direction since the early 2000s. However, the question how to develop rights-based review in the EU increasingly towards such a pluralistic form of review which would appropriately combine ex ante review of legislative proposals by EU legislative institutions with ex post review of legislation by courts with the CJEU at their apex is a multifaceted issue within the foundations of the EU constitutional system. Hence, it should be explored elsewhere.

3

Domestic Surveillance of Public Activities and Transactions with Third Parties: Melding European and American Approaches

CHRISTOPHER SLOBOGIN

I. Introduction

In most countries, government surveillance of activities that take place in public is not regulated or only lightly regulated. Similarly, in most countries, police efforts to obtain records of everyday transactions usually requires, at most, a finding that the record is 'relevant' to an investigation. It is time to rethink these rules, now that technology—cameras, drones, computers, and the like—has made monitoring our public activities and our transactions easier and cheaper. Because governments are increasingly relying on 'panvasive' surveillance—that is, surveillance that invasively and pervasively collects information across jurisdictional boundaries and wide swathes of the community[1]—and mining the accumulated data, rules designed for a non–technological era are insufficiently protective of civil liberties.

On the assumption that a new regulatory regime is necessary, this paper looks to European law as a model for regulating the creation of panvasive systems, and to American law as a model for regulating government uses of such systems to investigate individuals. It argues, following Europe's lead, that surveillance systems should not be established unless they are authorised by legislative bodies representative of the affected populace, through specific delegations that require mechanisms for overseeing even–handed implementation of the program. With

---

[1] See Christopher Slobogin, 'Rehnquist and Panvasive Searches' (2013) *82 Mississippi Law Journal* 307, 308.

respect to targeting, it argues, following suggestions in recent US Supreme Court caselaw, for implementation of 'mosaic theory' as a way of calibrating the justification required to access the activities or records of a particular individual.

Part II of this paper first discusses issues surrounding targeting and considers how mosaic theory might be implemented in a way that meaningfully protects the targets of government investigation. Part III addresses principles derived from European law that should govern the establishment of the panvasive programs that facilitate such targeting.

II. Targeted Investigations and Mosaic Theory

Because the Fourth Amendment to the US Constitution prohibits only 'unreasonable searches and seizures', the crucial threshold issue in American privacy jurisprudence is whether a government investigative action is a 'search' or 'seizure'. American courts have not construed these words the way lay people might, but rather declared that a search occurs only when government officials infringe 'an expectation of privacy' that 'society is prepared to recognise as reasonable'[2] and that a seizure only occurs when there is a 'meaningful interference with an individual's possessory interest'.[3] Furthermore, until recently courts have construed these narrow definitions of search and seizure narrowly. For instance, the US Supreme Court has held that neither exploring private property from the air[4] nor accessing personal information surrendered to a third party[5] is a search or seizure, because neither action infringes 'legitimate' expectations of privacy or affects a legitimate possessory interest.

If a government action *is* considered a search or seizure, then the Fourth Amendment's language commands that it be 'reasonable'. This requirement usually mandates that, in non-exigent circumstances, police obtain a judicially-issued warrant that is based on 'probable cause' (approaching a more-likely-than not level of certainty) and that describes with 'particularity' the place to be searched or person or item to be seized.[6] However, some lesser searches and seizures may be reasonable without a warrant or probable cause if, for instance, a police officer has 'reasonable suspicion' (a lesser justification than probable cause) that a person is about to commit a crime or is armed,[7] or if the government

---

[2] *Bond v United States* 529 U.S. 334, 338 (2000) (quoting *Katz v United States* 389 US 347 (1967) (Harlan, J, concurring).

[3] *United States v Jacobsen* 466 US 109, 113 (1984).

[4] *Florida v Riley* 488 US 445 (1989).

[5] *United States v Miller* 425 US 435 (1976).

[6] See generally Charles H Whitebread and Christopher Slobogin, *Criminal Procedure: An Analysis of Cases & Concept*, 6th edn (Foundation Press, 2014) at 122–26.

[7] *Terry v Ohio* 392 US 1 (1968).

can demonstrate that the search or seizure is necessary to achieve an important regulatory goal (as distinguished from the goal of detecting 'ordinary criminal wrongdoing').[8]

To the surprise of many, in the 2012 decision of *United States v Jones*[9] the Supreme Court held that month–long tracking using a device planted on a car is a 'search' triggering the Fourth Amendment's guarantee against unreasonable searches, and thus (probably)[10] requires a warrant based on probable cause before it can occur. The decision was big news in the United States for a number of reasons, two of which are important here.[11] Firstly, it introduced the possibility that, contrary to prior caselaw, surveillance of public spaces is governed by the Constitution. Second, it indicated that at least five justices of the Court are willing to consider some version of what has come to be called 'mosaic theory' as a way of figuring out when government information gathering that normally would not be considered a Fourth Amendment 'search' becomes one.

The mosaic idea is captured in Justice Alito's statement in *Jones*, made in a concurring opinion joined by three other justices, that 'relatively short-term monitoring' of a person's movements on public streets does not implicate the Fourth Amendment but that 'prolonged' GPS monitoring does.[12] Justice Sotomayor's separate concurrence went further, stating that the question should be 'whether people reasonably expect that their movements will be recorded and aggregated in a manner that enables the Government to ascertain, more or less at will, their political and religious beliefs, sexual habits and so on'.[13] These kinds of statements reflect a mosaic approach to the Fourth Amendment because they suggest that, while collecting isolated bits of publicly available information is not a constitutionally cognisable search, accumulation and assemblage of numerous discreet pieces can be, given the picture they provide of an individual's personal life.[14]

We all can intuit that this is true. Following someone for a few minutes probably won't reveal much, but tracking the person for 28 days, as occurred in *Jones*, probably will. As the lower court in *Jones* stated:

'Prolonged surveillance reveals types of information not revealed by short-term surveillance, such as what a person does repeatedly, what he does not do, and what he does [over time]. These types of information can each reveal more about a person than does any individual trip viewed in isolation. Repeated visits to a church, a gym, a bar, or a bookie

---

[8] *Edmond v Indianapolis* 531 US 32 (2000).

[9] 132 S Ct 945 (2012).

[10] ibid 954 (explaining that the court had 'no occasion to consider' the government's argument that something less than a warrant based on probable cause would have justified the search in *Jones*).

[11] A third aspect of *Jones* was its rejuvenation of trespass as a basis for Fourth Amendment protection. Above n 9 at 952 (stating that the dominant test for determining the scope of the Fourth Amendment—which focuses on whether a police action infringes 'reasonable expectations of privacy'—'has been added to, not substituted for, the common-law trespassory test').

[12] Above n 9 at 964 (Alito, J., concurring).

[13] See n 9 above at 956 (Sotomayor, J, concurring).

[14] The first court to apply this term in the Fourth Amendment context was *United States v Maynard* 615 F.3d 544, 562 (DC Cir 2010).

tell a story not told by any single visit, as does one's not visiting any of these places over the course of a month. The sequence of a person's movements can reveal still more; a single trip to a gynecologist's office tells little about a woman, but that trip followed a few weeks later by a visit to a baby supply store tells a different story. A person who knows all of another's travels can deduce whether he is a weekly church goer, a heavy drinker, a regular at the gym, an unfaithful husband, an outpatient receiving medical treatment, an associate of particular individuals or political groups—and not just one such fact about a person, but all such facts.'[15]

The same can be said for government perusals of records held by third parties, such as banks, phone companies, internet service providers and credit card agencies. Finding out that an individual has made a particular payment, phone call or email communication can provide some insight into what a person is up to. But a month's-worth of phone and email logs and credit card data is much more likely to reap a gold mine of detail about how one lives one's life.[16]

A number of courts have nonetheless rejected mosaic theory. The major resistance to the theory has not been conceptual, but rather practical. To wit: How is a court to figure out when surveillance is 'prolonged'? In the context of stored records, the analogous question might be: How much 'aggregation' must occur before the Fourth Amendment is implicated? For instance, has a search occurred when the government tracks a person for a week rather than a month, or accesses bank records for a couple of days? As a recent Florida Supreme Court opinion stated in refusing to endorse mosaic theory, this approach 'requires case-by-case, after-the-fact, ad hoc determinations about whether the length of the monitoring crossed the threshold of the Fourth Amendment in each case challenged'.[17]

Those who believe that this implementation problem is intractable could go in one of two directions. The first is to declare that the Fourth Amendment is usually not applicable in these cases, or at most requires a subpoena based on a showing that the information is 'relevant' to an investigation—an extremely easy standard to meet.[18] The second position, endorsed by the post-*Jones* cases noted above, is to state that even minimal surveillance requires a warrant, based on probable cause.[19]

---

[15] ibid. See also, Jeffrey M Skopek, 'Reasonable Expectations of Anonymity' (2015) 101 *Virginia Law Review* 691 (arguing that the more information the government gathers about individuals, the less anonymous they become, which undermines the right to anonymity).

[16] See Steven M Bellovin, Renee M Hutchins, Tony Jebara and Sebastian Zimmeck, 'When Enough is Enough: Location Tracking, Mosaic Theory and Machine Learning' (2014) 8 *New York University Journal of Law and Liberty* 556 (arguing that the science of machine learning demonstrates how longer-term data collection enhances predictions about behaviour and thus allows greater understanding of the person targeted).

[17] *Tracey v State* 2014 WL 5285929, *14 (Fl Sup Ct 2014). See also *United States v Wilford*, 961 F Supp 2d 740, 771 (D Md 2013) (noting that 'mosaic' theory has presented problems in practice); *United States v Graham* 846 F Supp 2d 384, 401 (D Md 2012) (same).

[18] Orin Kerr, 'The Mosaic Theory of the Fourth Amendment' (2012) 111 *Michigan Law Review* 311, 315 (arguing that, 'as a normative matter, courts should reject the mosaic theory' and intimating that the author favours a legislative approach).

[19] See cases cited above at n 17.

The problem with the first approach—which is in essence the Supreme Court's outside of the anomalous concurring opinions in *Jones*—is that it blinks at the privacy invasion and governmental abuse that can be associated with suspicion-less surveillance. Most of the Court's cases have insisted that we assume the risk that people will see us when we go into public spaces and that a third party to whom we surrender information will hand that information over to the government.[20] But that reasoning is bankrupt, both descriptively and normatively. Most of us don't expect to be subject to prolonged surveillance or monitoring, either visual or transactional.[21] Nor should we expect such invasions. As many commentators have argued, the Fourth Amendment's promise of 'the right to be secure against unreasonable searches' guarantees both a right to anonymity in public[22] and a right to expect that third party institutions to which we surrender information will use it only for its intended purpose.[23] Therefore, the government should not be able to monitor public movements for long periods or access transactions with banks, phone companies and the like without justification.[24] Many lower courts have agreed, both with respect to surveillance of public activities[25] and with respect to accessing records from third parties.[26]

The problem with the second approach—making every act of public or transactional surveillance a search requiring probable cause—is twofold. Firstly,

[20] See, eg, *United States v Knotts*, 460 US 276, 281–82 (1983) ('A person travelling in an automobile on public thoroughfares has no reasonable expectation of privacy in his movements from one place to another [because he] voluntarily convey[s] to anyone who want[s] to look the fact that he [is] travelling over particular roads in a particular direction …'.); *United States v Miller*, 425 US 435, 443 (1976) ('[T]he Fourth Amendment does not prohibit the obtaining of information revealed to a third party and conveyed by him to Government authorities, even if the information is revealed on the assumption that it will be used only for a limited purpose and the confidence placed in the third party will not be betrayed').

[21] See Christopher Slobogin, *Privacy at Risk: The New Government Surveillance and the Fourth Amendment* (Chicago, University of Chicago Press, 2007) 110–13, 180–86 (describing studies indicating that many types of public and transaction surveillance are viewed as more intrusive than inspections and frisks that have been held to infringe the Fourth Amendment).

[22] ibid 90–108; Skopek (n 15) 725.

[23] Daniel J Solove, 'Digital Dossiers and the Dissipation of Fourth Amendment Privacy' (2002) 75 *Southern California Law Review* 1083, 1167 (arguing for such a regime).

[24] See generally, Slobogin (n 21) Chs 5 and 7.

[25] See *Commonwealth v Rousseau* 990 NE2d, 543, 548 (Mass 2013) (passenger in the vehicle 'had a reasonable expectation that his movements would not be subjected to extended electronic surveillance by the government through use of GPS monitoring.'); *State v Zahn* 812 NW2d 490, 497 (S Dak 2012) ('When the use of a GPS device enables police to gather a wealth of highly-detailed information about an individual's life over an extended period of time, its use violates an expectation of privacy that society is prepared to recognise as reasonable'); *People v Weaver* 909 NE2d 1195, 1201 (NY 2009) (holding, prior to *Jones*, that '[t]he massive invasion of privacy entailed by the prolonged use of the GPS device was inconsistent with even the slightest reasonable expectation of privacy.').

[26] Stephen E Henderson, 'Learning from All Fifty States, How to Apply the Fourth Amendment and its State Analog to Protect Third Party Information from Unreasonable Search' (2006) 55 *Catholic University Law Review* 373, 424–25 (describing states that require reasonable suspicion or probable cause to obtain records considered particularly private).

it will often overestimate the privacy invasion; a single location, phone number, or credit charge is usually nowhere near as revealing as the invasions that are classically associated with the Fourth Amendment's probable cause requirement—ie, ransacking one's home or eavesdropping on phone calls.[27] Second, a rule requiring probable cause for every investigative activity that American law considers a 'search' impedes law enforcement efforts to *develop* probable cause. Much short-term surveillance and many subpoenas for records are designed to get information that will lead to arrest; if the police already had probable cause they wouldn't need the surveillance in the first place.[28] If probable cause were required for all searches, police would be prevented from carrying out even the relatively unintrusive preliminary investigative techniques necessary to develop that level of suspicion, such as tracking a person to see if he consorts with a known suspect, contacting a phone company to discover whether he called a suspected co-conspirator on the day of the crime, or acquiring store records to find out whether he purchased a particular type of gun or an item found at the crime scene.

Thus, mosaic theory—a middle ground between the extremes of no regulation and requiring probable cause for every police action—makes sense in theory. Moreover, it can be implemented effectively, albeit not perfectly.[29] For instance, for surveillance of public activities that endures longer than 48 hours, probable cause might be required. But for public surveillance that lasts less than 48 hours (and more than 20 minutes) police might only need to demonstrate reasonable suspicion (a well-known concept in US law that, as noted above, connotes a lower level of certainty than probable cause but still requires more than a hunch). Similarly, obtaining records that reflect activity over more than a 48-hour period might require probable cause, but accessing records of activities covering a shorter period of time only reasonable suspicion. Probable cause could be required to authorise access to phone or bank records covering more than two days or a record of medical or purchasing history, while obtaining information about a single credit card purchase or headers about a day-long email thread would require only reasonable suspicion.[30]

---

[27] See, eg, *Berger v New York* 388 US 41, 63 (1967) (stating that application of the Fourth Amendment's requirements to electronic surveillance 'is no formality ... but a fundamental rule that has long been recognised as basic to the privacy of every home in America').

[28] Nina Totenburg, 'Do Police Need Warrants for GPS Tracking Devices' *National Public Radio* (8 November 2011) www.npr.org/2011/11/08/142032419/do-police-need-warrants-for-gps-tracking-devices (quoting former assistant Attorney General asserting that GPS tracking is a useful device for following up leads necessary to develop probable cause); Howard W Goldstein, *Grand Jury Practice* (New York, Law Journal Press, 2005) 5–25 (noting that subpoenas are typically issued 'in the context of a preliminary investigation to determine whether any wrongdoing has occurred and whether probable cause exists to charge any individual with commission of any offence').

[29] Christopher Slobogin, 'Making the Most of United States v Jones in a Surveillance Society: A Statutory Implementation of Mosaic Theory' (2012) 8 *Duke Journal of Constitutional Law and Public Policy* 1, 24, 28.

[30] Interception of communications would be regulated in the traditional manner, requiring probable cause and a warrant. See 18 USC. § 2511.

This implementation of mosaic theory is based on what has been called a 'proportionality theory' of the Fourth Amendment.[31] Proportionality theory already plays a role in the US Supreme Court's seizure jurisprudence, which as a general matter requires only reasonable suspicion for a detention of up to 20 minutes but for any detention beyond that requires probable cause,[32] determined by a judge if the detention lasts more than 48 hours.[33] These distinctions between seizures are based in part on the idea that a stop is less intrusive than an arrest,[34] and in part on the realisation that police need something short of arrest—an investigatory detention—if they are to do their jobs well.[35] The court has been more reluctant to adopt proportionality reasoning in the context of investigatory searches,[36] but that approach is justified in the search context as well. Otherwise, we are left with the extremes: no constitutional regulation at all, or an impossible-to-meet or very watered-down probable cause standard.

Of course, durational limits of the sort proposed here are arbitrary means of delineating privacy protection. Even so, the US Supreme Court routinely uses time periods as a prophylactic method of implementing the Constitution.[37] Good examples come from the Court's decisions, just noted, that declare that individuals who are arrested do not need to be brought in front of magistrate unless they are held for longer than 48 hours, and that hold that 15 to 20 minutes is the presumptive threshold for determining when a detention transforms from an investigative stop into a full-blown arrest.[38] Statutes also often use duration as a dividing point for privacy protections. For instance, the Electronic Communications Privacy Act requires a warrant for records held on a server less than 180 days but only a showing of relevance after that period,[39] and Title III limits electronic eavesdropping warrants to 30 days.[40] In Europe, France provides several similar examples. For instance,

---

[31] Slobogin (n 21) 21.

[32] *United States v Sharpe* 470 US 675, 687–88 (1985) (finding a twenty-minute stop reasonable but only because the suspect was responsible for some of the delay). In a few cases a longer detention has been permitted on less than probable cause, but the police in those cases also had more than reasonable suspicion. See, eg, *Michigan v Summers* 452 US 692 (1981) (detention of house occupant during search of house pursuant to a search warrant).

[33] *County of Riverside v McLaughlin*, 500 US 44, 56 (1991) (requiring a judicial determination of probable cause within 48 hours).

[34] *Terry v Ohio* 392 US 1, 26 (1968) ('An arrest is a wholly different kind of intrusion upon individual freedom from a limited search for weapons').

[35] *Adams v Williams* 407 US 143, 145 (1972) ('The Fourth Amendment does not require a policeman who lacks the precise level of information necessary for probable cause to arrest to simply shrug his shoulders and allow a crime to occur or a criminal to escape.').

[36] Eg, *Arizona v. Hicks* 480 US 321 (1986) (requiring probable cause even though the search consisted merely of moving a stereo set a few inches). But see *TLO v New Jersey* 469 US 3325 (1984) (permitting search of high school student's purse on reasonable suspicion).

[37] In addition to the Fourth Amendment rules noted in the text, for instance, the Supreme Court has adopted durational rules in the interrogation context. See *Maryland v Shatzer* 559 US 98, 111 (2010) (holding that police may re-initiate questioning two weeks after a suspect requests counsel).

[38] See cases cited above nn 32, 33.

[39] 18 USC § 2703(a) (2006).

[40] ibid § 2518(5).

Christopher Slobogin

witnesses may be held only for 24 hours without judicial review, and detentions for identity checks are limited to four hours.[41] All of these rules calibrate legal requirements by reference to time periods that, in any given case, could be over or under inclusive. Indeed, in virtually every area of law, prophylactic rules that inexactly effectuate constitutional or legislative intent are common and necessary.[42]

A workable scheme governing investigatory targeting should have one other significant component as well: a danger exception that allows relaxation of the usual justification if necessary to *prevent* a serious, specified crime.[43] This exception is based on the idea—well accepted in Fourth Amendment cases[44]—that when the goal of government intervention is prevention, a somewhat relaxed standard is permissible. However, this exception should never apply if the police are trying to solve a crime that has already occurred, nor would it apply unless the crime sought to be prevented is serious and specified. An informant's tip that a bomb has been planted need not meet the usual standard, but a generalised fear of terrorist acts would not trigger this exception.

The proportionality principle, together with the danger exception, can produce a rational regulatory framework for targeted searches and seizures using surveillance technologies. Still unaddressed, however, is the issue of when panvasive surveillance *systems*, designed to facilitate targeting of individuals, may be established. For instance, when may the state install a city-wide camera system or a tracking regime for monitoring the movements of all vehicles? When may it create data collection systems like the National Security Agency programs exposed by Edward Snowden, or the 'fusion centers' that fill the same role for local law enforcement?[45] That is the subject to which we now turn.

III. Panvasive Systems and Political Process Theory

The two concepts introduced so far—a mosaic theory of privacy protection that requires proportionately greater justification for greater intrusions, and an

---

[41] See Richard Frase, 'Comparative Criminal Justice as a Guide to American Law Reform: How Do the French Do It, How Can We Find Out, and Why Should We Care?' (1990) 78 *California Law Review* 539, 574–575.

[42] See generally David A Strauss, 'The Ubiquity of Prophylactic Rules' (1988) 55 *University of Chicago Law Review* 190, 208.

[43] See Slobogin (n 20) 23 (permitting a search 'if a reasonable law enforcement officer would believe [the search] is necessary to help avert [a serious and specific danger]').

[44] *Terry v Ohio* 392 US 26–27 ('a perfectly reasonable apprehension of danger may arise long before the officer is possessed of adequate information to justify taking a person into custody for the purpose of prosecuting him for a crime').

[45] For a description of the NSA metadata program, see Glenn Greenwald, 'XKeyscore: NSA Tool Collects "Nearly Everything a User Does on the Internet"' *The Guardian* (London, 31 July 2013) www.theguardian.com/world/2013/jul/31/nsa-top-secret-program-online-data. For a description of fusion centers, see Constitution Project, 'Recommendations for Fusion Centers' (2012) www.constitution project.org/pdf/fusioncenterreport.pdf.

exception to that rule in cases involving a serious and specific danger—have parallels in European law. European countries recognise that the concept of proportionality is crucial in determining the scope of government's ability to infringe on fundamental rights.[46] Moreover, Germany at least, limits data mining aimed at persons of interest to those situations where the government can demonstrate the mining is in response to serious threat.[47] Generally speaking, however, European law is not as well developed as American law with respect to determining when an individual may be targeted by the government.[48]

In contrast, the European Union has been much more attentive, at least in theory, to the predicate issue of when a surveillance system or program may be created in an effort to collect information that can be used to target individuals. In *Digital Rights Ireland*,[49] the European Union Court of Justice held that large-scale retention of data implicates several rights guaranteed in the European Union Charter of Fundamental Rights. It further held that this type of panvasive action is justified only if the retention is 'strictly necessary' to fight terrorism, organised crime or other serious crime;[50] justified by a court or an administrative body that is implementing duly enacted legislation;[51] and limited durationally and securely.[52]

The *Digital Rights Ireland* case sets out a framework, but is not specific in its directives. German law provides an example of a more detailed approach. As Professor Francesca Bignami has noted, in Germany, and to a lesser extent some other European countries, a programme that indiscriminately vacuums up information about large segments of the domestic population must meet several requirements, even in the national security context. In Germany, such a programme has to be (1) 'authorised by a public law or regulation'; (2) 'reviewed, in advance, by an independent privacy agency' and monitored by that agency 'to guarantee that the programme [is] being run in accordance with the law' and (3) careful to mine the information acquired 'only for certain statutorily prescribed "serious" threats and, in the case of terrorism, only if there [is] an "imminent and specific endangerment" from the threat'.[53] Further, European law (4) does not permit prolonged detention of the data accumulated and (5) often permits individuals 'to check on

---

[46] See, eg, *Rotaru v Romania* App No 28341/95, 8 BHRC 449 para 43 (May 4, 2000) (construing the Council of Europe Convention and the European Convention on Human Rights, Article 8).

[47] See *Bundesverfassungsgericht* [BVerfG], 4 April 2006, 1 FVerfGE, para 158 (German Constitutional Court decision requiring an 'imminent and specific endangerment' of a serious offence, not simply an 'abstract endangerment').

[48] For instance, compared to United States law, the warrant and probable cause requirements are diluted and exclusion of evidence is a rarity. See Christopher Slobogin, 'Comparative Empiricism and Police Investigative Practices' (2011) 37 *North Carolina Journal of International Law and Commercial Regulation* 321, 323–26.

[49] Joined cases C-293/12, C-594/12 *Digital Rights Ireland and Seitlinger and Others* (EU: C: 2014:238).

[50] ibid § 56.

[51] ibid § 62.

[52] ibid § 63 and § 66.

[53] Francesca Bignami, 'European v American Liberty: A Comparative Privacy Analysis of AntiTerrorism Datamining' (2007) 48 *Boston College Law Review* 609, 610–11.

their personal data, to ensure that it [is] being used lawfully'.[54] Finally, if information is gathered by an intelligence agency, (6) it can only be passed on to domestic
law enforcement if a factual threshold of suspicion for a 'serious' offence is met.[55]

Compare all of this to the paltry regulation of American mass surveillance
programs. Many such programs are either not authorised by legislation or are
authorised by extremely vague statutory language. For instance, numerous state
police forces have established fusion centres, which function like mini-metadata
programs by collecting financial-transaction data, credit reports, car-rental data,
utility payments, vehicle identification numbers, phone numbers and other information from government and private records.[56] Yet in most of the states where
fusion centres operate there is no legislation even recognising their existence, and
in other states the relevant statute merely references the centres without indicating the type of information that may be gathered, the purpose for which it may
be obtained, how long it may be retained, means of ensuring its accuracy, or when
it may be passed on to officers in the street (in contrast with items 3–6 above
describing German law).[57] Camera surveillance, drone usage and systemic car
tracking systems are more likely to be authorised by the relevant legislative body,
but again often in vague terms that do not address many of the data collection and
retention issues that should be addressed.[58] At the federal level, while the well-
known NSA metadata programmes supposedly do have congressional authorisation,[59] the relevant statute places few limitations on the type of information that
may be gathered other than providing that it must be useful in protecting national
security;[60] in recognition of that fact, one important lower court has held that

[54] ibid.
[55] ibid.
[56] Constitution Project (n 46) 7.
[57] See, eg, Tenn Code Ann § 67-4-601(7)(b)(i) (in the sole reference to fusion centers in the entire code, stating that municipal tax funds may be used to establish 'high technology systems that collect and share data on criminal activity and historical data with other law enforcement agencies, including fusion centers …'). See generally, US Senate Permanent Subcommittee on Investigations, 'Federal Support for and Involvement in State and Local Fusion Centers' (3 October 2012) www.hsgac.senate.gov/download/report_federal-support-for-and-involvement-in-state-and-local-fusions-centers (detailing the absence of state regulation of fusion centers and the misuse of fusion center funds by the states, and recommending specific regulations).
[58] See Somini Sengupta, 'Privacy Fears Grow as Cities Increase Surveillance' *New York Times* (New York, 13 October 2013) www.nytimes.com/2013/10/14/technology/privacy-fears-as-surveillance-grows-in-cities.html (cameras and drones); Adam Clark Estes, 'Why the FAA Isn't Worried Drones Invading Your Privacy Right Now' *Gizmodo* (12 December 2014 www.gizmodo.com/why-the-faa-isnt-worried-about-drones-invading-your-pri-1665794268 (drones); Devlin Barrett, 'U.S. Spies on Millions of Drivers' *Wall Street Journal* (Washington, 25 January 2015) www.wsj.com/articles/u-s-spies-on-millions-of-cars-1422314779 (car tracking).
[59] 50 USC § 1861(a), (b) and (c) (authorising the NSA to collect 'any tangible thing' that is 'relevant to an authorized investigated … to protect against international terrorism or clandestine intelligence activities,' with the authorization to come from the Attorney General or his or her delegate).
[60] David S Kris, 'On the Bulk Collection of Tangible Things' (29 September 2013) 1(4) *Lawfare Research Paper Series*, 18–20 www.lawfare.s3-us-west-2.amazonaws.com/staging/s3fs-public/uploads/2013/09/Lawfare-Research-Paper-Series-No.-4-2.pdf.

the statute *fails* to provide adequate legislative authority for the bulk collection of metadata.[61]

Of particular note is the absence—in virtually every state and until recently at the federal level as well—of an independent privacy agency charged with monitoring the implementation of these laws (item 2 above). According to Bignami, European privacy agencies are 'policymakers first, enforcers second.... Their resources are devoted largely to vetting government proposals for proportionality and making policy recommendations in the face of new technological threats to privacy'.[62] These agencies also ensure that the public is told about the effect of any laws that are passed.[63] Although in the US the Privacy and Civil Liberties Oversight Board, reconstituted in 2012, now appears to be fulfilling these roles at the federal level, its oversight authority is limited to national security operations and the extent of its influence remains to be seen. To date, most of its recommendations have not been implemented fully.[64] Numerous federal agencies have privacy officers, but these officials do not have the power that other administrative agencies have to create and enforce rules.[65] Their principal enforcement mechanism is a complaint filed with the Inspector General.[66]

As commentators have documented, America's failure to institute meaningful oversight of panvasive programmes can have concrete repercussions, ranging from erroneous targeting to mission creep.[67] Perhaps of most concern, the know-it-all state tends to be a state that oppresses, because officials are tempted to use in any way they can the data they obtain. Congress recognised that fact when it defunded the unfortunately-named Total Information Awareness programme in 2003, undoubtedly influenced by the programme's icon, depicting an all-seeing eye atop a pyramid accompanied by the logo 'Knowledge is Power'.[68] Even the late Chief Justice William Rehnquist, no enemy of strong law enforcement, was leery of such panvasive investigative techniques; as he wrote in 1974 soon after he joined

---

[61] *ACLU v Clapper*, 785 F3d 787 (2d Cir 2015) (holding that the programme as operated by the NSA 'exceeds the scope of what Congress has authorised'). At about the same time, Congress passed the USA Freedom Act, Pub L No 114–23, 129 Stat 268 (2015), limiting some aspects of the programme but still authorising private companies to engage in bulk collection of information, which the government then can access.

[62] Bignami (n 54) 685.

[63] ibid 648.

[64] See Privacy and Civil Liberties Oversight Board, 'Recommendation Assessment Report' (29 January 2015) 3–15.

[65] Bignami (n 54) 686.

[66] See 50 USC § 3029(c).

[67] Christopher Slobogin, 'Is the Fourth Amendment Relevant in a Technological Age?' in Jeffrey Rosen and Benjamin Wittes (eds), *Constitution 3.0: Freedom and Technological Change* (Washington, Brookings Institution Press, 2011) 19–23; Kim A Taipale, 'Technology, Security and Privacy: The Fear of Frankenstein, the Mythology of Privacy and the Lessons of King Ludd' (2005) 7 *Yale Journal of Law & Technology* 123, 143–59.

[68] See Christopher Slobogin, 'Government Data Mining and the Fourth Amendment' (2008) 75 *University of Chicago Law Review* 317, 318–19 (describing the congressional vote and the influence of the icon).

the US Supreme Court, 'most of us would feel that ... a dossier on every citizen ought not to be compiled even if manpower were available to do it'.[69]

As with the targeting issue, there are at least three methods of regulating pan-vasive surveillance. The most draconian is to ban the creation and maintenance of databases devoted to ensuring the government can develop digital dossiers on its citizens; this would be the practical effect of requiring authorisation through a warrant and individualised suspicion, since panvasive surveillance by definition is not based on suspicion. The opposite extreme is the typical American scheme—either non-existent or loose authorisation that leaves virtually all important deci-sions about the scope and operation of the panvasive system to the executive branch or to the private sector. The third, intermediate, position is to adhere to some version of the European approach described above.

Relying on John Hart Ely's political process theory, which posits that only laws that are the product of a properly functioning political process should be con-sidered legitimate,[70] here it is contended that the third approach is constitution-ally required in the US.[71] More specifically, the legality of panvasive surveillance programs should be predicated on whether: (1) they have been authorised by a legislative body (federal, state or local) in a statute setting forth an 'intelligible principle' that meaningfully guides the executive branch;[72] (2) the legislature exercises oversight or requires the executive branch to do so; (3) the executive agency provides reasons for its implementation rules; (4) the rules it establishes are substantively reasonable and well-grounded in fact, and (5) the rules are devel-oped through a notice-and-comment procedure or similarly transparent process (taking into account the need to protect investigational methods).[73] Furthermore, courts should have the authority, under what American administrative law calls the 'hard look' doctrine,[74] to ensure that the enforcement agency's implementa-tion of those rules is equitable and fair, and not aimed, for instance, solely at ethnic or religious groups or dissidents.[75]

Consistent with this framework, a few American judicial decisions have inti-mated that, when a programme is panvasive, some version of an administrative regime is necessary to curb executive discretion. For instance, in its regulatory inspection cases the Supreme Court has stated that even though warrants and

---

[69] William H Rehnquist, 'Is an Expanded Right of Privacy Consistent with Fair and Effective law Enforcement? Or: Privacy, You've Come a Long Way, Baby' (1974) 23 *University of Kansas Law Review* 1, 10.

[70] See generally, John Hart Ely, *Democracy and Distrust: A Theory of Judicial Review* (Boston, Harvard University Press, 1980).

[71] Christopher Slobogin, 'Panvasive Surveillance, Political Process Theory and the Nondelegation Doctrine' (2014) 102 *Georgetown Law Journal* 1721.

[72] This is sometimes called the 'nondelegation doctrine.' ibid 1733–37.

[73] ibid 1758–65 (describing the nondelegation doctrine and its implications for surveillance programs).

[74] See Kevin Stack, 'Interpreting Regulations' (2012) 111 *Michigan Law Review* 355, 379.

[75] See n 71, 1758–59. See also Christopher Slobogin, 'Policing as Administration' (forthcoming) 165 *Pennsylvania Law Review* __.

individualised suspicion are not required, courts must ensure that there are 'reasonable legislative or administrative standards for conducting an ... inspection ...'.[76] As a Utah court succinctly put it, '[b]oth warrants and statutes originate outside the executive branch, serving to check abuses of that branch's law enforcement power. In the absence of either of these checks, leaving authority in the hands of police alone is constitutionally untenable'.[77] Application of political process theory and the hard look doctrine would provide content to these broad pronouncements.

Consider how a court applying political process theory would analyse a surveillance programme aimed at collecting information about the Internet activities of American citizens (the following is a much truncated version of a comprehensive discussion elsewhere).[78] The court would begin by looking at whether Congress has specifically authorised the programme; a programme created solely at the behest of the executive branch would immediately violate separation of powers doctrine. Assuming authorising legislation, the court would examine, in a general way, the scope of the programme. Of course, if on its face the law is aimed at a politically powerless minority, it would be constitutionally suspect.[79] If, instead, it contemplates gathering data on everyone, it would, perhaps counter-intuitively, be less vulnerable; if members of Congress pass legislation that will affect them and their constituents in addition to others, they presumably will have internalised the costs as well as the benefits of the programme.

Next, analogous to European law, the court would analyse the extent to which the statute creates independent oversight of the implementing agency and gives concrete direction to that agency about the types of data to collect. As indicated above, political process theory requires that legislation set out an 'intelligible principle' for agencies to follow. Although as interpreted by the courts this is not a particularly demanding requirement,[80] an omnibus statutory directive to law enforcement that states, for instance, that the agency should collect 'any and all information relevant to counter-terrorism' might violate even this vacuous maxim, especially in the absence of legislative oversight.

Finally, and most importantly, the court would examine the extent to which the relevant government agency develops implementation rules for targeting individuals that are reasonable and developed through a transparent procedure. This last aspect of the analysis would be pre-empted by the Fourth Amendment if, contrary

---

[76] *Marshal v Barlow's Inc* 436 US 307, 320, 323 (1978); See also *Colonnade Catering Corpn v United States* 397 US 72, 77 (1970) ('where Congress has authorised inspection but made no rules governing the procedure that inspectors must follow, the Fourth Amendment and its various restrictive rules apply'.).

[77] *State v Sims* 808 P2d 141, 149 (Utah Ct. App. 1991).

[78] See Slobogin, Panvasive Surveillance (2014) 1755–58, 1767–74.

[79] One robust indicator of whether a minority is powerlesss is whether there is a good reason for singling the affected group out for special treatment. *cf* Barry Friedman and Cynthia Stein, 'Redefining What's Reasonable: The Protections for Policing', (2016) 84 *George Washington Law Review* 281, 336–343 (advocating for strict scrutiny in such situations).

[80] See *Whiteman v Am Trucking Ass'ns*, 531 US 457, 472 (2001).

to the Supreme Court's current stance, that Amendment applies in the way outlined in the first part of this article. Even if the Fourth Amendment does not apply,
however, political process theory and the associated hard look doctrine entitle
the courts to evaluate how the statute and regulations are enforced. If, in practice, the programme targets only certain groups for collection, it is legally suspect
despite facially permissible legislative and regulatory authorisation. A central tenet
of hard look doctrine is that the enforcing agency must act even-handedly: 'It is
firmly established that an agency's unjustified discriminatory treatment of similarly situated parties constitutes arbitrary and capricious agency action.'[81] Thus,
courts have held that, unless the rationale for the rule signals a different result, all
potential targets of a programme should be treated in the same manner.[82] Following this rule is essential to a legally adequate panvasive surveillance effort, which
otherwise might unfairly focus on disfavoured groups.

Political process theory also has implications for American attempts to obtain
personal data about people who are not residing in the United States. As construed by the Supreme Court, the Fourth Amendment only applies to citizens and
to aliens who are within the United States and have a significant attachment to
it.[83] However, even if this doctrine continues to stand, political process theory
provides a basis for arguing that aliens outside the country who are affected by
American law can challenge uneven application of that law under other constitutional provisions. As explicated by Ely, process theory entitles citizens from other
states to the same guarantees enjoyed by citizens within the state.[84] Although this
stance is based on the Fourteenth Amendment's privileges and immunities clause
(which speaks of 'citizens of the United States') and the equal protection clause
(which speaks of persons 'within [a state's] jurisdiction'),[85] Ely also argued that, as
a general matter, courts should be particularly solicitous of discrimination claims

---

[81] Joseph T Small Jr and Robert A Burgoyne, 'Criminal Prosecutions Initiated by Administrative
Agencies: The FDA, the Accardi Doctrine, and the Requirement of Consistent Agency Treatment'
(1987) 78 *Journal of Criminal Law and Criminology* 87, 103–04.

[82] See, eg, *Green County Mobilephone v FCC* 765 F2d 235, 237 (DC Cir 1985) ('[w]e reverse the
Commission not because the strict rule it applied is inherently invalid, but rather because the Commission has invoked the rule inconsistently. We find that the Commissioner has not treated similar
cases similarly'); *Distrigas of Mass Corpn v Fed Power Commission* 517 F2d 761, 765 (1st Cir 1975) ('[An
administrative agency] has a duty to define and apply its policies in a minimally responsible and even-
handed way.'); *Crestline Memorial Hospital Association v NLRB* 668 F2d 243, 245 (6th Cir 1982) (the
NLRB cannot 'treat similar situations in dissimilar ways'); *Contractors Transport Corpn v United States*
537 F2d 1160, 1162 (4th Cir 1976) ('[p]atently inconsistent application of agency standards to similar
situations lacks rationality' and is prohibited under the Administrative Procedure Act's arbitrary and
capricious standard).

[83] *United States v Verdugo-Urquidez* (1990) 494 US 259, 274–75 (requiring an individual to have
a 'voluntary attachment' to the United States in order to be one of the 'people' referenced in the
Amendment).

[84] Ely, *Democracy and Distrust* (1980) 83–84.

[85] The relevant parts of the Fourteenth Amendment read: 'No state shall make or enforce any law
which shall abridge the privileges or immunities of citizens of the United States; ... nor deny to any
person within its jurisdiction the equal protection of the laws'.

by non-Americans unrepresented in the legislature, noting that 'hostility toward aliens is a time-honored American tradition'.[86]

Thus, it can be argued that even foreigners who are not within the United States ought to be accorded privacy protection equivalent to that enjoyed by American citizens.[87] While this protection may not be identical to that provided European citizens by their own countries,[88] it at least prevents Congress from passing laws that allow American law enforcement and national security agencies to infringe foreigners' civil liberties at will, given the protections afforded American citizens.[89] That prohibition would nullify those surveillance statutes that explicitly provide less protection to foreign citizens outside the country than to citizens of the United States.[90]

IV. Conclusion

The hysteria following 9/11 and the ready availability of mass surveillance technology have been a potent one-two punch that has damaged important civil liberties protecting privacy, autonomy, and self-expression. In working through how to respond to the resulting government enthusiasm for collecting and analysing any information it can get its hands on, European and American law each have something to offer. Specifically, European law, supplemented by American administrative law principles, provides a template for regulating the establishment of technologically-sophisticated panvasive surveillance systems, and American law provides a useful model for rules regulating use of those systems to target individuals. This chapter has summarised how political process theory strengthens the case for European-style rules governing programmatic surveillance and how proportionality/mosaic theory can improve on the United States' law governing surveillance of individuals.

---

[86] John Hart Ely, *War and Responsibility: Constitutional Lessons of Vietnam and Its Aftermath* (Princeton, Princeton University Press, 1993) 161. See also Laurence H Tribe, *American Constitutional Law*, 2nd edn (West Academic Publishing, 1988) 1548–50 (noting that the court has required the States to provide strong justification for discriminating against aliens within their jurisdiction).

[87] cf *Plyler v Doe* (1982) 457 US 202, 213 ('To permit a State to employ the phrase "within its jurisdiction" in order to identify subclasses of persons whom it would define as beyond its jurisdiction, thereby relieving itself of the obligation to assure that its laws are designed and applied equally to those persons, would undermine the principal purpose for which the Equal Protection Clause was incorporated in the Fourteenth Amendment'.).

[88] Convention for the Protection of Individuals with Regard to Automatic Processing of Personal Data, (opened for signature 28 January 1981, entered into force 1 October 1985) CETS No 108 art 2(a) (defining 'personal data' that is protected as '*any* information relating to an identified or identifiable individual') (emphasis added).

[89] This position is also consistent with the United Nations' position. See United Nations Human Rights Committee, 'Concluding Observations on the Fourth Report of the United States of America' (23 April 2014) UN Doc CCPR/C/USA/CO/4, para 22 www.state.gov/documents/organization/235641. pdf (concluding that the right to privacy under the International Covenant of Civil and Political Rights applies extraterritorially).

[90] See 50 USC § 1881a(b)(1)–(5) (permitting warrantless eavesdropping only if the target is a non-US person who is not located in the United States).

Part II

Comparative Perspective

4

Privacy Federalism in the United States and the European Union: The Role of State Institutions

BILYANA PETKOVA

I. Introduction

Federalism—a term not mentioned in the United States (US) Constitution—denotes ideas that have been central to the constitutional order in America and, increasingly, around the world. Federalism as such is a disputed notion. In the US, while it was associated with centralisation when the federation was still young, more recently it has come to signify preserving or enhancing the power of the states. Conversely, in the context of the European Union (EU), federalism tends to be used synonymously with directing more power to the EU institutions. This chapter follows prevailing usage in referring to the centralised institutions at the US national level as the 'federal' government, but uses the term 'federalism' to show how both in the US and in the EU, states and localities matter as conduits for national or European policy.[1]

The conventional wisdom is that neither central oversight nor fragmentation can serve data privacy any more. In the United States, there are concerns regarding the increased fragmentation of American data-privacy law and the lack of relevant federal consolidation of sector-specific law. In the EU, where an effort to introduce harmonised, EU-wide regulation has been going on for more than four years, there has been fear of over-centralisation of powers in the European institutions. In providing legal certainty, a level of consolidation of data-privacy laws can be beneficial to individuals, businesses and law enforcement alike, but how can a legal system arrive at the right level of regulation? The value of privacy

---

[1] This understanding is consistent with the school of 'new, new federalism' in the US. See Heather K Gerken, 'Federalism as the New Nationalism: An Overview' (2014) 123 *Yale Law Journal* 1889, 1890.

is constantly debated, as is the legal framework within which to protect it. As an alternative to fully-fledged decentralisation or centralisation of data privacy policies, a model of concurrent state-federal privacy governance for both the US and the EU is suggested. Government institutions at the level of American states and European Member States have an important role to play in the construction of such concurrent data–privacy governance.[2]

This chapter proceeds as follows: Section I briefly outlines the main argument; Sections II and III first describe the role of legislative and executive bodies, in the US and the EU respectively, before going into the role played by state courts and other institutions in shaping data-privacy governance. Part IV draws some tentative conclusions from the comparative institutional analysis developed in the previous sections.

II. Institutional Analysis of Data Privacy
in the United States

Although the *status quo* has been challenged in the legal scholarship and—to some extent—in case law, at present American law does not recognise a constitutional right to privacy in data.[3] In the US, before the advent of the digital age, data privacy stood comfortably within the remit of traditional state powers. For instance, responsibility for education records of high school students fitted into the province of state education and family law.[4] Yet the US Constitution gives Congress the power to regulate interstate commerce, and in the landmark case of *Gibbons v Ogden* (1824), Chief Justice John Marshall found that pursuant to this 'commerce clause', the federal government could regulate navigable waterways 'so far as that navigation may be, in any manner, connected with commerce with foreign nations, or among the several States.'[5] In 2016, to borrow from Professor Schwartz, '…the deep streams [of commerce] in the US are not the Hudson River and the Erie [Canal]….'[6] Clearly, the internet and other advanced communication

---

[2] The present chapter does not address the related issue of the interplay between law-making by the US public sector and private ordering by contract in the US private sector. For extended discussion of that issue and interview material providing an account of that regulatory interplay, see Bilyana Petkova, 'The Safeguards of Privacy Federalism' (2016) 20:2 *Lewis and Clark Law Review*.

[3] Generally, American constitutional law affords to the individual limited privacy protections against the government but none against private actors.

[4] Lauren Henry Scholz, 'Comparing American and German Consumer Privacy Federalisms', paper presented at a conference on Federalism(s) and Fundamental Rights: Europe and the United States Compared, held at the Yale Law School, 31 October 2015 (on file with the author).

[5] *Gibbons v Ogden* (1824) 22 US 1.

[6] Paul Schwartz, 'The Value of Privacy Federalism', in B Roessler and D Mokrosinska (eds), *Social Dimensions of Privacy: Interdisciplinary Perspectives* (Cambridge, Cambridge University Press, 2015) 324.

technologies, to which data privacy is closely tied, provide the channels of commerce today and make data privacy a candidate for federal regulation.

The US Congress, however, has been drifting away from a comprehensive statutory scheme. A proposal for a federal Consumer Privacy Bill of Rights failed twice, first in 2012 and then in 2015.[7] Whereas the checks and balances of US federal lawmaking could be understood as originally designed to guard the states from federal over-reach, at present Congress' acute gridlock raises democratic concerns on both sides of the political spectrum in the US. In a dynamic area of the law like data privacy, time is of the essence: when Congress cannot deliver, state policy makers are filling up the gap. Across a wide range of legislative concerns—protecting the private social media accounts of employees, identity theft, employment opportunities for constituents with criminal records incurred decades ago, the privacy and security of student records, security breach notification laws, bans on revenge porn and law enforcement access to personally identifiable information—state laws in the US have helped kick-off a nationwide debate.

A. The Role of Elected State Institutions: The Attorneys-General in the United States

State Attorneys General play an active role in the promotion and institutionalisation of privacy-friendly initiatives in the US states. Kamala Harris, California's Attorney-General (now running for a Senate seat) and her former Special Assistant Attorney-General Travis LeBlanc, now heading the Federal Communications Commission (FCC) Enforcement Bureau, have played a decisive role in establishing a new Privacy Enforcement and Protection Unit in California and doubling the number of prosecutors protecting privacy by enforcing state and federal privacy laws in their state. What is more, in 2012 Harris entered into an agreement with major industry players such as Google, Microsoft, Apple, Amazon.com, Hewlett-Packard, Research-In-Motion and later Facebook, requiring these companies to adopt privacy policies for their mobile applications (apps) in order to comply with California's Online Privacy Protection Act (CalOPPA). CalOPPA requires operators of commercial websites that collect data from Californian residents to detail the kinds of information gathered by the website, how the information may be shared with other parties, and, if such a process exists, describe the process that the user can use to review and make changes to their stored information. In order for the Act to have teeth, it has been designed to have a broad scope going well beyond California's borders: neither the web server nor the company that created the website has to be in California to fall under the scope of the law.[8]

---

[7] See, eg, the unsuccessful 2015 version of the White House proposal: Consumer Privacy Bill of Rights Act of 2015, www.whitehouse.gov/sites/default/files/omb/legislative/letters/cpbr-act-of-2015-discussion-draft.pdf.

[8] California Business and Professions Code, Sections 22575–22579 (2004).

Privacy policy adoption in mobile applications leapt from 19% in 2011 to 72% in 2013[9] while Harris, broadly interpreting CalOPPA, commenced enforcement actions against those companies that had not yet put such policies in place. Having visible data privacy policies on companies' websites gives the Federal Trade Commission (FTC) enforcement powers under Section 5 of the FTC Act.[10]

One of the most weighty legislative initiatives of the California's Attorney-General has been the 2014 minors'-protection privacy law requiring websites to give minors the possibility to erase information that they had posted on websites.[11] The law defined minors as under the age of 18 and not under the age of 13 like the federal Children's Online Privacy Protection Act (COPPA) does, and outright forbade providers from marketing to minors certain products including alcohol, firearms, cigarettes, tattoos and tanning devices.[12] Further, in addition to initiating the changes in California's law for the protection of the privacy of minors, the California Attorney-General has also sponsored the 'Do Not Track' amendment to CalOPPA, requiring that companies collecting 'personally identifiable information about an individual consumer's online activities over time and across third party websites or online services' must disclose how they respond to browser 'do not track' signals or 'other mechanisms that provide consumers the ability to exercise choice regarding such collection.'[13]

In addition to becoming agenda-setters on their own initiative, Attorneys General have statutory enforcement powers under both federal and state law,[14]—powers that they have exercised individually, for the sake of their own state, but also collectively—in cross-border actions, in conjunction with other Attorneys General. In 2013 the Attorney-General offices of 37 states and the District of Columbia signed a $17 million settlement with Google after allegations that it circumvented Safari's default privacy settings and allowed third parties to track the browsers of users without their knowledge or consent.[15] Moreover, in another

---

[9] Ganka Hadjipetrova and Hannah G Poteat, 6 'States are Coming to the Fore of Privacy Policies' (2014) *Landslide*.

[10] 15 USC § 45(a)(2): 'The Commission is hereby empowered and directed to prevent persons, partnerships, or corporations, except banks, savings and loan institutions… from using unfair methods of competition in or affecting commerce and unfair or deceptive acts or practices in or affecting commerce.'

[11] California Business and Professions Code 568 Privacy: Internet: minors (2013–2014).

[12] ibid, Chapter 22.1 (commencing with Section 22580) added to Division 8 of California Business and Professions Code.

[13] For a detailed overview of this and other US State Attorneys General initiatives, see Danielle K. Citron, 'Privacy Enforcement Pioneers: The Role of State Attorneys General in the Development of Privacy Law', *Notre Dame Law Review* (forthcoming), 2016.

[14] On the federal level, the Attorneys General have enforcement powers under the CAN-SPAM Act, the Children's Online Privacy Protection Act (COPPA), the Federal Credit Reporting Act (FCRA), the Health Insurance Portability and Accountability Act (HIPAA) and the Telephone Consumer Protection Act, see Bernard Nash, Anne-Marie Luciano and Bryan Mosca, 'Recent Developments in State Attorneys General Enforcement' (2014) 46 *Urban Lawyer* 901, 906–907, further enlisting 17 state data breach notification statutes that require notice to the Attorneys General and pointing to examples of successful actions brought by individual AGs under state statutes.

[15] Above at n 9.

multistate settlement, Google agreed to pay $7 million for improper collection of personal information through its Street View project.[16] As a part of the settlements, Google has committed itself to educating its employees on privacy protection and to executing pro-active monitoring of employees' actions. In 2013, Doug Gansler, the president of the National Association of Attorneys General (NAAG)—an established forum for Attorneys General in the US—declared privacy a central issue through the NAAG's Presidential Initiative called 'Data Privacy in the Digital Age.'[17] Professor Judith Resnik has emphasised the significance of such 'translocal organizations of government officials': 'generally organized not by an interest (such as climate control or women's rights) but by the political units of this federation—by the level of jurisdiction (federal, state, county, city) or the kind of office (governor, attorney general, legislator, mayor).'"[18] Voluntary organisations like NAAG or the National Conference of State Legislatures contribute to interweaving the strands of the US (privacy) federalism grid. State Attorneys General are also co-ordinating their actions to send comments to federal lawmakers, as in a recent letter that 47 NAAG members sent to Congress in order to express their views on federal data-security breach-notification proposals.[19] Such input could be valuable and perhaps have even greater impact if Attorneys General are invited to testify in Congress on pending data-privacy bills.

Importantly, the state Attorneys General have not only co-ordinated their actions horizontally but have also joined efforts with the FTC, which some argue has become 'the *de facto* US data protection authority'.[20] Gansler noted: 'We pay close attention to [the FTC's] efforts to inform privacy policy through reports and testimony, and we keep in contact with them on enforcement matters as well.'[21] He pointed out as an example the collaboration between the FTC and Maryland's Workgroup on Children's Online Privacy Protection.[22] In enforcement actions, however, state Attorneys General are able to draw on state statutory protections that are sometimes stronger than the federal counterpart. For instance, the California Confidentiality of Medical Information Act (CMIA) was designed to exempt some state health laws from federal pre-emption, sometimes even when the state provisions contradict federal law.[23] This allows state officials in California, when

---

[16] Above at n 13, B Nash, A-M Luciano and B Mosca.

[17] National Association of Attorneys General, 2012–13 Annual Report, 'Privacy in the Digital Age' (2013).

[18] Judith Resnik, 'New Federalism(s): Translocal Organizations of Government Actors (TOGAs) Reshaping Boundaries, Policies and Laws' (2010) *Why the Local Matters: Federalism, Localism, and Public Interest Advocacy* 83, 94 (Liman Public Interest Program at Yale Law School).

[19] Letter from Marty Jackley, President of the National Association of Attorneys General, to the Honorable Mitch McConnell, Senate Majority Leader (7 July 2015), www.naag.org/assets/redesign/files/sign-onletter/Final%20NAAG%20Data%20Breach%20Notification%20Letter.pdf.

[20] Above at n 18.

[21] ibid.

[22] Above at n 9.

[23] California Civil Code Section 56–56.07 (2005).

bringing an enforcement action, to choose whether to bring the action in federal court under the federal law—the Health Insurance Portability and Accountability Act (HIPAA)—or in state court under the Californian statute.[24] Often bringing a HIPAA action in a federal court might not be the preferred option because the penalties available under HIPAA are more limited.[25] Further, the wording of the applicable California statute is broader than that of the relevant federal law, so any violation of HIPAA, CMIA or another state or federal statute can serve as a hook to trigger California's state competition law that in turn, unlike the FTC's Section 5 Act, provides the possibility of claiming civil penalties of up to $ 2,500 for each violation (per consumer).

Moreover, even with respect to jurisdiction (as distinct from substantive requirements and penalties), the involvement of US state courts can benefit consumer privacy in the US. In that regard, Maryland's Attorney-General Gansler appealed to state legislators to make violations of the federal Children's Online Privacy Protection Act enforceable in the state courts.[26] The enforcement of federal law by the state courts would reinforce the vindication of federal rights in cases where there are issues of under-enforcement by the federal courts, for example due to lack of standing.[27]

B. The State Courts in the United States

The controversy around the adoption of the USA Freedom Act of 2015[28] and the slow pace of reform of laws governing the processing of personal data for purposes of national security and law enforcement (Electronic Communications Privacy Act, the Foreign Intelligence Surveillance Act, Privacy Act of 1974 and Executive Order 12,333) leave a vacuum that can be filled in to a certain extent only by legislative activity in the states. Many states have state constitutional analogues to the Fourth Amendment.[29] From 'Peeping Tom laws' and bans on two-way mirrors, to prohibitions on the interception of telegraph communications and on telephone

---

[24] California Business and Professions Code Section 17200: '…unfair competition shall mean and include any *unlawful*, unfair or fraudulent business act or practice', (emphasis added).

[25] One such case was *People v Kaiser Foundation State Plan, Inc* No RG14711370 (Cal Super Ct Alameda Cnty Feb 10, 2014).

[26] Above at n 9.

[27] Robert Shapiro, *Polyphonic Federalism: Toward the Protection of Fundamental Rights* (Chicago, University of Chicago Press, 2009) (making a general argument for federal rights to be claimed at state courts, including in other areas of the law).

[28] Charlie Savage, 'Surveillance Court Rules that N.S.A. Can Resume Bulk Data Collection' *NY Times* (30 June, 2015) http://www.nytimes.com/2015/07/01/us/politics/fisa-surveillance-court-rules-nsa-can-resume-bulk-data-collection.html.

[29] See, eg, Massachusetts Declaration of Rights, art XIV; Florida Constitution art I, §23; California Constitution art I, §19. For an overview, see Stephen E Henderson, 'Learning from All Fifty States: How to Apply the Fourth Amendment and its State Analogs to Protect Third Party Information from Unreasonable Search' (2006) 55 *Catholic University Law Review* 373, 427–38.

wiretapping,[30] the states were privacy frontrunners in the area of law enforcement long before the dawn of the digital era.

The aftermath of *United States v Jones*[31] and *Riley v California*[32] is now giving privacy advocates reason for measured optimism regarding a possible re-interpretation of the Fourth Amendment. Before these two cases, the Supreme Court's so-called 'third party doctrine' meant that the Amendment places no constitutional restriction on information shared with a telephone provider, a bank, a search engine or any other third party to which information has been made available, even for different purposes.[33] The doctrine has been criticised for not being up to speed with new technologies.[34] The two recent decisions just mentioned have inspired a lively debate: some scholars favour the gradual fall into obsolescence of the third-party doctrine, while others have focused on the workability of 'a mosaic theory' under which access to information held by a third party would be limited in time and scope to avoid comprehensive profiling, while allowing law enforcement to reconcile security with privacy interests.[35] Beyond the aspirations of legal academia, civil liberties organisations have also joined forces in specifically attacking location tracking and drug prescription disclosures, as these are areas of the Fourth Amendment perceived as important not only in their own right but also because of the potential they present to pierce the third party doctrine in key contexts, and perhaps lead to its gradual demise.

State courts have an important role to play in developing this area of the law. The interpretation of a reasonable expectation of privacy in the digital era by state court judges may generate a snowball effect that would lead to a convergence toward a common standard between state jurisdictions and the private sector,

---

[30] Daniel Solove, 'A Taxonomy of Privacy' (2006) 154 *University of Pennsylvania Law Review* 477, 491–92 (providing more examples of such state laws).

[31] *United States v Jones* 132 S Ct 945 (2012).

[32] *Riley v California* 134 S Ct 2473 (2014).

[33] *United States v Miller* 425 US 435, 443 (1976). *Smith v Maryland* 442 US 735, 741–42 (1979).

[34] Stephen E Henderson, 'After United States v. Jones, After the Fourth Amendment Third Party Doctrine' (2013) 14 *North Carolina Journal of Law and Technology* 431 (showing, moreover, that the Supreme Court did not apply a strong version of the third party doctrine even before *Jones*).

[35] The former argumentation has been triggered by Justice Sotomayor's concurring opinion in *Jones*, whereas the latter is based on Justice Alito's concurring opinion in the same case. See Stephen J Schulhofer, More Essential Than Ever: The Fourth Amendment in the Twenty-First Century 126–143 (2011). See also Orin Kerr, 'The Mosaic Theory of the Fourth Amendment' (2012) 111 *Michigan Law Review* 311 (arguing against the theory because of its problematic application in practice); Christopher Slobogin, 'Making the Most of United States v. Jones in a Surveillance Society: A Statutory Implementation of Mosaic Theory' (2012) 8 *Duke Journal of Constitutional Law and Public Policy* 1, 24 and 28; Christopher Slobogin, 'Domestic Surveillance of Public Activities and Transactions with Third Parties: Melding European and American Approaches' (in this volume) (suggesting a proportionality theory of the Fourth Amendment to apply the mosaic approach); for a similar idea see S Henderson, 'Real-time and Historic Location Surveillance after United States v. Jones: An Administrable, Mildly Mosaic Approach,' (2013) 103 *Journal of Criminal Law and Criminology* 803, 820 ('[t]he threshold protection would be that a single datum of location information is not protected, a day or less of location information is moderately protected, and more than a day of location information is highly protected').

and thus could then weigh on federal judges' and legislators' understanding of this 'reasonable expectation of privacy', the concept which is decisive for marking the reach of the Fourth Amendment. Moreover, state court decisions also offer substantively compelling reasoning that prepares the ground for a possible constitutional re-interpretation or statutory legislation. In other words, state court decisions matter on a federal scale, both quantitatively and qualitatively.

In the former sense, state court interpretations of state analogues of the Fourth Amendment not only potentially add constitutional rights to the Fourth Amendment floor[36] but also are themselves relevant in defining that floor. Horizontal adaptation through state-court spillovers can be discerned pre-*Jones* if one compares the Oregon Supreme Court[37] with that of the Supreme Courts of Washington,[38] New York[39] and Massachusetts:[40] All four courts quoted each other and eventually coincided in requiring law enforcement officers to obtain a warrant before installing radio transmitters or GPS tracking devices in cars. Moreover, in requiring a warrant, state courts both pre-and post-*Jones* specifically denounced the profiling effect of locational tracking and the dangers it presents for revealing potentially sensitive information.[41] Quoting the preceding judgments of the Supreme Courts of Washington and of Oregon, the New York judges stated: 'We find persuasive the conclusions of other state courts that have addressed this issue and have held that the warrantless use of a tracking device is inconsistent with the protections guaranteed by their state constitutions.'[42]

As when serving to shed light on the interpretation of other constitutional rights,[43] absolute consensus among state courts and legislatures is not necessary for such views to influence jurisprudence at the federal level. Thus, in *Mapp v Ohio*,[44] the Supreme Court overruled its own prior precedent, influenced in part by the fact that at the time many states had overruled their own precedents in order to require suppression of evidence obtained via an unconstitutional search or seizure. When *Jones* was being decided, the four state courts just mentioned restricted GPS tracking, while 10 others did not. Although the court in *Jones* decided the case

---

[36] Above n 31.

[37] *State v Campbell* 306 Or 157, 759 P2d 1040 (1988).

[38] *State v Jackson* 150 Washington 2d 251, 76 P3d 217 (2003) ('We find persuasive the analysis of the Oregon Supreme Court in a case involving a radio transmitter attached without a warrant to the exterior of a suspect's vehicle…').

[39] *People v Weaver* 12 NY3d 433, (2009).

[40] *Commonwealth v Connolly* 454 Mass 808 (2009).

[41] *Weaver* 12 NY3d at 362; *Jackson* 150 Wash 2d at 262–63; *State v Earls* 214 NJ 564, 569 (2013) (ruling that under the New Jersey Constitution cell phone real-time locational tracking three times in one day requires a warrant based on probable cause).

[42] *Weaver* 12 NY3d at 365–447.

[43] Bilyana Petkova, 'The Notion of Consensus as a Route to Democratic Adjudication?' (2011–2012) 14 *Cambridge Yearbook of European Legal Studies* 663 (discussing nuances in the application of the consensus method to fundamental rights by the Court of Justice of the European Union, the European Court of Human Rights and the US Supreme Court).

[44] *Mapp v Ohio* 367 US 643 (1961).

on narrower grounds than those raised by those four state courts,[45] the absence
of complete consensus at the state level did not deter the majority in *Jones* from con-
demning the practice under the US Constitution. Moreover, even if the Supreme
Court may hesitate to impose nationwide departure from the status quo before a
stronger national consensus emerges,[46] there can hardly be any similar concern
on the side of Congress. Drawing on each other's decisions, the state courts that
have reviewed cellphone locational tracking post-*Jones* have thus far all ruled
against giving free reign to the practice.[47] Congress can capitalise on this trend
by amending the Electronic Communications Privacy Act (ECPA) (or the Stored
Communications Act), or by introducing the proposed Geolocational Privacy and
Surveillance Act (GPS Act) and efforts are already under way.[48] This is not to say
that the strength of an emerging consensus does not matter. Civil rights organisations' state affiliates have realised the importance of the states and are working to
improve the count of privacy-protective jurisdictions by lobbying state legislatures
to pass statutory bans on locational tracking and drug-prescription disclosure, as
well as on surveillance drones.[49] To that effect, the American Civil Liberties Union
(ACLU) has provided draft state legislative bills on locational tracking, that by
2014 had been adopted or considered for adoption in about a dozen states.[50]

When looking into the qualitative impact of state law, it is worth mentioning the
reach it has into Supreme Court separate opinions that can later serve as building
blocks for eventual constitutional reinterpretation. State courts decide cases based
on the federal Constitution or on the respective state-constitutional analogues.

[45] Scalia's majority opinion in *Jones* decided the case under trespass theory (*Jones*, 132 S Ct) whereas
the concurring opinions and most state courts applied the reasonable expectations of privacy test, first
announced in *Katz v United States* 389 US 347 (1967).

[46] Roderick Hills, Jr 'Counting States' (2009) 32 *Harvard Journal of Law and Public Policy* 17
(arguing that the Supreme Court should at most, pressure outlier states into following the course taken
by the rest).

[47] See, eg, *Earls*, above n 40; *Commonwealth v Rousseau* 990 NE2d, 543, 553 (Massachusetts 2013)
(the third party doctrine does not apply to compelled disclosure of cell site location information);
Tracey v State 152 So 3d 504 (Florida 2014).

[48] Geolocation Privacy and Surveillance Act (GPS) of 2013, HR 1312, S 639, a bipartisan initiative
that requires the government to show probable cause and obtain a warrant before acquiring the geolocational information of a US person for both real-time tracking and the acquisition of records of past
movements (except in emergency situations), available at www.wyden.senate.gov/news/press-releases/
wyden-chaffetz-stand-up-for-privacy-with-gps.act. Cf Online Communications and Geolocation
Protection Act HR 983, a similar bipartisan initiative of 2013 to modernise the Electronic Communications Privacy Act by requiring law enforcement to obtain a warrant for disclosure of stored e-mail
and other private documents and to track the movements of a person through his or her cell phone,
available at www.congress.gov/bill/113th-congress/house-bill/983.

[49] Marc Jonathan Blitz, James Grimsley, Stephen E Henderson and Joseph Thai, 'Regulating Drones
under the First and Fourth Amendments', (2015) 57 *William & Mary Law Review* 1 (stating that,
depending on how one counts, bills regulating drone flights have been proposed at the federal level
and have been enacted in between 13 and 21 states).

[50] Allie Bohm, *Status of Location Privacy Legislation in the States* (2014), www.aclu.org/blog/
status-location-privacy-legislation-states?redirect=blog/technology-and-liberty-national-security/
status-location-privacy-legislation-states.

In the latter context, state courts' reasoning could inform the federal bench in factually similar situations, because the wording of state constitutional provisions often does not diverge significantly from the text of the Fourth Amendment. For example, the first sentence of Article I, § 12 of the New York Constitution follows that of the Fourth Amendment almost verbatim.[51] Although this is not the case for a number of other state constitutional analogues,[52] what matters for the relevance of a state judgment on a federal scale is whether the ratio decidendi of the case is based on the specific wording of a State Constitution or on arguments congruent with the Fourth Amendment.

III. Institutional Analysis of Data Privacy in the European Union

Having outlined the main features of institutional interaction between the federal and the state tier in American data-privacy law, here follows a comparison between those American features to those salient in the European context. Despite structural similarities, significant differences in positive law lead the two privacy regimes to collide at times.[53] Unlike in the United States, in Europe privacy is conceptualised as a fundamental right, enshrined in the constitutions and statutes of many of the EU Member States, as well as in the Charter of Fundamental Rights of the European Union and the European Convention of Human Rights. Alongside the established right to privacy in Article 7, the EU Charter includes a separate right to data protection in Article 8. (For convenience, I use the term 'data privacy' also when referring to the European context). Importantly, EU law extends constitutional protections to both the private and the public sector. Moreover, unlike in the US, also on the statutory level, EU data protection law has been harmonised to some extent at least for the past 20 years,[54] and with the final agreement on the passage of a General Data Protection Regulation (GDPR)[55] the laws of the 28 Member States are going to be further harmonised by 2018, when the GDPR enters into force.

---

[51] New York Constitution Art I, § 12.

[52] Washington Constitution Art. I, § 7, which can be deemed broader than that of the Fourth Amendment: 'No person shall be disturbed in his private affairs, or his home invaded, without authority of law.'

[53] See case C-131/12 *Google Spain SL, Google Inc v Agencia Española de Protección de Datos* (AEPD) [2014] and Case C-362/14 *Schrems v Data Protection Commissioner*, judgment 6 October 2015 (not yet reported).

[54] European Parliament and Council Directive 95/46/EC of 24 October 1995 on the protection of individuals with regard to the processing of personal data and on the free movement of such data [1995] OJ L281/23.

[55] Proposal for a Regulation of the European Parliament and of the Council on the Protection of Individuals with Regard to their Personal Data and on the Free Movement of Such Data, COM (2012) 11 final.

Despite these differences between the US and the EU however, there are several structural similarities that shed light on an emergent model of data-privacy governance: the first has to do with the fact that privacy protections level up from the state to the supranational or the federal level, and the second with the fact that in contrast to a model of federal or state-only data-privacy power, a model of shared state-federal (or European) competence works best in this area.

A. The Role of Elected State Institutions: The Member State Parliaments

Since the GDPR would not need to be implemented on the national level to have effect, the national parliaments of the EU Member States would lose their power of discretion in the implementation of data protection laws. However, they could instead rely on leverage in the European law-making process through the political control mechanism of the so-called 'Early Warning System' detailed in Protocol 2 of the Lisbon Treaty.[56] According to this procedure, draft legislative acts are first forwarded to national parliaments, which verify their compliance with the principle of subsidiarity. The principle of subsidiarity is one of the basic caveats of 'European' federalism. It postulates that the subsidiarity test (which must be met for valid law-making at the EU level) is satisfied only if the objectives of the proposed legislative action cannot be achieved sufficiently by the Member States and the action can, by reason of its scale or effects, be implemented more successfully on the EU level. In the case of GDPR, the European Parliament (EP) took on board several of the demands raised by national parliaments in consecutive amendments of the draft regulation.

The German Bundesrat, the Belgian House of Representatives, the French Senate, the Italian Chamber of Deputies, and the Swedish Parliament all submitted reasoned opinions objecting to the Commission's proposal for harmonised legislation. In addition, the Czech Senate, the German Bundestag (or lower chamber), the Dutch Senate, as well as the Romanian and the Slovenian Parliaments submitted statements commenting on the Commission's legislative proposal and asking concrete questions about it.[57] The number of reasoned opinions disputing the

---

[56] 'Any national parliament or any chamber of a national parliament may, within eight weeks from the date of transmission of a draft legislative act, in the official languages of the Union, send to the Presidents of the European Parliament, the Council and the Commission a reasoned opinion stating why it considers that the draft in question does not comply with the principle of subsidiarity', see Protocol No 2 on the Application of the Principles of Subsidiarity and Proportionality, TEU.

[57] Belgian Chambre des Représentants, Reasoned opinion of 6 April 2012 on COM (2012) 11, (Rapport fait au nom de la Commission de la Justice, DOC 53 2145/001), French Sénat, Reasoned opinion of 4 March 2012 on COM (2012) 11, German Bundesrat, Reasoned opinion of 30 March 2012 on COM (2012) 11, Italian Camera dei Deputati, Reasoned opinion of 4 April 2013on COM (2012) 11, Swedish Riksdag, Reasoned Opinion of 22 March 2012 on COM(2012) 11, Resolution of the Czech

---

proposal on grounds of subsidiarity[58] was insignificant in terms of erecting any legal barriers to the future adoption of the Regulation, but a common thread among the opinions and statements was concern about the European Commission's choice of a legal instrument. Most of the national parliaments stated a preference for a new or amended directive over a regulation. On a related note, national parliaments were preoccupied with preserving a high level of protection on the national level, which they feared a regulation would undermine (especially in the public sector, where detailed national legislation pre-dated the proposal). In something of a contradiction, the majority of the national parliaments demanded to retain legislative discretion but simultaneously called for the strengthening of common EU guarantees for data protection in international data transfers. Another frequent concern was the empowerment of the European Commission, most notably through the proposed exercise of delegated powers previewed by the regulation in many of the provisions in the Commission's first draft.

Rather than an exercise in the legal craft of splitting subsidiarity from proportionality,[59] the Early Warning System can be best understood in the context of data privacy as a part of a political dialogue between the European institutions and the national legislatures. Through the legislative process, the European Parliament (EP) concretised what may be described as high-level demands voiced by the national legislatures. First, most likely in response to concerns about pre-existing higher national standards in the public sector voiced by the German, Belgian and French legislatures, the European Parliament proposed an amendment that extended the application of general principles of data protection not only to the employment sector as first suggested by the Commission, but also in the context of social security benefits. The amended text specified that the regulation purported to establish EU law floors, not ceilings, in these domains.[60] Second, the EP was responsive to

---

Senate on the New Framework for Data Protection, 22 May 2014, Motion approved by the Plenary of the German Bundestag on the proposal for a General Data Protection Regulation of 13 December 2012, Questions about the General Data Protection Regulation and about the specific Personal Data Protection Directive in Criminal Matters by the Dutch Senate of the States General of 15 May 15 2012, Letter of the Romanian Parliament on the General Data Protection Regulation of 3 April 2012, Position of the Committee on EU Affairs of the Republic of Slovenia on the proposed General Data Protection Regulation of 20 March 2012.

[58] If the number of Member States voting in the negative does not reach a certain threshold, the Commission may take the parliamentary opinions into account at its own discretion, but no further consequences are formally triggered in the legislative process.

[59] For a critique of the manner in which the procedure is sometimes used as a check on the proportionality of the proposed Union measure instead of on subsidiarity grounds only, see Federico Fabbrini and Katarzyna Granat, '"Yellow card, but no foul": The role of the national parliaments under the subsidiarity protocol and the Commission Proposal for an EU regulation on the right to strike' (2013) 50 *Common Market Law Review* 115.

[60] The amendment uses the language of 'minimum standards', European Parliament Legislative Resolution of 12 March 2014 on the Proposal for a Regulation of the European Parliament and of the Council on the Protection of Individuals with Regard to their Personal Data and on the Free Movement of Such Data, amend 124, COM (2012) 11 final (25 January 2012).

demands that a high level of protection be guaranteed in international data transfers, something that both the Belgian House of Representatives and the German Bundestag insisted on.[61] It further elaborated on measures intended to compensate for the lack of protection in a third country pending an 'adequacy' decision,[62] by stipulating that any measures such as binding corporate rules, standard data protection clauses or contractual clauses should respect the data subject rights valid in intra-EU processing. In particular, the principles of purpose limitation, right to access, rectification, erasure and the possibility to claim compensation were endorsed in the EP amendments. Additionally, the Members of the European Parliament suggested that in the absence of an adequacy decision, the principles of data protection by design and by default need to be observed and that guarantees for the existence of data protection officers needed to be provided.

The unequivocal insistence of Parliament on strengthening the safeguards in international data transfers culminated in the recent EU-US Umbrella Agreement, which contemplates that EU citizens will have rights of redress in US courts.[63] Finally, in accordance with the demands of the majority of national parliaments, the EP proposed amendments that would substantially limit the Commission's powers to adopt implementing and delegated acts.[64] The Commission explained the provisions as motivated by a desire to provide a general legislative framework on data protection while leaving some of the details to be specified at a later stage to avoid rigidity and ossification.[65] The EP suggested that the Commission consult the newly established European Data Protection Board instead.[66] Under the EP amendments, the Data Protection Board would be authorised to issue opinions on a lead supervisory authority at the request of any of the competent national authorities and would serve as a dispute settlement mechanism.

The success of this strategy is likely to depend on the ability of the European Data Protection Board to function as an effective venue of horizontal co-ordination

---

[61] The EP amended the Preamble of the Regulation to read: 'any legislation which provides for extra-territorial access to personal data processed in the Union without authorization under Union or Member State law should be considered as an indication of a lack of adequacy', ibid, amend 55.

[62] Much like Article 25 of the General Data Protection Directive, the Regulation requires that data transfers to non-EU countries be made only if the level of protection in the third country is deemed 'adequate'. See Case C-362/14, *Schrems v Data Protection Commissioner* 6 October 2015, (not yet reported). (invalidating the adequacy decision of the Commission regarding data transfers to the US and defining adequate to mean essentially 'equivalent').

[63] EU-US data protection 'Umbrella Agreement' signed in Brussels on 8 September 2015. The Agreement remains subject to EP approval that in turn will depend on the adoption of a Judicial Redress Bill, introduced in US Congress on 18 March 2015. See Francesca Bignami, 'The US Legal System on Data Protection in the Field of Law Enforcement: Safeguards, Rights and Remedies for EU citizens', Study for the LIBE Committee of the European Parliament, May 2015 13, available at: www.europarl.europa.eu/RegData/etudes/STUD/2015/519215/IPOL_STU(2015)519215_EN.pdf.

[64] See n 58 above, amendment 91.

[65] Commission Reply of 21 February2013 to the Reasoned Opinion of the Italian Camera dei Deputati on COM (2012) 11.

[66] The EDPB replaces the former Article 29 Working Party.

between the data protection authorities.[67] The 'one-stop shop' (consistency mechanism) seems based on the EU principle of mutual recognition that permeates many other areas of EU law. Given possible divergences between the data protection authorities (DPAs) of the Member States when they interpret EU data protection law, horizontal co-ordination seems both promising and of possible importance to other areas of EU law.

By partly outsourcing the specifics to the European Data Protection Board and leaving regulatory details to be clarified later by the co-ordinated effort of national data-protection authorities with the involvement of the European Data Protection Supervisor, the EP aimed to keep pace with innovation while avoiding over-centralisation. Evidently, while some of the national demands for stronger data-privacy protections found place in the final version of the GDPR, others had to be accommodated through concurrent governance mechanisms. For instance, while Article 35 of the GDPR's last version obliges public authorities, government agencies and—in some limited circumstances—private companies to employ a data protection officer (DPO), the German legislation has more stringent requirements in this respect. However, more demanding national requirements on DPOs such as the German ones are preserved under GDPR Article 35.4.[68]

B. The Role of Other Member State Institutions: State Courts and Data Protection Authorities

In the context of law enforcement, the role of Member State constitutional courts in invalidating acts that implemented the former Data Retention Directive, has been well documented elsewhere.[69] In the end, the European Court of Justice, in *Digital Rights Ireland*, invalidated the Directive in its entirety.[70] The ratio decidendi resembled that of the national courts, just as in the US. Secisions by state courts have had impact at the US national level. Given the lack of EU-wide data-retention legislation for the moment, it is likely to once again be up to the national constitutional courts to hear first arguments against and in favour of some re-enacted

[67] See Council Position on the Proposal for a Regulation of the European Parliament and of the Council on the Protection of Individuals with Regard to the Processing of Personal Data and on the Free Movement of Such Data, 9565/15 (11 June 2015), paras. 97–106.

[68] Proposal for a Regulation of the European Parliament and of the Council on the Protection of Individuals with Regard to their Personal Data and on the Free Movement of Such Data, COM (2012) (final) 11 December 2015. Article 35.4 reads 'in cases other than those referred to in paragraph 1, the controller or processor … may or, where required by Union or Member State law shall, designate a data protection officer …'.

[69] Francisca Boehm and Mark De Cole, 'Data Retention after the Judgment of the Court of Justice of the European Union, Report for the Greens: European Free Alliance in the European Parliament', (2014) available at: www.janalbrecht.eu/fileadmin/material/Dokumente/Boehm_Cole_-_Data_Retention_Study_-_June_2014.pdf

[70] Joined cases Case C-293/12, Case C-594/12 *Digital Rights Ireland Ltd v Minister for Communications, Marine and Natural Resources and Kärntner Landesregierung and Others* 2014, ECLI 2014: 238.

national data-retention laws.[71] Moreover, it will be up to the national courts to refer questions on the interpretation of the General Data Protection Directive or the Regulation, when the latter enters into force. Especially relevant are issues on the intersection of secondary law with the EU Charter. In the light of highly disputed national surveillance measures in the UK, France and Finland,[72] interesting questions arise especially regarding the interpretation of derogations to the data-protection provisions. In that respect, the new Article 21 of the GDPR, based on Article 13 of the Directive in conjunction with the new case law of the Court of Justice, emphasises the requirement of necessity and proportionality in national laws which restrict rights under the Regulation.

Finally, the GDPR makes the role of national data-protection authorities (DPAs) particularly prominent, since in cases of serious infringements of the data-privacy provisions of the regulation, they are vested with powers to impose fines of up to 2% of the annual turnover of the respective private companies. The Regulation establishes novel governance mechanisms for the DPAs to enforce it. The consistency and one-stop-shop mechanisms are a unique expression of what can be understood as an institutionalised version of horizontal federalism:[73] the DPAs would need to adapt to one another's enforcement cultures in a compromise-driven fashion. For example, unless specific national laws apply, the so-called 'one-stop-shop' mechanism under the GDPR gets activated.[74] In order to avoid forum shopping on the one hand, and compliance costs for companies, on the other, the 'one-stop shop' mechanism contemplates that only one DPA (lead authority) would be responsible for taking legally binding decisions (including on fines) against a company. The site of the implicated company's main or single establishment in the EU determines the lead DPA. During negotiation of the GDPR, there were concerns that businesses would locate their main establishment in EU Member States where the DPAs have the weakest enforcement approach. However, the GDPR details a structure for co-operation between the DPAs so that decisions are taken jointly and processes are put into place for situations where the DPAs disagree with one another. To that effect, the GDPR establishes a new body—the

---

[71] For newly enacted national data retention legislation in the aftermath of *Digital Rights Ireland*, see Francesca Galli, 'Law enforcement data retention and EU constitutional principles—reinventing a common framework?', (forthcoming, 2016) *Maastricht Journal of European and Comparative Law*. See also request for a preliminary reference to the Court of Justice in C-203/15 from the *Kammarrätten i Stockholm* (Sweden).

[72] See Stephen J Schulhofer, 'A Transatlantic Privacy Pact?: A Skeptical View' (Chapter 10 of this volume). See also Juha Lapapuro, '"Finish Government and the Desire to Constitutionalize Mass Surveillance": Toward Permanent State of Emergency?', *Verfassungsblog*, 31 August 2015; A. Breeden, 'France Clears Final Hurdle to Expand Spying Power', *New York Times*, 25 July 2015. On the application of the EU Charter to Member State surveillance laws, see B Petkova, 'Data Privacy Rights and Citizenship: Notes on Federalism All the Way Up', in Dimitry Kochenov, *EU Citizenship and Federalism: The Role of Rights*, (Cambridge, Cambridge University Press, 2016, forthcoming).

[73] Heather K Gerken and Ari Holtzblatt, 'The Political Safeguards of Horizontal Federalism' (2014) 112 *Michigan Law Review*.

[74] See Article 54a, above at n 67.

European Data Protection Board (EDPB) that consists of all 28 DPAs[75] and a member of the European Commission (with no voting powers). The EDPB decides by a 2/3 majority and unlike the existing advisory body consisting of Member State DPAs (ie, the Article 29 Working Party), the EDPB would be able to issue legally binding decisions. Therefore, despite open questions about how horizontal co-operation between the different DPAs will function in practice, the GDPR introduces a new mechanism that is an interesting experiment in horizontal federalism. The requirement of the Regulation for co-operation between the Member State DPAs significantly minimises the risk of a 'race to the bottom' whereby the less rigorous national enforcement standard could prevail. In addition, it potentially minimises also rigidity in enforcement—since the national DPA that espouses the strictest enforcement standard might well find itself wanting of a sufficient coalition among the rest of the DPAs.

IV. Concluding Remarks

The American experience with state leadership in privacy-friendly models promoted by the state Attorneys General can be taken as a template for federal-wide regulation, consistent with the American political economy. Data-privacy governance in the private sector (also referred to as consumer privacy), even if somewhat structurally similar to the dynamic interplay between the US private sector and the US state and national tiers is however markedly different in the European context, where the law (at least on the books)[76] places an emphasis on fundamental rights and substantive protections. In turn, both federal and state US law places emphasis mainly on the legal requirements for disclosure. It remains to be seen whether horizontal co-operation between the national DPAs in Europe can to a certain extent serve as a model for further institutionalising enforcement actions by the state Attorneys General in the US In any event, the European experience in light of both the final outcome of the GDPR that clearly does not provide for full harmonisation, as well as the *Schrems* case's insistence on the national DPAs independence[77] shows that even when consolidated, privacy laws can leave breathing space for the overlapping jurisdiction of the state tier. Finally, in the law

---

[75] Note that federal countries such as Germany, where there are more than one DPAs on the domestic level, would have to decide on their representations.

[76] Kenneth A Bamberger and Deirdre K. Mulligan, 'Privacy on the Ground: Driving Corporate Behaviour in the United States and Europe' (2015, *MIT Press*).

[77] L Azoulai and M van der Sluis, 'Institutionalizing personal data protection in times of institutional distrust within a global context: Schrems', *CML Rev*, (forthcoming).

enforcement arena, the potential role of state courts in safeguarding data privacy in both the EU and the US is notable.

To summarise, in the American and the European context, state and federal (or supranational) institutions regulate data privacy simultaneously. Rather than an anomaly, this state of affairs should be credited for the potential it carries to prevent regulatory ossification in data privacy while achieving some degree of simplification and legal certainty across jurisdictions.

5

From DRD to PNR: Looking for a New Balance Between Privacy and Security

ARIANNA VEDASCHI AND GABRIELE MARINO NOBERASCO*

I. Introduction

Since the entry into force of the Treaty of Lisbon, Article 218 TFEU has granted the European Parliament (EP) and the Court of Justice (ECJ) increased powers with respect to international treaties concluded by the European Union (EU). On the one hand, international agreements, in most cases, need to gain the approval of the EP before the Council can adopt a final decision and ratify the agreements. On the other hand, Article 218(11) entitles the EP (as well as the Council, the Commission and any Member State) to seek the preliminary opinion of the ECJ on the compatibility of the agreement with the EU Treaties.[1] Thus, in the event of an adverse opinion, the agreement cannot be concluded unless it is amended to comply with European fundamental law. Such a provision entrusts to the EP (and—albeit indirectly—to the ECJ) a new and reinforced role in overseeing and influencing the foreign policy of the Union, assessing its compatibility with the *acquis communautaire*.

It is worth noting that members of the EP have viewed this role with increasing seriousness. On 25 November 2014,[2] the EP decided to refer the Passenger Name

---

* Arianna Vedaschi wrote sections IV and V; Gabriele Marino Noberasco wrote sections II and III. The Introduction and Conclusions were written in conjunction between the authors.

[1] See Article 218(11) TFEU.

[2] EP Resolution of 25 November 2014 on seeking an opinion from the ECJ on the compatibility with the Treaties of the Agreement between Canada and the EU on the transfer and processing of Passenger Name Record data P8_TA(2014)0058.

Record (PNR) agreement between the EU and Canada—the text of which was negotiated with the Canadian authorities and approved by the Council—to the ECJ, in order to obtain an opinion on its compatibility with the Treaties and the EU Charter of Fundamental Rights.[3] The EP Resolution came a few months after the ECJ, with a landmark judgment in the *Digital Rights Ireland* case, which had declared the so-called Data Retention Directive (DRD)[4] to be in violation of EU constitutional law,[5] and set forth a number of fundamental principles with regard to data protection and the right to privacy, vis-à-vis security needs and counter-terrorism measures.

In fact, in the above-mentioned Resolution, the EP made explicit reference to this ECJ judgment, casting serious doubts on the legitimacy of the PNR agreement in the light of Article 16 TFEU (protection of personal data by EU institutions), as well as Articles 7 (protection of private and family life), 8 (data protection) and 52 (scope of protected rights) of the EU Charter of Fundamental Rights.

Indeed, in October 2015, the principles clearly set forth in *Digital Rights Ireland* were further confirmed and developed by the ECJ in the *Schrems* judgment,[6] which led to the invalidation of the Safe Harbour agreement,[7] concluded by the EU and the US in 2000.[8]

Starting from the general remarks made by the EP around the 'uncertain' legitimacy of the agreement, this chapter analyses PNR agreements concluded by the EU, with the US and Canada[9] respectively (as well as proposed legislation at EU

---

[3] Case A-1/15, pending.

[4] Directive 2006/24/EC of the European Parliament and of the Council of 15 March 2006 [2006] OJ L105/54.

[5] Joined Cases C-293/12 and C-594/12 *Digital Rights Ireland v Minister of Communication, Marine and Natural Resources et al* [2013] ECR I-845. For an in depth analysis of Directive 2006/24/EC and the court judgment see, eg, A Vedaschi and V Lubello, 'Data Retention and its Implications for the Fundamental Right to Privacy. A European perspective' (2014) 20 *Tilburg Law Review* 14; F Fabbrini, 'Human Rights in the Digital Age: The European Court of Justice Ruling in the Data Retention Case and its Lessons for Privacy and Surveillance in the U.S.' (2015) 28 *Harvard Human Rights Journal* 65. For different perspectives on the potential effects of the court judgment see also E Guild and S Carrera, 'The Political and Judicial Life of Metadata: Digital Rights Ireland and the Trail of the Data Retention Directive' (2014) 65 *CEPS Papers in Liberty and Security in Europe*; MH Murphy, 'Data Retention in the Aftermath of Digital Rights Ireland and Seitlinger' (2014) 24 *Irish Criminal Law Journal* 105; N Vainio and S Miettinen, 'Telecommunications data retention after Digital Rights Ireland: legislative and judicial reactions in the Member States' (2015) 23 *International Journal of Law and Information Technology* 290; MP Granger and K Irion, 'The Court of Justice and the Data Retention Directive in Digital Rights Ireland: Telling Off the EU Legislator and Teaching a Lesson in Privacy and Data Protection' (2014) 39 *European Law Review* 835.

[6] Case C-362/14 *Schrems v Data Protection Commissioner*, judgment 6 October 2015 (not yet reported).

[7] The so-called Safe Harbour agreement between the US and the EU introduced a common European legal framework to allow the transfer of EU citizens' data to US companies, for commercial purposes. Safe Harbour was mainly based on a self-certification process by US companies, which committed to comply with data protection standards provided by the agreement.

[8] Commission Decision 2000/520/EC of 26 July 2000, [2000] OJ L215/7.

[9] It should be pointed out that the EU entered into analogous agreements with Australia in 2008 and ultimately in 2012. The EU Commission is currently negotiating a similar instrument with Mexico,

level), in order to assess their compatibility with the principles set out by the ECJ in *Digital Rights Ireland*, and further confirmed in *Schrems*. In particular, this chapter aims at understanding the predictable outcome of the judgment demanded from the ECJ, and its potential effects on the PNR agreement between the EU and the US. Moreover, it discusses the path that should be followed to draft a PNR Directive, after the proposal by the Commission[10] was firstly rejected en bloc by the EP Committee on Civil Liberties, Justice and Home Affairs (LIBE Committee) in April 2013,[11] and a significant number of amendments were barely approved by the Committee itself in July 2015.[12] The analysis will also take into account the strong 'emotional legacy' left behind by the terrorist attacks which occurred in Paris in January and November 2015, arguing that it should not influence the ECJ's ruling and further decision-making by European institutions and Member States.

In conclusion, the chapter expresses the wish that, through the action of the EP and the ECJ, the EU might find a reasonable and proportionate balance between privacy and security, acting more as a data protector than as a data collector.

The chapter is divided as follows: section II and III provide an essential analysis of PNR agreements between the EU and the US and Canada respectively. Section IV outlines the main criticalities of such agreements in the light of the legitimacy doubts raised by the EP and the principles set forth by the ECJ. Section V is dedicated to discussing the possible outcome of the ECJ judgment and its influence on existing PNR agreements as well as on the forthcoming PNR Directive. Some brief concluding remarks follow.

---

whose final text will expectedly be influenced by the Court's opinion on the EU-Canada agreement. Far from being an encyclopaedic discussion on existing PNR agreements, this analysis will be purposely limited to the cases of Canada and the US, due to the specific relevance of the first one with regard to the Resolution at stake and—by contrast—to the global relevance of the second one as the first example of 'aggressive' PNR policy.

[10] European Commission, Proposal for a Directive of the European Parliament and of the Council on the use of Passenger Name Record data for the prevention, detection, investigation and prosecution of terrorist offences and serious crime, COM (2011) 32.

[11] On 24 April 2013 the LIBE Committee rejected the Proposal drafted by the Commission by 30 to 25 votes.

[12] On 15 July 2015 the LIBE Committee approved a wide set of amendments to the initial draft, by a vote of 32 to 27. The Committee also voted to open negotiations with the Council of Ministers to reach an agreement on the final text. While this book was being published, Directive 2016/681/EU of the European Parliament and of the Council of 27 April 2016 on the use of passenger name record (PNR) data for the prevention, detection, investigation and prosecution of terrorist offences and serious crime, [2016] OJ L119/132, was definitively approved by the EP (final vote occurred on 14 April 2016) and by the Council (final vote occurred on 21 April 2016).

II. The EU–US PNR Agreements

The pressing need to reach an agreement for the transfer of PNR data from the EU to the other side of the Atlantic has emerged clearly since the 9/11 attacks. In the wake of these atrocities, by means of the US Aviation and Transportation Security Act of 2001,[13] the US Congress obliged airline carriers flying into the US to provide the US Customs and Border Control in advance with passengers' data, collected by means of the airlines reservation systems, with the threat of severe sanctions envisioned.

Such an obligation immediately appeared to be incompatible with European law and in particular with Article 25 of the Data Protection Directive (DPD), which prohibits personal data originated within Member States to be transferred to third countries unless they provide 'an adequate level of protection'.[14]

Consequently, European airline carriers found themselves facing an insurmountable problem, ie, that of being required by US domestic law to behave in breach of EU law, should they wish to maintain their routes towards the US. At the time, the EP[15] and the Article 29 Working Party[16] expressed serious concerns on the unilateral initiative taken by the US, calling into question the effectiveness and necessity of the indiscriminate collection of PNR data in the name of the fight against international terrorism. These dissenting voices, however, went mostly unheeded.

Having obtained a prorogation of the entry into force of the obligations provided by the US Aviation and Transportation Security Act, until March 2003, the Commission initiated negotiations with US authorities to reach a consensus on the transfer of PNR data.[17] The agreement was officially signed on 28 May 2004.[18]

---

[13] Public Law 107–71 of 19 November 2001 and, in particular, s 115. The Act inter al established a new law enforcement body: the Transportation Security Administration (TSA), within the Department of Transportation. TSA was later transferred under the responsibility of the Department of Homeland Security by the Homeland Security Act of 2002, Public Law 107–296 of 25 November 2002.

[14] Directive 95/46/EC of the European Parliament and of the Council of 24 October 1995 on the protection of individuals with regard to the processing of personal data and on the free movement of such data [1995] OJ L281/31.

[15] EP Resolution of 13 March 2003 on transfer of personal data by airlines in the case of transatlantic flights [2004] OJ C61/381; EP Resolution of 9 October 2003 on transfer of personal data by airlines in the case of transatlantic flights: state of negotiations with the USA [2004] OJ C81/105.

[16] The Article 29 Working Party is an independent advisory board within the EU, established by Directive 95/46/EC, which includes: (i) a representative for data protection authorities set up in each Member State; (ii) a representative for the European Data Protection Supervisor and (iii) a representative for the European Commission. See, in particular, Opinion 4/2003, adopted 13 June 2003, on the Level of Protection ensured in the US for the Transfer of Passengers' Data.

[17] On the one side, undertakings were given by the US Customs and Border Protection as to the use and retention of PNR data: Undertakings of the US Bureau of Customs and Border Protection and the US Transportation Security Administration of 11 May 2004. On the other side, the Commission formally recognised the adequacy of US undertakings with regard to the protection standards set forth by Directive 95/46: Commission Decision 2004/535/EC, of 14 May 2004, on the adequate protection of personal data contained in the Passenger Name Record of air passengers transferred to the US Bureau of Customs and Border Protection [2004] OJ L235/11.

[18] See Council Decision 2004/496/CE, of 17 May 2004, on the conclusion of an Agreement between the European Community and the United States on the processing and transfer of PNR data by Air

The reason for the PNR data transfer to the US was given as being an essential element in the fight against terrorist-related offences and other serious crimes, including organised crime. Pursuant to the agreement, 34 different categories of passenger data (with the exclusion, under normal circumstances, of sensitive data) were to be transferred from airline carriers to US authorities, by means of a 'pull' system: customs officers were authorised to directly access airline carriers' databases and extract data, without the need for the carriers themselves to actively co-operate in the transfer. The retention period by the US Customs and Border Protection was identified as three and a half years (possibly extended by a further eight years in the case of an investigation), followed by complete destruction of the records.

The EP expressed its concerns about the dangerous restriction of fundamental rights entailed by the agreement. In particular, stronger criticism was directed at the extreme vagueness of the purposes declared by the agreement itself, regarded as a violation of the 'specific purpose' principle, that requires the clear identification of the aims to be pursued by means of legislation that restricts fundamental rights. Moreover, the enormous amount of data transferred and the extended retention period were called severely into question as regards the necessity and proportionality to pursue the purpose of the agreement itself.[19]

It is for these reasons that the EP and the European Data Protection Supervisor applied to the ECJ to obtain the annulment of the Commission's Decision on the adequacy of US undertakings and the Council's Decision on the conclusion of the agreement.[20]

In favour of the application filed by the EP and the European Data Protection Supervisor, the Advocate General (AG) of the ECJ outlined how the Decision, taken by the Council to conclude the PNR agreement with the US, lacked any legal basis.[21] In fact, the Decision was adopted pursuant to then Article 95 TEC (now Article 114 TFUE), which explicitly recalled the provisions of then Article 14 TEC (now Article 26 TFUE), aimed at 'establishing or ensuring the functioning of the internal market'. According to the AG, while the agreement certainly involved the actions of economic players (ie, airline carriers), nonetheless its declared purpose was clearly to enhance public security and reinforce inter-state co-operation in the field of criminal law. Such matters, however, were absolutely excluded from the scope of the DPD.

Carriers to the United States Department of Homeland Security, Bureau of Customs and Border Protection [2004] OJ L183/84.

[19] On the critical issues related to the agreement see also B Siemen, 'The EU-US Agreement on Passenger Name Records and EC-Law: Data Protection Competences and Human Rights Issues in International Agreement of the Community' (2005) 47 *German Yearbook of International Law* 629.

[20] According to Article 230 TEC (now Article 263 TFUE).

[21] See Opinion of Advocate General Léger, delivered on 22 November 2005 in Case C-317/04.

On 30 May 2006,[22] the ECJ annulled the challenged Decisions, ruling in favour of the EP and the European Data Protection Supervisor. To support its judgment, the ECJ wholly adhered to the formal reasoning made by the AG, without scrutinising the merits of the severe restrictions on basic rights and civil liberties, denounced by the EP and the European Data Protection Supervisor. As a consequence, while the first EU-US PNR agreement was struck down by the ECJ, European lawmakers still lacked any guidance or advice to engage in the drafting of a new one.[23]

Such a lack of guidance is evident in the interim PNR agreement between the EU and the US approved by the Council on 19 October 2006,[24] and aimed at replacing the previous agreement, while waiting for the negotiation and drafting of a new text. The interim agreement possibly aggravated the restriction placed on fundamental rights, such as the right to privacy and data protection, by the PNR programme and raised even more concerns with respect to its consistency with EU Treaties and the Charter of Fundamental Rights. In particular, in the interim agreement, no precise definition could be found as to the type and amount of shared PNR data. In addition, the 'pull' collection system was significantly extended to include US Immigration and Customs Enforcement and—in general—every office or agency within the US Department of Homeland Security. In so doing, the agreement considerably heightened the risk of data dissemination, data loss and abuses. According to the interim agreement, moreover, the only law applicable to data retention and data processing was that of the US.

Upon the expiry of the interim agreement, a new text for a final PNR agreement was approved by the Council on 23 July 2007.[25] The text was accompanied by a letter from the US administration to the EU, clearly stating that shared PNR data could be used to pursue any (legitimate) purpose whatsoever, in accordance to US law, which would have resulted in further indiscriminately widening the scope of

---

[22] Joined Cases C-317/04 and C-318/04 *European Parliament v Council of the European Union and Commission of the European Communities* [2006] ECR I-04721. A complete analysis of the case is provided by F Casolari, L'incorporazione del diritto internazionale nell'ordinamento dell'Unione Europea (Milano, Giuffrè, 2008) 146; G Gilmore and G Rijpma, 'Joined Cases C-317/04 and C-318/04, European Parliament v. Council and Commission, Judgment of the Grand Chamber of 30 May 2006 [2006], ECR I-04721' (2007) 44 *Common Market Law Review* 1081; CC Murphy, 'Fundamental Rights and Security: The Difficult Place of the European Judiciary' (2010) 16 *European Public Law* 289.

[23] In fact, while it adjudicates on the compatibility of EU legislation with the Treaties (and the EU Charter of Fundamental Rights), the ECJ has gained an increasingly central role in shaping future legislation (or, at least, influencing legislators), by setting forth the guidelines and principles it should follow and safeguard.

[24] Agreement between the European Union and the United States on the processing and transfer of passenger name record (PNR) data by air carriers to the United States Department of Homeland Security [2006] OJ L298/29.

[25] Council Decision 2007/551/CFSP/JHA of 23 July 2007 on the signing, on behalf of the European Union, of an Agreement between the European Union and the United States on the processing and transfer of Passenger Name Record (PNR) data by air carriers to the United States Department of Homeland Security (DHS) [2007] OJ L204/16.

the agreement itself. While the proposed text did reduce the amount of PNR to be shared by airline carriers, it 'enriched' their variety by including some categories of 'potentially' sensitive data, to be filtered in case they might reveal 'racial or ethnic origin, political opinions, religious or philosophical beliefs, trade union membership, and [information] concerning the health or sex life of the individual'.[26] The retention period by US authorities was considerably extended to seven years (plus a further eight years in a 'dormant' database), and access was granted to the entire Department of Homeland Security.

By contrast—and in what can probably be considered the only positive element of the new text—the data sharing system switched from 'pull' to 'push', excluding direct access of US officials to airlines' databases, but demanding active cooperation of the carriers in transmitting requested data to federal authorities.

While the proposed agreement was, in any case, to be applied provisionally, the EP suspended its final approval and passed a Resolution,[27] asking for a complete re-negotiation of the agreement itself, a decision which cast more than a doubt on its compatibility with the Treaties and the EU Charter of Fundamental Rights.

As a consequence, a new agreement was negotiated with the US, and approved by the Council on 13 December 2011.[28] Eventually, after a contested positive opinion given by the LIBE Committee on 27 March 2012, the EP gave its consent to the conclusion of the agreement on 19 April 2012.[29]

According to the last agreement (currently in force), the retention period was reduced from seven to five years, with a partial 'de-personalisation' (by masking some relevant information such as name and contact details) after six months only. At the end of the first five years, PNR data are transferred to a 'dormant' database, where they can remain from five to 10 years, before they are completely 'anonymised' (but not destroyed) by deleting any information that could allow personal identification. Moreover, should PNR data be used in criminal investigations by US authorities, they can be kept in the active database until the end of the investigation in question (and possibly well beyond five years, at the complete discretion of federal bodies). Ultimately, PNR data can be retained by US

---

[26] Para III of the letter sent by the US Secretary of Homeland Security to the President of the European Council on the collection of PNR data by US authorities, as attached to Dec 2007/551/CFSP/JHA.

[27] European Parliament Resolution of 5 May 2010 on the launch of negotiations for Passenger Name Record (PNR) agreements with the United States, Australia and Canada [2011] OJ C81/70.

[28] Council Decision 2012/381/EU, of 13 December 2011, on the conclusion of the Agreement between the European Union and Australia on the processing and transfer of Passenger Name Record (PNR) data by air carriers to the Australian Customs and Border Protection Service [2012] OJ L 186/3.

[29] European Parliament Legislative Resolution of 19 April 2012 on the draft Council decision on the conclusion of the Agreement between the United States and the European Union on the use and transfer of Passenger Name Records to the United States Department of Homeland Security [2013] OJ C258/132, 7 September 2013. The much-debated Resolution was approved by a majority vote of 409 to 226 and 33 abstentions. The rapporteur Sophie in't Veld voted against the agreement and withdrew her name from the proposal.

authorities for 15 years (and even more)[30] which—given the reversible nature of the 'de-personalisation' process—still appears to be unnecessary and disproportionate to the purpose of the agreement.

In fact, the agreement provided data to be (mainly) used to fight international terrorism and transnational organised crime, defined as the range of offences punishable by US law with more than three years in prison and being 'transnational in nature'. Furthermore, data could be used—on a case-by-case basis—to prevent situations of 'serious threat and for the protection of vital interests of any individual or if ordered by a court' or to identify persons that would be subject to 'closer questioning or examination upon arrival to or departure from the United States'. Resort to sensitive data is limited to those cases in which a life is in danger.

Such a general statement of purpose allows wide discretion to US authorities in determining the 'exceptional cases' in which data could be used, making the extended retention period a subject of even greater concern. If the question of the supreme importance of saving lives is not raised, it is still unclear who can decide when such a need, in fact, occurs.

The only positive innovation introduced by the 2012 agreement is the provision of some safeguards offered to citizens against US authorities. In particular, irrespective of their nationality, people whose data were transferred by carriers to the US Department of Homeland Security are entitled to file administrative complaints and judicial claims in the US, against any illegal dissemination or misuse related to their data. In addition, citizens are entitled to ask the Department of Homeland Security for full access to their data and to request correction in case of errors. While the provision of such minimal safeguards should certainly be welcomed, given the low level of attention paid to the rights of the individual, it nonetheless seems highly unlikely that a European citizen could bear the burden and costs of judicial proceedings in the US to protect his or her PNR data from disclosure and misuse.[31]

III The EU–Canada PNR Agreements

The systematic analysis of PNR data of inbound passengers was introduced in Canada following the Anti-Terrorism Act (2001).[32] The so-called PAXIS system,

---

[30] See Article 8 of the Agreement.

[31] See the Opinion given by the European Data Protection Supervisor, P Hustinx: Opinion of the European Data Protection Supervisor of 9 December 2011 on the proposal for a Council Decision on the conclusion of the Agreement between the United States and the European Union on the use and transfer of Passenger Name Records to the United States Department of Homeland Security [2012] OJ C35/16.

[32] Anti-Terrorism Act, SC 2001, C 41.

by receiving data from airline carriers, is able to perform an automated risk assessment and bring potential risks to the attention of Canada Border Services Agency officers in charge of the final security evaluation. Such national legislation, as happened with the US, forced the EU to reach an agreement with Canada, in order to prevent airline carriers from transferring PNR data in breach of EU law.

Negotiations to reach an agreement between the EU Commission and the Canada Border Services Agency started in March 2005 and resulted in a Decision[33] taken by the Council on 25 July 2005. This Decision, which approved the text of the agreement, made repeated and explicit reference to official Commitments,[34] issued by Canadian border authorities, on the rules and procedures for data transmission and protection. Subsequently, on 6 September 2005 the Commission issued a Decision[35] assessing the adequacy of these Commitments with respect to protection standards set forth by the DPD. The agreement was henceforth concluded and entered into force in March 2006, and is currently still in force.

Pursuant to the agreement, a set of 25 categories of PNR data is to be collected by airline carriers and electronically transferred to the Canada Border Services Agency, once the flight has departed, by means of a 'push' system. While in its statement of purpose the agreement explicitly refers to the need to ensure that PNR data are transferred in full 'respect of fundamental rights and freedoms, in particular the right to privacy', the commitments, issued by Canadian authorities, clearly state the aim of the PNR programme as 'identify[ing] persons at risk to import goods related to, or persons who are inadmissible to Canada because of their potential relationship to, terrorism or terrorism-related crimes, or other serious crimes, including organised crime, that are transnational in nature'.[36] If the wording of the latter clause appears straightforward (at least in comparison with the EU-US PNR agreement), no explicit definition of terrorism and 'serious transnational crimes' can be found, either in the agreement or in the commitments, thus permitting wide leeway for interpretation that appears—prima facie—inconsistent with a serious enforcement of the principle of purpose. However, Canadian authorities agreed not to take enforcement decisions on the sole basis of automated PNR analysis processes.

Rules governing the retention period for PNR data are set forth in the commitments only and divide data into two macro-categories. One category is for

---

[33] Council Decision 2006/230/EC of 18 July 2005 on the conclusion of an Agreement between the European Community and the Government of Canada on the processing of API/PNR data [2006] OJ L82/14. For an in-depth analysis of the agreement see P Hobbing, 'Tracing Terrorists: The EU-Canada Agreement in PNR Matters', Special Report, *Center for European Policy Studies*, 17 November 2008, available at www.ceps.eu.

[34] Commitments by the Canada Border Service Agency in Relation to the Application of its PNR Program, 11 May 2004.

[35] Commission Decision 2006/253/EC of 6 September 2005 on the adequate protection of personal data contained in the Passenger Name Record of air passengers transferred to the Canada Border Services Agency [2006] OJ L91.

[36] See the Commitments by the Canada Border Service Agency, above at n 34.

PNR data related to passengers who are not under investigation which are retained in the PAXIS database for a maximum of three years and six months, undergoing progressive de-personalisation.[37] After two years, PNR data are wholly de-personalised and personal information can be obtained by investigating officers only with the authorisation of the President of the Canada Border Services Agency. The other category, for PNR data related to passengers who are under investigation, is stored in a separate enforcement database and retained for a maximum of six years. At the end of the retention period any PNR data is destroyed.

The retention rules outlined above undoubtedly show a closer attention to proportionality requirements, when it comes to restricting individual rights such as privacy. However, re-personalisation of PNR data—during the first two years— seems to rely on the sole reasonable assessment of the investigating officer, without any proper guidance as to how to evaluate the actual necessity for accessing personal information. In addition, data relating to passengers under investigation remain available for a considerable period, with no specific rules providing de-personalisation if the investigation is closed before the expiry of the six-year term.

As regards protections and safeguards offered to EU and other non-Canadian citizens by the agreement (beside the right to access, correction and notation), the commitments seem to admit judicial redress for possible abuses or misconducts by means of a general reference to Section 8 and 24 of the Canadian Charter of Rights and Freedoms,[38] with no further specification. By contrast, the commitments provide a quite complex procedure to file administrative complaints, involving the Canadian Privacy Commissioner and EU data protection authorities. This procedure appears excessively burdensome, the outcome uncertain and—in practice— unfeasible without dedicated legal assistance.

In March 2010, as the adequacy decision taken by the Commission had formally expired in 2009,[39] the Council decided to re-open negotiations with the government of Canada, in order to reach a new long-term agreement on the transfer of PNR data. These negotiations took place following the Commission's Communication of 21 September 2010[40] and the EP Resolution of 11 November 2010[41] on the global approach to transfers of PNR data to third countries, adopted in the aftermath of the Parliament's call for re-negotiation of the EU-US 2007 agreement.

---

[37] After the first 72 hours the passenger's name is masked out and cannot be accessed unless it is deemed necessary for investigative purposes.

[38] Part I, Constitution Act, 1982, enacted as Schedule B to the Canada Act 1982—1982, c. 11 (UK).

[39] The Canada Border Service Agency has, nevertheless, undertaken to respect its Commitments until a new agreement has been reached.

[40] Communication from the Commission of 21 September 2010 on the global approach to transfers of Passenger Name Record (PNR) data to third countries, COM (2010) 492, not published in the Official Journal. See also the Opinion of the European Data Protection Supervisor of 19 October 2010 on the Commission's communication on the global approach to transfers of Passenger Name Record (PNR) data to third countries [2010] OJ C357/7.

[41] EP Resolution of 11 November 2010 on the global approach to transfers of passenger name record (PNR) data to third countries, P7_TA(2010)0397.

A first draft of the Decision[42] to conclude the new agreement was approved by the Council on 5 December 2013, and the agreement was eventually signed on 25 June 2014.

The main difference with the 2006 agreement clearly lies in the statement of purpose: the new text dropped any reference to the necessary protection of fundamental rights, such as privacy; in favour of setting out the conditions for the transfer and retention of PNR data, to ensure 'the security and the safety of the public'. A cursory reference to human rights and civil liberties protection is confined to the introductory remarks and lacks the necessary prescriptive value. Such a choice evidently reflects the changes that have occurred in EU privacy policy, from a data protection approach, enshrined in the DPD, to a data retention, security-inspired approach, whose symbol was then the DRD.

As to the legitimate use of transferred PNR data, the agreement allows Canadian authorities to process such information 'for the purpose of preventing, detecting, investigating or prosecuting terrorist offences or serious transnational crime'.[43] While it provides at least some embryonic definition of 'terrorist offences', including material and moral support to terrorism, the agreement identifies 'serious transnational crime' as any offence punishable in Canada with at least four years imprisonment, provided that it is transnational in nature. Furthermore, according to the new agreement, PNR data can exceptionally be processed, on a case-by-case basis, to protect 'the vital interests of any individual' or to 'comply with the subpoena or warrant issued or an order made by a court'.[44]

It is easy to understand how the proposed agreement considerably widens the scope of PNR collection and retention by Canadian authorities, leaving significant room for discretionary interpretations.

The new text maintains the 'push' transmission system but, departing from the 2006 agreement, it provides for a general retention period of five years, for any collected PNR data, regardless of whether the passenger is under investigation or not. After the first 30 days, PRN data should be anonymised by masking passengers' names and completely de-personalised after two years by masking any information that could lead to personal identification. However, PNR de-personalisation is a reversible process that can be authorised for investigative reasons.

In addition, according to the new text, 'Canada may retain PNR data, required for any specific action, review, investigation, enforcement action, judicial proceeding, prosecution or enforcement of penalties, until concluded'.[45] At the end of the retention period data shall be destroyed. In so doing, the new agreement causes

---

[42] See the opinion of the European Data Protection Supervisor of 30 September 2013 on the proposals for Council decisions on the conclusion and signing of the Agreement between Canada and the European Union on the transfer and processing of Passenger Name Record data [2014] OJ C51/12.

[43] See Article 3, para 1.

[44] See Article 3, para 5.

[45] See Article 16, para 5.

complete PNR data to be potentially retained well beyond the initial five years, following the needs and discretionary interpretation of Canadian authorities.

Any reference to judicial redress was scrapped in the new text that generally refers to an 'independent public authority' to oversee the compliance of Canadian officers, with the conditions set forth by the agreement and domestic law and to receive administrative complaints. The only individual right enshrined in the agreement is a (limited) right to access one's own PNR data, with no explicit mention for correction or notation.

Furthermore, the new text completely changed the Canadian approach to PNR data collection and retention, clearly altering the delicate balance between human rights and security needs that the agreement currently in force was aimed at reaching. The new text seems very much closer to the 2012 EU-US agreement described above and reflects the change of direction that the Canadian government has imposed since 2007. Indeed, from 2001 to 2007, Canadian policy with regard to PNR data rarely encountered serious criticism. Such appreciation was most probably a consequence of the absence of unreliable automated enforcement mechanisms, such as no-fly and watch lists; the common-sense adjustment of automated risk 'flagging', usually performed by Canada Border Services Agency officers; and the relatively high transparency of the processes involving PNR data and the guarantees offered for judicial and administrative redress. By contrast, since 2007 the government regulation on the *Passenger Protect Programme* has introduced fully automated controls and no-fly lists to be enforced by airline carriers, moving towards general preventive security screening, largely modelled on the one adopted by the US.

IV. Applying the ECJ Privacy Doctrine to PNR

In adopting its Resolution to refer the proposed EU-Canada PNR agreement to the ECJ, the EP expressed concerns over its compatibility with Article 16 TFEU and Articles 7 and 8 of the EU Charter of Fundamental Rights, as regards the rights to privacy and data protection. The EP further questioned the choice of Articles 82 and 87 TFEU as the legal basis for the agreement.

The EP explicitly stated that its decision was adopted in the light of the judgment of the ECJ in *Digital Rights Ireland* that declared the DRD to be invalid.[46]

As outlined above, this is not the first time the EP has called for the ECJ to assess the legitimacy of a PNR agreement with a non-EU country on the basis of a potential violation of human rights. However, with regard to the 2004 EU-US PNR agreement, the ECJ refrained from evaluating the merits of the agreement and ruled in favour of the annulment of the Council and Commission Decisions

---

[46] See above at n 5.

that concluded the agreement, on the sole assumption that they were adopted on an erroneous legal basis and—as a consequence—followed the wrong decision-making procedure. In that case, perhaps compelled by reasons of political expediency, the ECJ failed to fully perform its role of 'Guardian of the Treaties', leaving the Council and the Parliament itself without any precise indication on the path to be followed in re-drafting a fundamental piece of international legislation, as the PNR agreement with the US certainly is. The results of such 'judicial shyness' are plain to see in the PNR saga related above.[47]

In 2012 the EP was de facto forced to give its consent (which was granted by a majority vote) to the new EU-US PNR agreement, after a lively debate both within the LIBE Committee and the EP Plenary, under alleged pressures by the US Administration, threatening to suspend the Visa Waiver Program for EU countries.[48]

Since the entry into force of the Treaty of Lisbon that made the EU Charter of Fundamental Rights an integral part of the Union's basic law, the ECJ has boldly taken a firmer stance on the protection of human rights and civil liberties in the field of security policies. The judgment adopted by the ECJ in *Digital Rights Ireland* undoubtedly represents a milestone in European data-protection case-law. One which has given added impetus to a new era of stricter judicial scrutiny, the principles of which were recently confirmed—and further developed—in *Schrems*.

In what follows, the main principles outlined by the ECJ in *Digital Rights Ireland* and *Schrems* will be compared with some major points of contention that can be found in the last PNR agreements with the US[49] and Canada.[50]

---

[47] By contrast, the latest practice in EU law-making has shown an increasing overlap between the traditional role played by the ECJ as the supreme interpreter of the Treaties and its new role, as the 'wise advisor' of the EP (and European institutions at large) on the guidelines and principles to be followed, to comply with the Treaties and the Charter of Fundamental Rights in future. In a certain way, the court has agreed to 'share the burden of legislation', by making clear—with sufficient detail—its auspices on the law to come. Such an attitude by the ECJ has made the separation of powers at the EU level even less distinct. On the one hand, judicial activism in influencing lawmakers could undoubtedly improve the quality of legislation and ensure a better balance between the various interests at stake; on the other hand, it can be argued that the court has gone well beyond its institutional role under the Treaties, creating a potential imbalance for democracy itself.

[48] As rapporteur Sophie in't Veld made clear immediately after the Parliament's vote. See BBC News, MEPs back deal to give air passenger data to US, 19 April 2012, available at www.bbc.com.

[49] On the EU-US PNR Agreement, before *Digital Rights Ireland*, see E Fahey, 'Law and Governance as Checks and Balances in Transatlantic Security: Rights, Redress and Remedies in EU-US Passenger Name Records and the Terrorist Finance Tracking Program' (2013) 31 *Yearbook of European Law* 1. See also G Hornung and F Bohem, Comparative Study on the 2011 draft Agreement between the Unites States of America and the European Union on the use and transfer of Passenger Name Records (PNR) to the United States Department of Homeland Security, Study for the Green-EFA Group in the European Parliament, 14 March 2012.

[50] A comprehensive study of the effect of the court judgment in *Digital Rights Ireland* can be found in F Bohem and MD Cole, Data Retention after the Judgement of the European Court of Justice of the European Union, Study for the Green-EFA Group in the European Parliament, 30 June 2014. See also E Guild and S Carrera, 'The Political and Judicial Life of Metadata: Digital Rights Ireland and the Trail of the Data Retention Directive'. Paper 65 in *Liberty and Security in Europe* (Center for European Policy Studies, 5 May 2014, available at www.ceps.eu).

The first clear principle, set out by the ECJ, is the necessary precision of EU legislation, restricting or dealing with fundamental human rights, such as the right to privacy and data protection. According to the ECJ, clear and strict rules must be laid down as to the scope of data retention and to the legitimate use of retained data by public authorities.[51] Special attention should be paid when retained data have to be processed for a purpose that is different from the initial purpose of collection. Particularly, in *Schrems* the ECJ criticised the possibility that personal data, initially collected, transferred and retained by private entities, could end up being indiscriminately accessed by security services and law enforcement bodies, by generally referring to 'national security needs' and relying indiscriminately on the US domestic legal framework alone.[52]

The above-mentioned principle seems to apply to PNR data: in fact, such data are collected by airline carriers for commercial purposes and are eventually processed by public authorities for security purposes.

In addition, the 2012 EU-US agreement and the proposed EU-Canada agreement do not seem to identify clear and precise rules as to the scope of PNR collection and retention, thus leaving the data open to a great variety of different purposes. Although both agreements identify the fight against terrorism (and terrorism-related offences, including material and moral support) as the main purpose for collecting and processing PNR data, they both add a reference to the prosecution of 'transnational serious crimes', without adequately identifying the offences that should be included in that definition. Indeed, the meaning of the word 'transnational' is very broadly intended as the concrete or potential involvement of more than one country in the criminal activity (ie, if the suspected individual is 'planning' to escape overseas). At the same time, the 'serious' nature of the crime is linked to the minimum term of imprisonment provided by US or Canadian law for such offences.[53]

What is more, both the US and Canada reserved the right to process PNR data, irrespective of the purposes set forth by the agreements, to protect the 'vital interests' of an individual or to comply with a court order.[54]

The wide scope of PNR collection and retention provided by the agreements, along with the extreme vagueness of the wording, undoubtedly grant US and Canadian authorities a broad interpretative discretion, which overtly clashes with the grade of precision demanded by the ECJ, when it comes to sacrificing privacy in the name of security. In fact, protection of the fundamental rights to privacy

---

[51] See *Digital Rights Ireland*, para 54.
[52] See, inter al *Schrems*, para 90.
[53] Specifically, three years in the case of the US, four years in the case of Canada.
[54] In this regard, see the Opinion of the European Data Protection Supervisor, above at 31.

and private life at EU level 'requires derogations and limitations in relation to the protection of personal data to apply only in so far as is strictly necessary'.[55]

The firm stance taken by the ECJ in *Schrems* clearly reflects the core of the right to privacy from a European perspective, as the result of long-standing national traditions and the interpretation of domestic and regional courts. In fact, within the EU legal system, protection of personal data from collection, retention and utilisation by third parties (either within the private or the public sector) is generally recognised as a self-standing right, regardless of the actual harmfulness of such collection, retention and utilisation. In this perspective, the peoples' right to deny access to their own data should be granted per se; any assessment of the individual's material interest in denying such access being completely irrelevant to the protection afforded.[56]

As to the retention period, the ECJ unambiguously stressed the need to find a proportionate balance between the interest of unsuspected individuals, whose personal data are retained, and the need to effectively combat and prevent international terrorism and serious crime.[57] In this regard, both the PNR agreement with the US and the proposed agreement with Canada apparently fail to adequately protect the rights of those individuals who are not under investigation for the offences that the agreements aim at fighting and preventing. Under each of the agreements, passengers' data can be retained for a minimum of five years and, although this information is subject to progressive 'de-personalisation' and 'anonymisation', such processes are fully reversible and do not afford any real protection against data dissemination and abuses. Furthermore, by reason of investigation, prosecution or enforcement needs, generally outlined within the agreements (and whose evaluation is the sole responsibility of US or Canadian authorities) the retention period can be extended indefinitely. In the particular case of the US agreement, at the end of the retention period, PNR data are 'completely' and 'irreversibly' anonymised, but not actually destroyed.

To this extent, it is useful to consider that, as the European Data Protection Supervisor has recently pointed out,[58] no factual evidence has been advanced to

---

[55] See *Schrems*, para 92. In the words of the court, at para 93, 'Legislation is not limited to what is strictly necessary where it authorises, on a generalised basis, storage of all the personal data of all the persons whose data has been transferred from the European Union to the United States without any differentiation, limitation or exception being made in the light of the objective pursued and without an objective criterion being laid down by which to determine the limits of the access of the public authorities to the data, and of its subsequent use, for purposes which are specific, strictly restricted and capable of justifying the interference which both access to that data and its use entail.'

[56] One can consider the merely potential harmfulness of data collection: the more personal data are collected, retained and utilised, the higher is the risk of illegal dissemination and misuse (and such assumption can be true, regardless of the private or public nature of the collector).

[57] See *Digital Rights Ireland*, para 63.

[58] See Opinion 5/2015, adopted on 24 September 2015; Second Opinion on the Proposal for a Directive of the European Parliament and of the Council on the use of Passenger Name Record data for the prevention, detection, investigation and prosecution of terrorist offences and serious crime.

demonstrate the effectiveness of massive PNR collection and long-term retention, in the fight against terrorism and serious organised crime. Furthermore, no operational reason has been explicitly set out to justify PNR data retention up to five years (and more), regardless of the actual use (which, in the case of investigation, usually occurs within a reasonably short period of time from collection).[59]

There is therefore a disproportion between the extended retention period provided by the agreements and the purpose that such retention should serve. The agreements lack objective criteria to justify the wholesale retention of PNR data, irrespective of their usefulness for the purpose of fighting terrorism and with no distinction between suspected and unsuspected people, giving rise to an indiscriminate mass-surveillance system, which carries a consistent 'risk of stigmatisation'.[60]

In this sense, the 2006 EU-Canada agreement currently in force is far more protective of human rights than the new draft agreement, providing at least some distinction between subjects under investigation and 'general passengers', with different retention periods. As regards access to collected data, the 'push' systems— which requires airline carriers to actively transmit a certain data set to US and Canadian authorities—ensures that only PNR data provided by the agreements are made available for processing and retention. However, once such data have reached their destination, no clear procedure is established as to limiting access only to information that can be deemed strictly necessary in each specific case, with the obvious consequence of granting wide and indiscriminate access to a significant amount of personal data. By contrast, the ECJ clearly described access to personal data—originally collected for commercial purposes—by public authorities, as an exceptional circumstance rather than a general rule, which should be restricted to the specific purpose of preventing or prosecuting a particular serious offence.[61] This is a restriction that is nowhere to be found, either in the current EU-US agreement or in the proposed EU-Canada agreement.

Lastly, both in *Digital Rights Ireland* and in *Schrems*, the ECJ pointed out the crucial role of effective remedies in order to protect individuals against the risk of abuses and unlawful disclosure of their personal data. In this regard, independent bodies, by overseeing the day-to-day processing of PNR data, as well as judicial authorities, capable of granting prompt redress to citizens whose rights have been violated, have a fundamental responsibility in maintaining a reasonable balance between the interests at stake.[62] Notably, in *Schrems* the ECJ stressed the role of European national supervisory authorities, in investigating 'any claim concerning the protection of a person's right and freedoms in regard to the processing of

---

[59] In addition, on the practical level, indiscriminate collection of an exorbitant amount of data in order to identify a relatively small number of subjects, bears the real risk of compromising the effectiveness of the analysis itself.

[60] See also *S and Marper v UK* (2009) 48 EHRR 50; F Bohem and MD Cole, *Data Retention* (2014) 62.

[61] See *Digital Rights Ireland*, para 59.

[62] See *Digital Rights Ireland*, para 54 and *Schrems*, para 95.

personal data', without any restriction to their powers being imposed by means of a Commission Decision under Article 25 of the DPD.[63] As outlined above, however, no such review is guaranteed by the agreements. In both cases the right to file administrative complaints or judicial claims (in the sole case of the EU-US agreement) is regulated by domestic laws and involves US and Canadian bodies only, with the plausible effect of discouraging any action by foreign nationals.

As this brief analysis has shown, both the 2012 EU-US PNR agreement and the proposed EU-Canada PNR agreement are overtly at odds with the principles set forth by the ECJ in its privacy case-law. The following paragraph looks at what is considered to be the desirable outcome of the ECJ opinion on the legality of the EU-Canada PNR agreement, and discusses its potential effects on the PNR system as a whole, in the aftermath of the attacks which occurred in Paris in January and November 2015.

V. From DRD to PNR: Which Balance between Privacy and Security?

The Resolution adopted by the EP presented the ECJ with an opportunity to shape the future of European policy in a field as sensitive as public security, vis-à-vis privacy, family life and data protection. In this respect, Article 218(11) TFUE recognises the crucial role of the ECJ as the highest interpreter of the Treaties, whose opinions—whether demanded by the EP, the Council or the Commission—have a decisive influence in the law-making process.

As argued in the previous section, the proposed EU-Canada PNR agreement presents several contentious points, with respect to the principles outlined by the ECJ in *Digital Rights Ireland*, and *Schrems*, especially in the light of Article 16 TFUE, as well as Articles 7 and 8 of the EU Charter of Fundamental Rights. On the one hand, the scope of the agreement is too broad and, on the other, the reasons that would justify full access to passengers' data are subjected to a wide discretionary interpretation. Both of these aspects are in breach of the principle of precision, which is of the utmost importance when legislation comes to restricting basic rights. Cases in which intrusion into the private sphere of an individual can be legitimised by security needs should represent a *numerus clausus*, without any room for extensive interpretation.

In addition, systematic retention of an inordinate amount of PNR data, for a considerable period of time (five years or more), without any necessary correlation between the retention period and the categories of data and no distinction between suspected and unsuspected individuals, clashes with the principles of necessity and proportionality that the ECJ strenuously affirmed.

---

[63] See *Schrems*, para 99.

Furthermore, no conditions or restrictions whatsoever are provided for accessing retained data, which can be consulted and processed without any preventive independent or judicial review of the reasons for gaining access and the type and quality of information provided.

Lastly, individuals concerned do not have any effective (and reasonably feasible) judicial or administrative remedy to take action against possible abuses and to seek redress. Concerned individual citizens remain without any effective control over their own data, with no realistic chance to know where such data will be ultimately stored, by whom they can be accessed and whether or not they will be communicated to third parties, other than the original collector. In this respect, the profound difference between the level of data protection afforded in the EU and that given in the US and Canada becomes even more relevant.

In making explicit reference to the ECJ judgment on the DRD, the EP seems to have implicitly asked the ECJ to analyse the PNR agreement in the light of the principles that the same Court had set forth. In so doing, the EP decided to keep the debate on a strictly legal ground, and avoid the 'political question' that a *de plano* parliamentary rejection of the agreement would have brought along.

Nevertheless, the terrorist attack that occurred in Paris in January 2015 and the more recent outrages that occurred in the same city in November 2015, combined with disturbing trend of the so-called Islamic State to actively recruit new combatants in Europe, has urged governments to look for new and effective ways to identify potential jihadists travelling to or returning from Syria, Iraq and the Middle East in general. As a consequence, the 'PNR issue' returned to the top of the news agenda as, supposedly, the only way to exert an effective control over the movements of suspected terrorists and to develop an accurate profile of potential jihadists, in order to intercept them before they reach their final destination. Such an idea has undoubtedly influenced public opinion with regard to the necessity of a European PNR system, modelled on the one adopted by foreign countries such as the US or Canada. The Commission has been actively working on the project for a European PNR framework since 2006, but EU legislation on the matter has yet to see the light, encountering the opposition of the EP. The draft of the PNR Directive[64] was rejected by the LIBE Committee in April 2013 and the EP plenary decided to refer the project back to the Committee for further analysis.[65]

---

[64] European Commission, Proposal for a Directive of the European Parliament and of the Council on the use of Passenger Name Record for the prevention, detection, investigation and prosecution of terrorist offences and serious crime, COM(2011) 32.

[65] The draft PNR Directive (which is not analysed within this paper) substantially invoked the 2012 EU-US PNR agreement and the proposed EU-Canada PNR agreement, and therefore gave rise to the very same critical questions outlined above. In addition, the draft Directive left Member States broad discretion in widening the scope of PNR collection, retention and processing, which may result in substantial differences between national legislations. The new report on the draft Directive was presented by the rapporteur, Timothy Kirkhope, on 26 February 2015. The proposal included several amendments to ensure better compliance with the principles set forth by the ECJ in *Digital Rights Ireland*.

On 15 July 2015 the same Committee approved a wide set of amendments to the original proposal, with the declared aim of providing higher protection standards for PNR data in the light of the *Digital Rights Ireland* judgment by the ECJ. On the one hand, the scope of the new PNR Directive was limited to flights between the EU and third countries, with the relevant exclusion of intra-EU flights. On the other, however, the Committee introduced further restrictions as to the reasons for justifying the retention and processing of PNR data, which are limited to the 'prevention, detection, investigation and prosecution of terrorist offences and certain types of serious transnational crime', listed by the LIBE Committee, with each access to PNR data being duly justified and traced.

However, besides a few relevant improvements, the new PNR Directive still provides PNR data to be retained for a period of four or five years respectively—with regard to terrorist offences and other serious crimes—although it prescribes identifying information to be completely masked out 30 days after collection. According to the new framework, masked-out data will still be accessible to a limited number of competent officials and complete erasure will occur after the four or five year retention period, unless the PNR data concerned are being used for specific criminal investigations or prosecutions.

Therefore, although the efforts made by the LIBE Committee in re-drafting the PNR Directive are to be applauded, the new proposed framework for a European PNR system still contains some of the points of criticisms outlined above, with respect to the EU-US and the proposed EU-Canada PNR agreements.[66] Insofar as the new PNR Directive refers partially to the PNR agreements discussed within this chapter, the forthcoming opinion of the ECJ will necessarily exert a great deal of influence on the fate of any such Directive and the PNR system as a whole.

In spite of the particularly strong political pressure, if the ECJ were to act in accordance with the clear principles it set out in *Digital Rights Ireland*, its opinion on the proposed EU-Canada PNR agreement should probably be an adverse one. This would entail the agreement being renegotiated, following the path recommended by the ECJ itself. The scope of PNR data collection and retention should be narrowly and precisely defined by providing a specific list of offences, without any room for interpretation by law enforcement authorities. Retention periods should be generally reduced and unequivocally limited to the strict minimum, with respect to the type and quality of the information at stake. As the ECJ has outlined, bulk retention of an undifferentiated amount of data overtly clashes with the principle of necessity.[67] Moreover, clear distinctions should be introduced, as to retention period and access requirements, between data related to suspected

---

[66] See Part III above. In particular, no distinction is envisaged between PNR data related to suspected or unsuspected individuals, while the overall retention period still seems disproportionate with regard to the purposes that the new Directive aims at pursuing (and can be extended according to investigative or prosecution needs).

[67] See also A Vedaschi 'I programmi di sorveglianza di massa nello Stato di diritto. La "data retention" al test di legittimità' (2014) 3 *Diritto Pubblico Comparato ed Europeo* 1224.

or unsuspected individuals, ensuring the latter data be completely destroyed (and not only 'anonymised') after a reasonable lapse of time. Lastly, independent administrative oversight or judicial review should be granted over the activities of competent authorities, to prevent unlawful or unjustified access to PNR data and effective remedies should be established, for individuals concerned, to seek redress in case of abuses or unlawful disclosure of their data.

Such guidelines would not undermine governments' ability to deal effectively with suspected terrorists and international criminals; rather, they would ensure that an instrument to fight terrorism and prevent serious crime such as PNR data, is only used in full compliance with the necessary protection of fundamental rights.

Keeping these principles in mind, the EP should champion a comprehensive reworking of the whole PNR system, taking as the first necessary step the adoption of an EU-PNR framework, fully compliant with the Treaties and the Charter of Fundamental Rights of the EU. In particular, precise rules should be set out to allow a thorough independent (administrative or judicial) review of access requirements and conditions, as well as effective remedies to ensure prompt redress in cases of abuse or unlawful disclosure.

Only the adoption of a well-balanced EU-PNR framework would lay the necessary foundations to seek a far-reaching renegotiation of the 2012 EU-US PNR agreement, whose legitimacy would be seriously undermined by the ECJ's potentially adverse opinion on the proposed EU-Canada PNR agreement.[68]

---

[68] As noted above (see n 12), Directive 16/681, establishing the EU PNR system was eventually approved in April 2016. The adopted text has substantially retained much of the amendments passed by the LIBE Committee. Nonetheless some of the criticalities outlined within this paper remain unresolved. First of all, the scope of PNR collection and retention is generally limited to flights between EU and third countries, but each Member State enjoys the right to extend it, to include intra-EU flights, by simply notifying the Commission about such a decision. Stricter provisions proposed by the LIBE Committee, as regards the reasons justifying the processing of PNR data, were largely accepted by the EP and the Council and a specific list of offences was provided in Annex II; by contrast, any reference to the transnational nature of such offences was unfortunately lost. Pursuant to the new PNR Directive, data can be retained for a maximum period of five years, after which they have to be irreversibly deleted. Furthermore, after six months from collection, PNR data need to undergo a process of comprehensive anonymisation, with passengers' identities being available only upon request of a judge or another 'competent national authority', in conformity with the purposes of the Directive. While it contains a number of positive innovations, still Directive 16/681 fails to address some crucial issues pointed out within this paper as regards PNR collection and processing in general. First, the period of retention seems far too long to be consistent with the ECJ case-law in *Digital Rights Ireland*; second, no effective form of redress is provided by the new legislation, with the exception of the right to file administrative complaints with national supervisory authorities, to be identified or established by each of the Member States pursuant to Article 25 of Framework Decision 2008/977/JHA (which largely relies on States' diligence in establishing such authorities); third, the possibility for Member States to extend PNR collection to intra-EU flights at will appears disproportionate for the purpose of the Directive and ultimately risks jeopardising the harmonising effect of the Directive itself and the effectiveness (if any) of PNR collection.

VI. Concluding Remarks

Our analysis has shown that the proposed EU-Canada PNR agreement contains a number of inconsistencies with the principles set out by the ECJ and—ultimately—with Article 16 TFEU as well as Articles 7 and 8 of the Charter of Fundamental Rights of the EU. In particular, the proposed agreement fails to precisely and unequivocally identify the purpose of PNR retention and collection; sets an indiscriminate and excessively long retention period; and does not provide for effective judicial (or administrative) review systems, aimed both at preventing and at ensuring redress against abuses or unlawful data disclosure.[69]

The new Article 218 TFEU has given EU political institutions (namely the EP, the Council and the Commission) and Member States the chance to preventively refer proposed agreements to the ECJ, in order to seek a binding opinion. In this respect, the ECJ is called to guide legislators through the law-making process, in order to ensure EU international obligations are fully compliant with the Treaties and the EU Charter of Fundamental Rights.

As outlined above, the EP decided to avoid a potential impasse, and forestalled any political debate, asking the ECJ to rule on the legitimacy of the EU-Canada PNR agreement, on a strictly legal basis. While seemingly giving up its 'responsibility to decide' to a judicial body, in fact the EP made a reasonable choice: such a sensitive issue as PNR demands a clear legal stance, free from political influences and repercussions, capable of setting a solid ground for future law-making. Be that as it may, in making explicit reference to the ECJ judgment on the DRD, the EP seems to have asked European judges to uphold the principles that they themselves had set out, notably in *Digital Rights Ireland* and *Schrems*.

The step taken by the EP is welcomed as a positive example of inter-institutional dialogue, aimed at establishing a new and wiser balance between the right to privacy and security needs and giving shape to future EU policies and actions in this field. Therefore, there are calls for the ECJ to rule consistently with its recent case-law and to reject the proposed agreement. In times when the fear of international terrorism risks endangering democratic societies more than the terrorism itself, judges have the responsibility to preserve the rule of law from the danger of a 'securitarian drift'. In this respect, the ECJ has the chance to continue influencing European data policy, and to redraw the Union's role as a data protector rather than a data collector.

---

[69] During the final editing stages of the current chapter, on 8 September 2016, Advocate General Paolo Mengozzi issued his opinion in Case A-1/15 (on the EU-Canada PNR Agreement), identifying the same criticalities outlined by the authors and recommending the Agreement not be entered into.

VI. Concluding Remarks

Part III

Perspective of Private Corporations

6

The Possibilities and Limits of Corporations as Privacy Protectors in the Digital Age

JONATHAN HAFETZ

I. Introduction

The revelations by former National Security Agency (NSA) contractor Edward J Snowden have generated significant controversy over corporate involvement in various bulk data collection programmes developed since 9/11. On 5 June 2013, the *Guardian* reported that the NSA had been collecting from Verizon, a major US telecommunication company, the metadata of every telephone call made in the United States.[1] The following day, the *Washington Post* reported that the US government had direct access to the servers of Google, Yahoo, Facebook, and other leading US Internet companies as part of another bulk collection initiative known as PRISM, which was designed to obtain the content of certain international communications.[2] News stories also appeared about a separate 'upstream' collection programme that swept up communications—including both metadata and content—sent from a computer or network as they passed through undersea fibre-optic cables.[3] Technology companies responded with outrage and denied the government had direct access to their servers.[4] Some private sector participation was knowing, if not willing. Snowden's revelations about upstream collection

[1] G Greenwald, 'NSA collecting phone records of millions of Verizon customers daily' (2001) *Guardian* (London, 5 June).

[2] B Gellman and L Poitras, 'U.S., British Intelligence Mining Data from Nine U.S. Internet Companies in Broad Secret Program' (2013) *Washington Post* (Washington DC, 7 June). While directed at foreign targets, PRSIM also swept in the communications of US persons.

[3] J Ball, 'NSA's Prism Surveillance program: how it works and what it can do' (2013) *Guardian* (London, 8 June).

[4] R O'Harrow Jr et al, 'U.S. company officials: Internet surveillance does not indiscriminately mine data' (2013) *Washington Post* (Washington DC, 8 June); TB Lee, 'Here's everything we know about PRISM to date' (2013) *Washington Post* (Washington DC, 12 June).

supported an earlier claim by an AT&T whistleblower that the company had installed a fibre optic splitter at an AT&T facility in San Francisco that enabled it to make and provide the NSA with copies of all the domestic and international Internet activities of its customers.[5] The NSA also paid various companies millions of dollars for turning over global communications data.[6] These examples highlight a pattern, dating back decades, of the government using the private sector to help implement secret surveillance programmes.

During the Cold War, for example, the US government obtained international telegraphic traffic from major companies that originated in or passed through the United States through a programme known as Project SHAMROCK.[7] While earlier private sector co-operation was largely voluntary, it has come under increased legal regulation. Federal statutes authorise the interception and storage of wire, oral, and electronic communications, including in circumstances that do not require probable cause or a warrant.[8] The Foreign Intelligence Surveillance Act of 1978 (FISA), designed for foreign intelligence gathering, and the Electronic Communications Privacy Act of 1986 (ECPA), designed for domestic surveillance, form the heart of electronic surveillance law in the US.[9] Additionally, the Communications Assistance for Law Enforcement Act of 1994 (CALEA) mandates that telephone and Internet service providers and manufacturers of telecommunications equipment design their technology so that the government can access communications pursuant to a lawful authorisation or court order.[10]

The rise of the Internet and big data has caused the government to rely more heavily on the private sector for intelligence gathering.[11] This reliance on telecommunication companies and Internet service providers to carry out surveillance programmes intensified after 9/11.[12] Congress has facilitated private-sector participation by amending FISA on multiple occasions[13] to expand the government's authority to conduct national security surveillance.[14] The government has relied

---

[5] J Bamford, *The Shadow Factory: The Ultra-Secret NSA from 9/11 to the Eavesdropping on America* (New York, Doubleday Publishing, 2008), 188–90, 193.

[6] C Timberg and B Gellman, 'NSA paying US companies for access to communications networks' (2013) *Washington Post* (Washington DC 29 August).

[7] L Donohue, 'Bulk Metadata Collection: Statutory and Constitutional Considerations' (2014) 37 *Harvard Journal of Law and Public Policy* 757, 774–75.

[8] KN Brown, 'Outsourcing, Data Insourcing, and the Irrelevant Constitution' (2015) 49 *Georgia Law Review* 607, 638–39.

[9] DJ Solove, 'Reconstructing Electronic Surveillance Law' (2004), 72 *George Washington Law Review* 1264, 1266.

[10] Communications Assistance for Law Enforcement Act of 1994 (CALEA), Pub L No 103–414, 108 Stat 4279) (codified at 47 USC §§ 1001–10 (2006)).

[11] Brown, 'Outsourcing, Data Insourcing,' above n 11 at 620–21.

[12] See GA Singha, 'NSA Surveillance Since 9/11 and the Right to Privacy' (2014) 59 *Loyola Law Review* 861, 876–92.

[13] M Schlanger, 'Intelligence Legalism and the National Security Agency's Civil Liberties Gap' (2015) 6 *Harvard National Journal* 112, 179–80.

[14] Donohue, above n 7, at 868–69; S Schulhofer, 'The New World of Foreign Intelligence Surveillance' (2006) 17 *Stanford Law and Policy Review* 531, 548–49.

on this expanded legal authority, which dispenses with FISA's traditional requirement of individualised suspicion, to justify new bulk data collection programmes
and compel private-sector co-operation. Companies, moreover, may be operating
in grey areas, where it is unclear whether, or to what extent, they must provide user
data to the government under broad legal authorisations that they would otherwise be prohibited from sharing. Secrecy exacerbates this uncertainty by limiting
public debate and posing barriers to judicial review.[15]

The Snowden revelations prompted a backlash against technology companies,
with significant reputational and financial consequences. Several US companies lost valuable contracts and business opportunities overseas.[16] A number of
companies responded by stepping up efforts to protect their customers' privacy
through litigation, lobbying, and changes to internal policies, and launched public relations campaigns touting their efforts. This increased corporate attention
to privacy protection accelerated a process that was already underway before the
Snowden revelations. US corporations have, since the mid-1990s, devoted greater
resources to privacy, creating a more privacy-protective corporate culture in the
shadow of legal regulation, as illustrated by the employment of chief privacy officers and other privacy professionals, increased privacy training, and the growth
of new privacy practices in large law firms and audit firms.[17] At the same time,
however, corporations, particularly in the technology sector, depend significantly on revenue generated from their access to and acquisition of user data. The
Snowden revelations highlight how corporate entanglement in government surveillance programmes—whether voluntary, mandated, or within a zone of legal
uncertainty—threatens individual privacy.

This paper examines the evolving role of corporations as protectors of privacy.
The paper describes how financial and public pressures are forcing companies to
be more responsive to individual privacy concerns. It explores the ways companies
have sought to protect privacy, including by opposing government demands that
jeopardise users' privacy, issuing transparency reports, and implementing privacy
enhancing technologies, while also highlighting variations in their approaches.
The paper then examines these developments through the lens of 'Corporate
Social Responsibility' (CSR), suggesting how CSR principles map onto developing
privacy norms in this area. The paper concludes that technology companies will
face increasing pressure to protect privacy rights, but that other incentives, including corporations' own reliance on user data, will limit the scope of their efforts.

---

[15] See, eg, *Jewel v NSA* No C 08–04373, 2015 WL 545925 (ND Cal, Feb 10, 2015) (dismissing Fourth
Amendment challenge to the NSA's upstream collection of Internet traffic through installation of a
fibre optic tap at AT&T's San Francisco office based on state secrets).

[16] CC Miller, 'Revelations of NSA Spying Cost U.S. Tech Companies' (2014) *New York Times* (New
York, 21 March); M Eoyang and D Forscey, 'Beyond Privacy and Security: The Role of the Telecommunications Industry in Electronic Surveillance' (2016) *Lawfare* (11 April), www.lawfareblog.com/
beyond-privacy-security-role-telecommunications-industry-electronic-surveillance-0.

[17] KA Bamberger and DK Mulligan, 'Privacy on the Books and on the Ground' (2011) 63 *Stanford
Law Review* 247, 251.

II. Corporations and the Rise of Big Data

The quantity of data collected, stored, and analysed has exploded since the mid-1990s,[18] and the process of 'datafication' continues to intensify.[19] By one estimate, 90% of the data that exists today has been generated in the past two years, and the world creates 2.5 quintillion bites of data on a daily basis—equivalent to a new Google every four days. Much of the data generated is controlled by corporations, who use it to aggregate, analyse, and track individual preferences, offer more targeted consumer experiences, and increase their bottom line.[20] As one analysis of private sector data gathering observers, 'The more and more daily activities are mediated by technology, private sector organizations have gained the ability to conduct surveillance at an unprecedented scale, meticulously documenting individuals' communications, online and offline purchases, financial activities, travel, energy consumption, geo-location, and health.'[21] Companies such as Google, Apple, and Facebook have become 'vertically integrated up and down the digital value chain', enabling them to capture a continually increasing quantity of individuals' personal information and devices.[22] Companies generate enormous sums from the collection, use, and sale of personal data. As Neil Richards observes, 'At the broadest level, we are building an Internet that is on its face free to use, but is in reality funded by billions of transactions where advertisements are individually targeted at Internet users based upon detailed profiles of their reading and consumer habits.'[23] Through behavioural advertising and other forms of private surveillance, companies now track people's basic daily movements online.[24]

The sharing of aggregated corporate data accumulated through tweets, online purchases, sensor data (information culled from road cameras, satellites, and other recording devices), and call data records, does offer significant opportunities to improve public policy and the delivery of public goods and services.[25] But it also poses significant risks, including the disclosure of personally identifiable information that can lead not only to identity theft, but also to discrimination,

---

[18] C Slobogin, 'Government Data Mining and the Fourth Amendment' (2008) 75 *University of Chicago Law Review* 317 (noting that since at least the mid-1990s, the quantity of the world's recorded data has doubled every year).

[19] S Verhulst, 'Mapping the Next Frontier of Open Data: Corporate Data Sharing' (2014) *GovLab* (16 September) www.thegovlab.org/mapping-the-next-frontier-of-open-data-corporate-data-sharing/.

[20] S Verhulst, 'OpenUp Corporate Data while Protecting Privacy' (2014) *GovLab* (6 November) www.thegovlab.org/openup-corporate-data-while-protecting-privacy/.

[21] C Diaz, O Tene, and S Gürses, 'Hero or Villain: The Data Controller in Privacy Laws and Technologies' (2013) 74 *Ohio State Law Journal* 923, 934.

[22] ibid, 935.

[23] NM Richards, 'The Dangers of Surveillance' (2013) 126 *Harvard Law Review* 1934, 1938.

[24] ibid, 938–39; CJ Hoofnagle et al, 'Behavioral Advertising: The Offer You Cannot Refuse' (2012) 6 *Harvard Law and Policy Review* 273, 279.

[25] Verhulst, 'OpenUp Corporate Data' above n 20 (citing, for example, efforts to combat Ebola).

profiling, and other infringements on individual rights and freedoms.[26] These latter risks are particularly salient when data controlled by private companies is shared with the government. That sharing can occur in various ways, including through voluntary requests, pursuant to legal or quasi-legal process, or via commercial sale. Commercial data brokers, for example, provide an increasing array of personal information about individuals to the government for use in fusion centres and other data mining initiatives focused both on counter-terrorism and ordinary law enforcement.[27] Additionally, some companies do not merely sell data to the government, but also create and reshape their products to meet the needs of government security agencies.[28]

Focusing on data sharing is important because, even as companies collect unprecedented quantities of data, governments still possess unique power to suppress or chill dissent, association, and public debate.[29] A report by President Obama's Review Group on Intelligence and Communications Technologies (PRG), created in response to the Snowden disclosures, emphasised this chilling effect. It cited the Church Committee's warning issued 35 years earlier, when 'the capacity of government to collect massive amounts of data about individual Americans was still in its infancy'.[30] The report cautioned that the vast centralisation of information creates a temptation to use that information for improper purposes.[31] States alone have the power to conduct investigations, engage in profiling, and, ultimately, impose constraints on personal liberty, whether through incarceration or non-custodial restrictions such as the placement of individuals on watch lists or the freezing of assets.[32]

Following the Snowden revelations, the Obama administration proposed in 2014 that the telephony metadata the US government had been collecting from domestic calls remain with the phone companies, which the US could then access with enhanced safeguards.[33] The subsequent passage in June 2015 of the USA Freedom Act now requires that the phone companies maintain domestic call records and that the government obtain an order from the Foreign Intelligence

---

[26] ibid.

[27] See Slobogin, above n 18 at 319.

[28] See American Civil Liberties Union, 'The Surveillance-Industrial Complex: How the American Government Is Conscripting Businesses and Individuals in the Construction of a Surveillance Society' (2004), 26, www.aclu.org/files/FilesPDFs/surveillance_report.pdf.

[29] *United States v US Dist Ct (Keith)*, 407 US 297 (1972); DJ Solove, 'Fourth Amendment Pragmatism' (2010) 51 *Boston College Law Review* 1511, 1526.

[30] 'Liberty and Security in a Changing World: The Report and Recommendations of the President's Review Group on Intelligence and Communications Technologies' (12 December 2013), 114, www.whitehouse.gov/sites/default/files/docs/2013-12-12_rg_final_report.pdf [hereinafter President's Review Group].

[31] ibid.

[32] JC Daskal, 'Pre-crime Restraints: The Explosion of Targeted, Non-Custodial Prevention' (2014) 99 *Cornell Law Review* 327; AM Fromkin, 'The Death of Privacy' (2000) 52 *Stanford Law Review* 1461, 1470–72.

[33] C Savage, 'Obama to Call for End to N.S.A.'s Bulk Data Collection' (2014) *New York Times* (New York, 24 March).

Surveillance Court in order to access them.[34] While the US can no longer engage in bulk domestic telephony metadata collection, it can continue to require phone companies to share customer data in response to legally authorised requests. The legislative reform, moreover, affects only the bulk metadata collection programme adopted pursuant to the USA PATRIOT Act; it does not affect different programmes adopted pursuant to other legislative or executive authorities.[35]

In addition to minimising political controversy over storing vast quantities of personal data, governments can harness private sector market incentives to improve data collection and aggregation technology when data remains in the private sector's hands. In the United States, the private sector remains an attractive repository for information for surveillance purposes because private data gathering is subject to less stringent and comprehensive regulation than government data collection.[36] Individuals, moreover, generally interface with the private sector in different ways and with greater frequency than with public authorities, thus providing a richer repository of data for the government to access.[37]

Commentators have termed the growth of state surveillance powers in connection with private sector entities as the 'surveillant assemblage'.[38] They have similarly described the convergence of state and private sector interests as an 'invisible handshake', with the former seeking to enhance its ability to monitor individuals and the latter eager for government assistance in addressing threats such as fraud and piracy.[39] In short, today's conception of Jeremy Bentham's Panopticon—the all-seeing eye used to control individual behaviour[40]—encompasses the pervasive gathering, mining, and sharing of data by corporations as well as by the state.

In the United States, the expansion of corporate data sharing is facilitated by regulatory gaps. Privacy laws in the United States are commonly described as sectoral.[41] A patchwork of federal and state laws regulate specific industries, particularly those that handle sensitive private data.[42] Critics have emphasised the gaps and inconsistencies resulting from the United States' failure to enact a comprehensive legal framework to safeguard privacy rights and establish an agency dedicated

---

[34] See Uniting and Strengthening America by Fulfilling Rights and Ensuring Effective Discipline Over Monitoring Act of 2015, Pub L No 114–23, 129 Stat 268.

[35] P Eddington, 'The Minimalist Surveillance Reforms of USA Freedom' (29 April 2015) *Just Security*, www.justsecurity.org/22553/usa-freedom-surveillance-reform-minimalism/.

[36] See JD Michaels, 'All the President's Spies: Private-Public Intelligence Partnerships in the War on Terror' (2008) 96 *California Law Review* 901, 908.

[37] ibid.

[38] See KD Haggerty and RV Ericson, 'The Surveillant Assemblage' (2000) 51 *British Journal of Sociology* 605, 608–09.

[39] See MD Birnhack and N Elkin-Koren, 'The Invisible Handshake: The Reemergence of the State in the Digital Environment' (2012) 8 *Virginia Journal of Law and Technology* 1, 3–4.

[40] J Bentham, *The Panopticon Writings* (Brooklyn, Verso, Miran Bozovic ed, 1995).

[41] FH Cate, 'The Changing Face of Privacy Protection in the European Union and the United States' (1999) 33 *Indiana Law Review* 173, 176.

[42] See, eg, DJ Solove, *The Digital Person* (New York, NYU Press, 2004) 56; M Cunningham, 'Privacy in the Age of the Hacker: Balancing Global Privacy and Data Security Law' (2012) 44 *George Washington International Law Review* 643, 664.

to data protection.[43] Current doctrine limits constitutional privacy protections by denying an expectation of privacy under the Fourth Amendment in information given voluntarily to third parties and thus facilitates the government's collection and assemblage of 'digital dossiers' about individuals.[44]

The US approach to privacy law differs from Europe's more comprehensive data protection regime and more rigorous application of Fair Information Practice Principles, the set of concepts underlying modern privacy regulation and the implementation of the right of informational self-determination. Informational self-determination has been described as 'the claim of individuals ... to determine for themselves when, how, and to what extent information about them is communicated to others'.[45] The European Union Data Protection Directive seeks uniformity in Member States' protection of privacy by imposing uniform standards for the collection and use of personal data.[46] The Directive is comprehensive, defining its scope of application broadly and requiring across-the-board safeguards in the private sector's collection, processing, and use of personal data.[47] Europe's cohesive data protection regime, which treats privacy as a human right, is often contrasted with the US reliance on industry self-regulation.[48] Yet, recent scholarship suggests that the divergence in legal approaches must take account of shifts on the ground, with the increased attention and resources devoted to privacy by US companies as well as evidence of the limitations of Europe's approach of mandating highly specific procedures.[49]

The Snowden revelations underscore that the current approach on both sides of Atlantic remains vulnerable to the substantial invasions of privacy that can result from bulk data collection. In its October 2015 ruling in *Schrems v Data Protection Commissioner*,[50] the European Court of Justice (ECJ) invalidated the European Commission's 2000 decision that the US Safe Harbour Privacy Principles

---

[43] M Rotenberg, 'Fair Information Practices and the Architecture of Privacy (What Larry Doesn't Get)' (2001) *Stan Tech L Rev* 1, 48; NM Richards, 'The Perils of Social Reading' (2013) 101 *Georgetown Law Journal* 689, 702.

[44] DJ Solove, 'Digital Dossiers and the Dissipation of Fourth Amendment Privacy' (2002) 75 *Southern California Law Review* 1083, 1086.

[45] AF Westin, *Privacy and Freedom* (1967) 7. See also *Bundesverfassungsgericht* [BVerfG] [Federal Constitutional Court] 15 December 1983, Entscheidungen des Bundesverfassungsgerichts [BVerfGE] 65, 1984.

[46] Council Directive 95/46 [1995] OJ L281/31.

[47] FH Cate, 'Privacy and Telecommunications' (1998) 33 *Wake Forest L Rev* 1, 7–13.

[48] JR Reidenberg, 'E-Commerce and Trans-Atlantic Privacy' (2001) 38 *Houston Law Review* 717, 718; PM Schwartz, 'Privacy and Democracy in Cyberspace' (1999) 52 *Vanderbilt Law Review* 1609, 1627, 1629.

[49] Bamberger and Mulligan, above n 17 at 307 ('a focus on specific mandated process "risks creating an organisational culture that focuses on meeting formalities to create paper regulatory compliance (via check boxes, policies, notifications, contracts, ...), rather than promoting effective good data protection practices"') (quoting N Robinson et al, *RAND Eur, Review of the European Data Protection Directive* (2009) 39).

[50] Case C-362/14 *Maximillian Schrems v Data Protection Commissioner* judgment 6 October 2015 (not yet reported).

adequately protect the privacy of EU citizens' personal data. *Schrems* involved data transfers that Facebook's Irish subsidiary sought to make to Facebook's US servers. The Commission's 2000 decision had permitted data transfers from the EU based on a certification by US entities that their privacy protections conformed to those of the EU, including to the EU Data Protection Directive on data transfers to third countries and the EU Charter of Fundamental Rights. In invaliding the 2000 decision, *Schrems* noted the ease with which the NSA accessed the data held by US companies. (*Schrems* involved data transfers by Facebook's Irish subsidiary to Facebook's US servers).

Schrems followed the ECJ's ruling the previous year in *Digital Rights Ireland Ltd v Minister for Communications* invalidating the EU's Data Retention Directive, which had required private companies to store metadata from telephone and Internet communications.[51] The ECJ recognised the importance of protecting the public against terrorism and other serious crimes, but it concluded that the collection of metadata constituted a serious interference with privacy and that the Data Retention Directive was disproportionate and lacked adequate safeguards.[52] *Digital Rights Ireland* establishes that the retention of data itself infringes the right to privacy, regardless of whether public authorities or private companies retain the data. It thus underscores how private data collection implicates privacy concerns, independent of whether (and on what basis) that information is shared with the government.[53]

The Snowden revelations have thus focused attention both on the private sector's acquisition of data and on the vulnerability of that data to acquisition by government authorities. Not surprisingly, non-government organisations traditionally concerned with protecting privacy from government intrusion are paying closer attention to corporate conduct. The Electronic Frontier Foundation (EFF), a leading not-for-profit organisation dedicated to protecting civil liberties in the digital world, now issues annual reports evaluating major technology companies on the basis of their resistance to improper government demands for user information.[54] The American Civil Liberties Union, which has brought leading challenges to government surveillance, also focuses increasingly on encouraging companies to incorporate privacy and free speech protections into their activities, and assisting them in doing so.[55] The Constitution Project, a non-partisan organisation,

[51] Joined cases C-293/12, C-594/12 *Digital Rights Ireland and Seitlinger and Others* (EU: C: 2014:238).
[52] ibid, paras 56–66.
[53] F Fabbrini, 'Human Rights in the Digital Age: The European Court of Justice Ruling in the Data Retention Case and Its Lessons for Privacy and Surveillance in the United States' (2015) 28 *Harvard Human Rights Journal* 65, 93.
[54] Electronic Frontier Foundation, 'Who Has Your Back: Protecting Your Data from Government Requests' (2014) www.eff.org/who-has-your-back-2014#executive-summary.
[55] American Civil Liberties Union of California, 'Privacy & Free Speech: It's Good for Business' (2012) www.aclunc.org/sites/default/files/privacy_free_speech_good_for_business.pdf.

recently honored Twitter for its leadership on First Amendment and privacy issues, a sign of civil society's growing recognition of the private sector's importance in securing digital privacy.[56] As described below, companies have responded to the Snowden revelations in various ways that demonstrate an enhanced attention to user privacy, but that also suggest the limits of corporate-led privacy efforts.

III. Corporation as Privacy Protectors

Snowden's revelations of government access to corporate data, whether through broad legal authorisation, voluntary co-operation, or without corporate knowledge, have spurred companies to reinvigorate their commitment to user privacy. These efforts have taken various forms, including transparency initiatives, resistance to the disclosure of customer data, greater use of encryption techniques and other privacy enhancing devices, and public advocacy and education. Often, these initiatives overlap: a company, for example, may engage in litigation not only to increase transparency, but also to burnish its privacy-protecting credentials. While technology companies engaged in these measures before, the Snowden revelations have driven home the financial and reputational harms that can result from the perception that technology companies are inattentive to privacy concerns or insufficiently proactive in the face of expanded government data collection programmes. One study, for example, estimates the US cloud computing industry could lose $180 billion as a result of alienating users and foreign legislation discouraging their citizens from using services from American Internet companies.[57] As Microsoft's general counsel, Brad Smith, warned, 'People won't use technology they don't trust'.[58]

A. Resisting Government Requests for User Data

One way that technology companies can protect privacy is by resisting government demands for user data. In the United States, secrecy and restrictions on standing to bring suit have combined to make it exceedingly difficult, if not impossible, for individuals to oppose government surveillance orders. In *Clapper v Amnesty International*, the Supreme Court ordered the dismissal of a suit by a coalition of human rights activists, journalists, and media organisations that challenged

---

[56] The Constitution Project, 'Eighth Annual Constitutional Gala Champions' (22 April 2015), www.constitutionproject.org/events/8th-annual-constitutional-champions-gala/.

[57] E Wyatt and CC Miller, 'Tech Giants Issue Call for Limits on Government Surveillance of Users' (2014) *New York Times* (New York, 9 December 2014).

[58] ibid.

section 702 of the FISA Amendments Act of 2008 (FAA) because the plaintiffs could not establish with sufficient certainty that they had been subjected to surveillance, despite strong evidence that such surveillance was likely occurring.[59] FISA provides that recipients of directives may bring challenges under certain circumstances.[60] In one prominent case, Yahoo brought suit in the Foreign Intelligence Surveillance Court (FISC) to challenge an order seeking foreign intelligence that targeted Yahoo's customers reasonably believed to be located outside the United States.[61] While Yahoo's challenge was rejected,[62] the company sought—and eventually obtained—public release of the FISC opinions and other litigation documents.[63] In another high profile dispute, Microsoft moved to quash a warrant issued under the Stored Communications Act of 1986 (SCA)[64] seeking customer data stored on its servers in Ireland, arguing that SCA warrants do not extend to data stored overseas. The district court ordered Microsoft to produce the materials sought by the warrant and, following Microsoft's refusal, held the company in contempt.[65] The U.S. Court of Appeals for the Second Circuit reversed that decision, ruling that the SCA does not authorize courts to issue and enforce warrants against U.S.-based service providers for the seizure of customer email content that is stored exclusively on foreign servers.[66] The ruling thus requires the United States to make a diplomatic request for data located outside the country through a mutual legal assistance treaty (or another mechanism if no treaty exists), and then await the foreign partner's response.[67]

Whether, and to what extent, companies are resisting government requests to turn over user data is difficult to determine because of the secrecy surrounding the issuance of and litigation over surveillance orders. There is, however, increased pressure on companies to defend user privacy and avoid the perception of complicity with government data collection that results from acquiescing in orders based on broad legal authorisations.

---

[59] *Clapper v Amnesty International USA* 133 S Ct 1138 (2013). See also SI Vladeck, 'Standing and Secret Surveillance' (2014) 10 *I/S: Journal of Law and Policy for the Information Society* 551.

[60] See 50 USC § 1861(f)(2)(A); 50 USC § 1881a(h)(4).

[61] See *In re Directives Pursuant to Section 105B of the Foreign Intelligence Surveillance Act* 551 F3d 1004 (FISA Ct Rev 2008).

[62] ibid, 1012. It was only recently revealed that the challenge was brought by Yahoo, as the recipient of the directive.

[63] See W Bennett, 'In re Directive Documents Released' (2014) *Lawfare* (11 September) www.lawfareblog.com/2014/09/in-re-directives-documents-released/.

[64] 18 USC §§ 2701–2712.

[65] *In re Warrant to Search a Certain Email Account Controlled and Maintained by Microsoft Corporation* 15 F Supp 3d 466 (SDNY 2014) (upholding issuance of the SCA warrant); A Ely, 'Second Circuit Oral Argument in the Microsoft-Ireland Case: An Overview' (10 September 2015) *Lawfare*, https://www.lawfareblog.com/second-circuit-oral-argument-microsoft-ireland-case-overview.

[66] *Microsoft v. United States,* __ F.3d __, 2016 WL 3770056 (2d. Cir. July 14, 2016).

[67] J Daskal, 'Three Key Takeaways: The 2d Circuit Ruling in The Microsoft Warrant Case' (14 July 2016) *Just Security*, https://www.justsecurity.org/32041/key-takeaways-2d-circuit-ruling-microsoft-warrant-case.

B. Transparency

The US government not only seeks user data from companies, but also attempts to prevent companies from disclosing receipt of those efforts. The FBI, for example, commonly issues National Security Letters (NSLs), an administrative subpoena, demanding information from companies for foreign intelligence investigations, including customer records from financial institutions, telephone companies, and Internet service providers.[68] NSL demands typically include gag orders barring recipients from disclosing both the letter's contents and existence.[69] The use of NSLs has grown significantly since 9/11,[70] prompting civil liberties organisations to bring suit over gag orders on behalf of anonymous Internet service providers who receive NSLs.[71] Technology companies have responded to criticisms of their handing over user data to the government by more aggressively challenging the gag orders that accompany NSLs and other secret surveillance orders requesting customer data, such as orders issued under Section 215 of the USA PATRIOT Act.[72]

Companies have responded, for example, by expanding publication of transparency reports documenting the number of requests for customer data. In June 2013, Google, Microsoft, Facebook, Apple, and other major technology companies brought suit in the FISC, claiming a right to publish information about NSL requests they had received. In January 2014, the government agreed to permit these companies to publish the aggregate number of NSLs received over a prior six-month period.[73] Companies previously could publish only the aggregate total of surveillance requests from within a specific period, a figure that encompassed requests by state and local law enforcement for garden-variety crimes as well as by the FBI for national security investigations.[74] The settlement agreement now permits companies to report the number of national security requests in bands of 1000 (from 0–999, 1,000–1,999, etc.). But companies can issue reports only every

---

[68] 18 USC § 2709.

[69] *Id* § 2709(c)(1).

[70] See Electronic Privacy Info. Center, 'Foreign Intelligence Surveillance Act Court Orders 1979–2014', www.epic.org/privacy/wiretap/stats/fisa_ stats.html#background [http://perma.cc/RK47-8LEG].

[71] See *Doe v Mukasey* 549 F3d 861 (2d Cir 2008) (holding that NSL gag was an unconstitutional prior restraint, but upholding statute by construing it to provide procedure for recipients to contest their gag order). See also PP Garlinger, Note, 'Privacy, Free Speech, and the PATRIOT Act: First and Fourth Amendment Limits on National Security Letters' (2009), 84 *New York University Law Review* 1105, 1117–23.

[72] R Wexler, 'Warrant Canaries and Disclosure by Design: The Real Threat to National Security Letter Gag Orders' (2014) 124 *Yale Law Journal Forum* 158, 159.

[73] Letter from James M Cole, Deputy Attorney General, to Colin Stretch et al, General Counsels of Technology Cos (17 January 2014) www.washingtonpost.com/r/2010-2019/WashingtonPost/2014/10/07/National-Security/Graphics/dagletter.pdf.

[74] BM Kaufman, 'Twitter's First Amendment Suit & the Warrant Canary Question' (10 October 2014) *Just Security* www.justsecurity.org/16221/twitters-amendment-suit-warrant-canary-question/.

six months (with a six-month publication delay), and cannot say anything for two years about an order that involved a new technological capability.[75] Despite these limitations, the companies have trumpeted the agreement as proof of their concern for the handling of user data.[76]

Some companies have also started issuing 'warrant canaries', or regularly published statements that the particular company has not received an NSL or other secret surveillance order that it would be prevented from saying it had received.[77] If the company receives a surveillance request with a gag order, it terminates the canary, thus informing its customers and the public that it received such an order. In October 2014, Twitter filed suit, claiming that it had a First Amendment right to disclose that it had not received specific surveillance orders during a given period,[78] a right not given to Google, Facebook and the other companies party to the January 2014 settlement agreement with the Justice Department, which requires them to report in bands, such as 0–999.[79]

More recently, Microsoft sued the Justice Department to prevent authorities from obtaining customers' e-mails through warrants without their knowledge. Microsoft asserts that permanent or indefinite bans on companies' informing their customers whether the government has accessed their electronic communications, as authorised under the Electronic Communications Privacy Act of 1986, violates Microsoft's free speech rights and its customers' Fourth Amendment rights.[80] Like Twitter's suit over warrant canaries, Microsoft's challenge to data gag orders highlights the increased pressure on companies to reveal more details about government demands for users' information and resist the perception of voluntary cooperation. Technology companies' increased reliance on cloud computing systems have heightened concerns about secrecy orders because these systems allow investigators to bypass individuals and obtain information directly from the company that hosts the information. Not only have the number of secrecy orders increased, but it is increasingly unlikely a person will ever know that he or she was the target of an investigation as long as there is a permanent electronic gag order in place.[81]

---

[75] Letter from James M Cole, above n 73.

[76] N Bilton, 'Tech Companies Update on Government Data Requests' (2014) *New York Times: Bits* (New York, 3 February) wwwbits.blogs.nytimes.com/2014/02/03/tech-companies-release-government-data-requests/?_r=0.

[77] K Opsahl, 'Warrant Canary Frequently Asked Questions' *Electronic Frontier Foundation*, www.eff.org/deeplinks/2014/04/warrant-canary-faq.

[78] Ellen Nakashima, 'Twitter Sues U.S. Government Over Limits on Ability To Disclose Surveillance Orders' (2014) *Washington Post* (Washington DC: 7 October) www.washingtonpost.com/world/national-security/twitter-sues-us-government-over-limits-on-ability-to-disclose-surveillance-orders/2014/10/07/5cc39ba0-4dd4-11e4-babe-e91da079cb8a_story.html; Kaufman, above n 74.

[79] Letter from James M Cole, above n 73.

[80] *Microsoft Corpn v United States Department of Justice* 16-cv-00538 (US Dist Ct West D Wash, *filed* 14 April 2016).

[81] S Lohr, 'Microsoft Sues Justice Department to Protest Electronic Gag Order Statute,' (2016) *New York Times* (New York, 16 April).

Other initiatives, labelled by one commentator as 'disclosure by design', boost transparency through the creation of a privacy-protection mechanism—a kind of electronic tripwire—to signal receipt of surveillance orders.[82] Such mechanisms can include partially automated canary services that send regular prompts to post a manual message stating that no secret orders have yet been received; a warrant canary metatag built into web browsers; and a tool informing users if their computers are compromised by known surveillance spyware typically employed by governments.[83] Alternatively, companies can engage in less automated forms of disclosure, such as when Lavabit founder Ladar Levison, after receiving government orders for customer records accompanied by nondisclosure requirements, tipped off users that Lavabit's servers had been compromised by shutting them down and indirectly signaling the lack of continued security in statements to his users.[84] These less formal types of disclosure depend on sophisticated users who track privacy indicators and are more capable of inferring privacy breaches from a company's public statements.

C. Privacy Enhancing Technologies

An increasingly important way in which technology companies can protect privacy is through encryption software and other privacy enhancing technologies (PETs). PETs attempt to protect personal privacy by limiting or eliminating the collection or further processing of identifiable data.[85] PETs vary widely, and can include advanced cryptographic protocols; communication anonymisers that hide a person's real online identity; identity theft monitoring software; and advertising blocking technologies.[86] PETs are also used as marketing tools, allowing companies to tout the latest protections, such as 'surveillance proof' smart phone applications.[87]

---

[82] Wexler, above n 72, at 173–77.

[83] ibid, 174–75.

[84] ibid, 176–77 (explaining how users might infer that the private messenger service Wickr's security had been breached if Wickr were to withdraw the statement that its 'architecture eliminates backdoors; if someone was to come to us with a subpoena, we have nothing to give them').

[85] See GW van Blarkom, JJ Borking and JGE Olk, *Handbook of Privacy and Privacy-Enhancing Technologies: The Case of Intelligent Software Agents* (2003) 33 www.andrewpatrick.ca/pisa/handbook/ Handbook_Privacy_and_PET_final.pdf. See also H Burkert, 'Privacy-Enhancing Technologies: Typology, Critique, Vision' in Philip E Agre and Marc Rotenberg (eds), *Technology and Privacy: The New Landscape* (Cambridge, Massachusetts, MIT Press, 1997) 125.

[86] Information and Privacy Comm'r/Ontario, Canada and Registratiekamer [Dutch Data Protection Authority], The Netherlands (1995) 1 *Privacy-Enhancing Technologies: The Path to Anonymity*, www.ipc.on.ca/web_ site.ups/matters/sum_pap/papers/anon-e.htm; A Thierer, A Framework for Benefit-Cost Analysis in Digital Privacy Debates (2013) 20 *George Mason Law Rev.* 1055, 1095.

[87] R Gallagher, 'The Threat of Silence' (4 February 2013) *Slate*, www.slate.com/articles/technology/ future_tense/2013/02/silent_circle_s_latest_app_democratizes_encryption_governments_won_t_ be.single.html.

The assumption underlying PETs is that data collectors may be forced to use data in unforeseen ways, to the detriment of affected individuals.[88] The US government has largely resisted PETs because of a concern that they could impede law enforcement or intelligence investigations.[89] European data protection authorities have been more supportive of PETs, stressing their importance in fostering compliance with data protection legislation.[90]

The Snowden revelations demonstrate the success of US and British intelligence agencies in penetrating the online encryption systems utilised by most individuals to secure the privacy of their personal data.[91] President Obama's Review Group on surveillance reform took a strong position in support of encryption technologies, recommending that the NSA and other government agencies not undermine efforts to create encryption standards or subvert generally available commercial software, for example by engineering vulnerabilities into encryption algorithms or demanding changes in any commercial product for the purpose of undermining its integrity.[92] The President did not adopt any of the group's recommendations on encryption or on not exploiting backdoors in networks, prompting criticism from the technology sector.[93]

Some technology companies are increasing their use of PETs and taking steps to eliminate backdoors. Apple and Google, for example, unveiled encryption improvements on their latest smartphones and tablets.[94] Describing his company's enhanced data protection measures, Google's executive chairman announced that 'no one believes the NSA can break [its encryption] during our lifetime'.[95] Whether accurate, such statements underscore how important it has become for leading technology companies to show they are protecting user privacy in the face of expansive government surveillance. The Snowden revelations have also boosted

---

[88] Diaz et al, above n 21, at 931.

[89] Fromkin, above n 32, at 976–77. See also R Simmons, 'Why 2007 Is Not Like 1984: A Broader Perspective on Technology's Effect on Privacy and Fourth Amendment Jurisprudence' (2007) 97 *Journal of Criminal Law and Criminology* 531, 544–47.

[90] Communication from the Commission to the European Parliament and the Council on Promoting Data Protection by Privacy Enhancing Technologies, COM (2 May 2007) 228 (recommending that PETs 'should be developed and more widely used, in particular where personal data are processed through information and communication technology (ICT) networks').

[91] J Larson, 'Revealed: The NSA's Secret Campaign to Crack, Undermine Internet Security' (2013) *Pro Publica* (5 September) www.propublica.org/article/the-nsas-secret-campaign-to-crack-undermine-internet-encryption.

[92] President's Review Group, above n 30 at 36, 220.

[93] G Gross, 'Obama fails to address NSA encryption-defeating methods, backdoors' (2014) *Techworld.com* (17 January) www.techworld.com/news/apps/obama-fails-to-address-nsa-encryption-defeating-methods-backdoors-3497844/.

[94] T Timm, 'Your iPhone is Now Encrypted' (2014) *Guardian* (London, 30 September) www.theguardian.com/commentisfree/2014/sep/30/iphone-6-encrypted-phone-data-default.

[95] H Kuchler, 'Tech companies step up encryption in wake of Snowden' (2015) *Financial Times* (London, 14 November).

privacy-focused start-ups that emphasise increased data security as a selling point, particularly in Europe.[96]

The practice of embedding privacy protections into products and services at the design phase, rather than after the fact, highlights the growing recognition of technology's power to resolve and implement privacy policy.[97] US officials, particularly the FBI and other law enforcement agencies, launched a public campaign to demonstrate the dangers of 'going dark'—not having access to encrypted communications—which they said would undermine investigations and threaten national security.[98] Leading technology companies vigorously resisted giving the government a backdoor to encrypted data through access to source codes and encryption keys.[99] So did leading technology experts, who warned that exceptional access systems would necessarily make private data vulnerable to hacking by foreign intelligence agents, cybercriminals, and terrorist groups. Experts also cautioned that such systems would threaten the openness of the Internet because authoritarian states would demand similar access.[100] After much debate, President Obama sided against forcing companies to create a backdoor,[101] but then signaled he might revisit that decision following the mass shooting in San Bernardino, California, in December 2015 that killed 14 people.[102]

Apple's subsequent stand-off against the Justice Department represents the most prominent instance of corporate defense of individual privacy to date. Apple had opposed the government's attempt to force it to create a back door to defeat the encryption on the iPhone in order to provide access to the iPhone of one of the shooters in the San Bernardino attack, who was killed by the police and left behind a locked encrypted iPhone 5C.[103] Apple CEO Tim Cook underscored the threat posed by the government's demand that Apple create a back door in a letter

---

[96] S Dorner, 'For German, Swiss Privacy Start-Ups, a Post-Snowden Boom' (2014) *Wall St Journal Blog* (20 August) www.blogs.wsj.com/digits/2014/08/20/for-german-swiss-privacy-start-ups-a-post-snowden-boon/.

[97] See DK Mulligan and J King, 'Bridging the Gap Between Privacy and Design' (2012) 14 *University of Pennsylvania Journal of Constitutional Law* 989, 992.

[98] I Bobic and RJ Reilly, 'FBI Director James Comey 'Very Concerned' about New Apple, Google Privacy Features' (2014) *Huffington Post* (25 September) www.huffingtonpost.com/2014/09/25/james-comey-apple-encryption_n_5882874.html.

[99] DE Sanger and N Perlroth, 'Obama Heads to Tech Security Talks Amid Tensions' (2015) *New York Times* (New York, 12 February).

[100] H Abelson et al., Computer Science and Artificial Intelligence Laboratory Technical Report, 'Keys Under Doormats: Mandating insecurity by requiring government access to all data and communications' (6 July 2015), www.dspace.mit.edu/bitstream/handle/1721.1/97690/MIT-CSAIL-TR-2015-026.pdf?sequence=8.

[101] N Perlroth and DE Sanger, 'Obama Won't Seek Access to Encrypted User Data' (2015) *New York Times* (New York, 10 October).

[102] Evan Halper, 'After San Bernardino attack, tech firms are urged to do more to fight terrorism' (2015) *Los Angeles Times* (Los Angeles, 8 December).

[103] M Apuzzo, J Goldstein and E Lichtblau, 'Line in the Sand Over iPhones Was Over a Year in the Making' (2016) *New York Times* (New York, 19 February).

to Apple customers[104] and described data privacy as a 'fundamental human right' in public statements.[105] Apple further stressed its refusal to become 'an agent of law enforcement', thus distancing itself from the government's effort to ensure access to users' data.[106] Other major technology companies rallied in support of Apple's defense of encryption as a bulwark of individual privacy.[107] Apple's stand, however, was also calculated to serve its bottom line, which it believed would be strengthened through a high-profile defence of individual privacy.[108] The Justice Department ultimately dropped its demand against Apple in the San Bernardino case, announcing that it had found a way to open the shooter's iPhone.[109] It then ended a second court battle with Apple, stating that it no longer needed Apple's assistance to unlock the iPhone of a suspected drug dealer in New York.[110] Resolution of these cases, however, has not settled the underlying battle in the US between technology companies like Apple and the federal government over back doors to encryption.

In the UK, former Prime Minister David Cameron proposed banning secure messaging applications if they fail to install backdoors that allow for government access.[111] Recently proposed UK surveillance legislation does not include a ban on encryption, but does require communications companies to retain customer data for at least one year and allows for government access to metadata without a judicial warrant in most cases.[112] The bill imposes stricter requirements in order for the government to access the content of communications.[113] The debate over access to encrypted communications suggests the significant role design-based protections will play in securing privacy rights from government interference in the future.

Yet, there are reasons to remain sceptical of relying on corporations to protect privacy. Large Internet and telecommunications companies remain under both legal obligation and informal pressure to co-operate with the govern-

---

[104] T Cook, 'A Message to Our Customers' (16 February 2016) www.apple.com/customer-letter/.

[105] D Pierson, 'Tim Cook's stance on privacy could define his Apple legacy' (2016) *Los Angeles Times* (Los Angeles, 18 February).

[106] Apuzzo, Goldstein and Lichtblau, above n 103.

[107] B Barrett, 'Tech Giants Agree: The FBI's Case against Apple is a Joke' (2016) *Wired* (13 March) www.wired.com/2016/03/apple-fbi-tech-industry-support-amicus-brief/.

[108] EJ Fox, 'Apple Challenges Court Order to Unlock San Bernardino Shooter's iPhone' (2016) *Vanity Fair* (17 February) www.vanityfair.com/news/2016/02/apple-court-order-san-bernardino-tim-cook.

[109] K Benner and E Lichtblau, 'U.S. Says It Has Unlocked iPhone without Apple' (2016) *New York Times* (16 March).

[110] C Smythe, 'Second U.S. Bid to Force Apple to Unlock Phone Ends in a Whimper' (2016) *Bloomberg* (22 April) www.bloomberg.com/news/articles/2016-04-23/u-s-drops-appeal-seeking-apple-help-in-brooklyn-iphone-case-incgxa37.

[111] W Oremus, 'Obama Wants Tech Companies to Install Backdoors for Government Spying' (2015) *Slate* (19 January), www.slate.com/blogs/future_tense/2015/01/19/obama_wants_backdoors_in_encrypted_messaging_to_allow_government_spying.html.

[112] S Castle, 'Britain Announces Plans to Update Surveillance Laws' (2015) *New York Times* (New York, 4 November) (describing the Investigatory Powers Bill).

[113] CC Murphy and N Simonsen, 'Interception, Authorisation and Redress in the Draft Investigatory Powers Bill' (2015) *UK Human Rights Blog* (5 November).

ment, and the strength of measures intended to enhance privacy norms varies widely.[114] Smaller companies still suffer from gaps in data security due to both lack of knowledge about security measures and a concern about their perceived costs.[115] Additionally, businesses that benefit from the collection and use of personal information have competing incentives not to deploy technological tools that curtail information flow.[116]

Perhaps most significantly, even major technology companies that take steps to protect private user data from outside interference, continue to gather data for their own commercial purposes. Private big data companies, such as Google and Facebook, as well as giant data brokers, such as Acxiom and Bluekai, are involved in equal if not greater collection of data than government agencies.[117] Neither the 'terms of service' companies thrust on consumers nor the 'privacy settings' that leading companies offer them can reasonably be expected to provide meaningful privacy protection.[118] The financial incentives driving the collection of data will remain a strong counterweight to any corporate-led privacy efforts.

Thus, while companies may be increasingly intent on demonstrating their commitment to user privacy, the level of that commitment can vary widely. New technology companies generally remain more dedicated to protecting privacy than older companies, such as telecommunications firms, which have a long history of co-operation with government surveillance.[119] Further, among new technology firms, the level of commitment to privacy protection can differ significantly. The Snowden revelations have accentuated these differences by expanding niche markets for companies that make privacy protection central to their products and services, including by making it burdensome, if not technologically infeasible, for the government to access user information through surveillance orders.[120]

[114] See, eg, Lucian Constantine, 'Yahoo starts encrypting all email, but implementation is inconsistent' (2014) *PCWorld* (8 January), www.pcworld.com/article/2085700/as-yahoo-makes-encryption-standard-for-email-weak-implementation-seen.html (describing shortcomings in Yahoo's new email encryption technology).

[115] S Ramanan, 'The 7 deadly sins of startup security' (2014) *CSO Online* (10 November), www.csoonline.com/article/2845332/cloud-security/the-7-deadly-sins-of-startup-security.html.

[116] Diaz, above n 21 at 934; Fromkin, above n 32 at 1524 (noting that the prevalence of privacy-destroying technologies will necessarily limit the reach of PETs).

[117] F Pasquale, *The Black Box Society: The Secret Algorithms that Control Money and Information* (Cambridge, Massachusetts, Harvard University Press, 2015).

[118] F Pasquale, 'Privacy, Antitrust, and Power' (2013) 20 *George Mason Law Review* 1009, 1012 ('The prospect of altering the terms of service for an intermediary like Facebook or Google is beyond the ambition of almost all users.').

[119] See Westin, above n 45 at 119–32; S Dash, RF Schwartz and RE Knowlton, *The Eavesdroppers* (Rutgers, New Jersey, Rutgers University Press, 1959) 34–35, 43–57, 79–95.

[120] JVJ Van Hoboken and IS Rubenstein, 'Privacy and Security in the Cloud: Some Realism about Technical Solutions to Transnational Surveillance in the Post-Snowden Era' (2014) 66 *Maine. Law Review* 487, 530.

IV. Corporate Social Responsibility and Privacy

Corporate Social Responsibility (CSR) offers another window into post-Snowden developments and the implications for privacy protections. CSR supplies a framework for understanding the expansion of voluntary actions by corporations to strengthen privacy as well as the limits of corporate-directed privacy efforts. It also sheds light on the interplay between corporate privacy initiatives and human rights.

The traditional view, often associated with the work of Milton Friedman, posits that a corporation's sole responsibility is to further the interests of its stockholders or members by maximising wealth and profits.[121] But this narrow conception of CSR has been supplanted by a broader understanding of corporate obligation. While CSR lacks a single definition, it generally describes how companies balance or integrate economic, environmental, and social considerations within their sphere of influence as they pursue traditional profit-maximising activities.[122] The proliferation of constituency statutes and corporate codes of conduct demonstrate the growing influence of CSR in recent decades.[123] CSR commonly addresses concerns about wages, working conditions, and the environmental effects of investment in developing countries. Despite its voluntary nature, scholars have noted the degree to which CSR's principles can affect not only corporate behaviour but also the development of human rights. The more the behaviour of multinationals becomes consistent with emerging human-rights norms, the more that behaviour reinforces those norms.[124] In particular, CSR has bolstered efforts to expand human rights obligations, which have traditionally focused on states, to private actors.[125] CSR has gained traction from a recent UN initiative to transform its principles into a more comprehensive and workable framework.[126]

Critics maintain that CSR often amounts to little more than window-dressing or sloganeering designed for public relations and marketing purposes. It allows

---

[121] See, eg, M Friedman, *Capitalism and Freedom* (Chicago: University of Chicago Press, 1962) 133.

[122] For representative definitions, see United Nations Industrial Development Organization, *What is CSR?: Defining the Concept*, www.unido.org/en/what-we-do/trade/csr/what-is-csr.html; EM Epstein, 'The Good Company: Rhetoric or Reality?: Corporate Social Responsibility and Business Ethics Redux' (2007) 44 *American Business Law Journal* 207, 218.

[123] Constituency statutes allow or require directors to consider the interests of other corporate constituencies, such as employees, creditors, consumers, suppliers, and communities, in their decision-making process. ME Van Der Weide, 'Against Fiduciary Duties to Corporate Stakeholders' (1996) 21 *Delaware Journal of Corporate Law* 27, 30.

[124] CM Dickerson, 'Human Rights: The Emerging Norm of Corporate Social Responsibility' (2002) 76 *Tulane Law Review* 1431, 1433.

[125] ibid, 1456–57; LC Backer, 'Realizing Socio-Economic Rights under Emerging Global Regulatory Frameworks: The Potential Impact of Privatization and the Role of Companies in China and India' (2013) 45 *George Washshington International Law Review* 615, 621.

[126] See W Bradford, 'Beyond Good and Evil: The Commensurability of Corporate Profits and Human Rights' (2012) 26 *Notre Dame Journal of Law, Ethics & Public Policy* 141, 177–79.

companies to enhance their reputations without keeping their commitments or bearing any costs.[127] Critics emphasise that CSR is not a substitute for regulation.[128]

CSR principles have not addressed privacy interests directly, but CSR, which urges the protection and promotion of human rights within a corporation's sphere of influence,[129] could encompass a technology company's users and possibly others with whom those users communicate. The more outspoken privacy positions recently adopted by technology companies, such as Apple's defence of encryption and resistance to government demands for backdoors, suggest an implicit recognition of CSR's potential relevance to digital privacy, even if they do not draw on CSR expressly.

Application of CSR principles to the collection and use of personal data could have implications for digital privacy rights. Enhanced corporate commitment to user privacy could support the application of human rights norms to government data collection by strengthening expectations of privacy. Conversely, corporate complicity or acquiescence in the type of bulk data collection programmes detailed in the documents provided by Snowden undercuts those norms.

The right to privacy is enshrined in the International Covenant on Civil and Political Rights (ICCPR)[130] and the European Convention on Human Rights and Fundamental Freedoms (ECHR).[131] In 1988, the UN Human Rights Committee outlined the contours of a right to privacy under the ICCPR, noting that an arbitrary or unlawful interference with the right to privacy would include situations where there was no law authorising the interference or the interference was unreasonable under the circumstances.[132] The European Court of Human Rights (ECtHR) has applied the right in the context of national security surveillance, requiring that there are effective guarantees against abuse.[133] In 2013, the UN General Assembly adopted Resolution 68/167, reaffirming that the right to privacy applies to mass digital surveillance and that the prohibition against arbitrary and unlawful interference with that right applies domestically and

---

[127] JW Pitts III , 'Corporate Social Responsibility: Current Status and Future Evolution' (2009) 6 *Rutgers J L & Pub Pol'y* 334, 374.

[128] *Resolution on Corporate Social Responsibility: A New Partnership,* European ParliamentDocumentP_6TA (2007) www.europarl.europa.eu/sides/getDoc.do?pubRef=//EP//TEXT+TA+P6-TA-2007-0062+0+DOC+XML+V0//EN.

[129] See UN Economic and Social Council, Subcommittee on the Promotion and Protection of Human Rights, Economic Social and Cultural Rights, *Norms on the Responsibilities of Transnational Corporations and Other Business Enterprises with Regard to Human Rights,* U.N Document E/CN.4/Sub.2/2003/12/Rev.2 (13 Aug. 2003), www1.umn.edu/humanrts/links/norms-Aug2003.html.

[130] International Covenant on Civil and Political Rights (ICCPR), 19 December 1966, art 17, 99 UNTS 171.

[131] European Convention for the Protection of Human Rights and Fundamental Freedoms (ECHR), 4 November 1950, art 8, 213 UNTS 222.

[132] General Comment 16, *The Right to Respect Privacy, Family, Home and Correspondence, and Protection of Honour and Reputation* (Art 17), UN GAOR Human Rights. Committee, 32d Sess (1988), UN Document CCPR/C/21/Rev1 (1989), http://www1.umn.edu/humanrts/gencomm/hrcom16.htm.

[133] See, eg, *Klass v Germany* Application No 20605/92, (1992) 2 EHRR 214.

extraterritorially.[134] Yet, how privacy protections apply extraterritorially to mass surveillance remains a subject of debate.[135] It is uncertain, for example, how privacy rights could apply extraterritorially under a standard such as that employed by the ECtHR, which obliges governments to respect treaty obligations only with respect to territories or persons over which they exercise effective control.[136] The ECtHR, moreover, has upheld the collection and querying of communications of foreign nationals abroad without particular suspicion of wrongdoing, suggesting some limits on privacy protections against bulk data collection and deference to surveillance measures adopted to protect public security.[137] Even the ECJ's recent ruling in *Schrems* on cross-border data sharing acknowledges the importance of national security and rests instead on the lack of safeguards to correct over-reaching.[138]

Following the *Schrems* ruling, European and American officials sought a new trans-Atlantic data sharing agreement that would allow the sharing of data between private sector companies in different jurisdictions. In February 2016, after months of negotiations, officials reached a new agreement—known as the EU-US Privacy Shield—that will allow companies to move individuals' data back and forth, across the Atlantic, with additional safeguards, including written annual assurances by US officials that Europeans' personal data is being protected. The deal, however, remains subject to legal challenge by privacy advocates and scrutiny by national privacy agencies in Europe, which can investigate and fine companies for mishandling individuals' personal information.[139] EU data protection authorities subsequently issued an analysis of the Privacy Shield which, while acknowledging the agreement's enhanced privacy protections, expressed concern about the continuing vulnerability of Europeans' personal information due to broad US data collection power over foreign nationals under section 702 of the FAA.[140]

The United States takes a highly circumscribed view of the extraterritorial application of human rights, including the right to privacy. It maintains, for example, that the right to privacy under the ICCPR does not apply extraterritorially,[141] a position recently rejected by the UN Human Rights

---

[134] UN General Assembly Resolution, *The Right to Privacy in the Digital Age*, A/RES/68/167, *adopted on* 18 Dec. 2013, www.un.org/ga/search/view_doc.asp?symbol=A/RES/68/167.

[135] See, eg, M Milanovic, 'Foreign Surveillance and Human Rights' (2013) *EJIL: Talk!* (25 November) www.ejiltalk.org/foreign-surveillance-and-human-rights-introduction/.

[136] See, eg, *Al-Skeini v United Kingdom*, Application No 55721/07, 53 (2011) EHRR 589, 647–50.

[137] See *Weber v Germany* 2006-XI ECtHR 309. See also P Margulies, 'The NSA in Global Perspective: Surveillance, Human Rights, and International Counterterrorism' (2014) 82 *Fordham Law Review* 2137, 2158–59 (describing attempts by the ECtHR to apply a right of privacy to mass surveillance).

[138] *Schrems*, above n 50.

[139] M Scott, 'U.S. and Europe in "Safe Harbor" Data Deal, but Legal Fight May Await' (2016) *New York Times* (New York, 2 February).

[140] Article 29 Data Protection Working Party, 'Opinion on 01/2016 on the EU-US Privacy Shield draft adequacy decision,' 16/EN WP 238, adopted 13 April 2016, http://ec.europa.eu/justice/data-protection/article-29/documentation/opinion-recommendation/files/2016/wp238_en.pdf.

[141] Margulies, above n 137 at 1 and n 8.

Committee.[142] Obama's Presidential Policy Directive on Signals Intelligence Activities (PPD–28) does recognise that all individuals have legitimate privacy interests in their personal information, regardless of where they are located, and that US signals intelligence activities accordingly must include safeguards for the protection of foreign nationals abroad.[143] The Directive also precludes surveillance for such purposes as suppressing speech critical of the United States, discriminating against racial, religious or ethnic groups, or gaining a competitive advantage for US companies.[144] PPD–28, however, leaves significant gaps in protections for individuals, whether they are US citizens or foreign nationals. It permits, for example, 'vacuum cleaner' signals intelligence collection and analysis under Executive Order 12,333 and its implementing procedures, which apply to surveillance measures effectuated outside US borders.[145] Even where private individuals are ostensibly protected against surveillance, US law imposes obstacles to such individuals' ability to prove 'standing' to bring suit.[146] These gaps increase pressure on companies to take the lead in protecting the privacy of their customers from government interference, whether by avoiding voluntary co-operation or pushing back against overbroad legal demands.

Application of CSR principles could help reinforce emerging human rights norms by eroding territorial limits on privacy protections. It could strengthen corporate respect for personal data and strengthen corporate resistance to overbroad government data collection programmes. Additionally, CSR could facilitate implementation of privacy-enhancing measures, which, in turn, would strengthen privacy protections on the ground.

However, the impact of extending CSR principles to digital privacy would likely encounter opposing forces that could limit their privacy-enhancing impact. Companies will continue to gather data for their own commercial purposes. The magnitude of the financial incentives driving private collection in an era of big data will constrain the degree to which market forces can promote privacy.[147] Further, companies will face continuing government pressure to co-operate in data collection programmes, and the latitude they have to protect user privacy from government interference will itself be shaped partly by the scope of the government's surveillance powers under any given legal and regulatory landscape.

---

[142] UN Human Rights Committee, *Concluding observations on the fourth report of the United States of America*, P 22, http://justsecurity.org/wp-content/uploads/2014/03/UN-ICCPR-Concluding-Observations-USA.pdf.

[143] The White House, Presidential Policy Directive/PPD-28, 17 January2014, www.whitehouse.gov/the-press-office/2014/01/17/presidential-policy-directive-signals-intelligence-activities.

[144] ibid.

[145] M Schlanger, 'U.S. Intelligence Reforms Still Allow Plenty of Suspicionless Spying on Americans' (2015) *Just Security* (13 February) http://justsecurity.org/20033/guest-post-intelligence-reforms-plenty-suspicionless-surveillance-americans/.

[146] *Clapper v Amnesty* (2013) 133 S Ct 1138; *Wikimedia v NSA* No 15–662, 2015 WL 6460364 (D Md 23 October 2015).

[147] Pasquale, above n 118 at 1010.

V. Conclusion

While technology companies will continue to gather and aggregate data to enhance profits, they will also face countervailing pressure to protect privacy and avoid the perception of complicity in government surveillance and data collection programmes. The degree to which companies can contribute to the development of privacy protections will depend on a number of factors, particularly the extent to which they perceive it is important to their bottom line. CSR principles suggest areas of convergence between enhanced privacy safeguards and corporate self-interest. But despite a flurry of pro-privacy initiatives following the Snowden revelations, there are reasons to remain sceptical of relying on corporations to protect privacy in the digital age.

7

The Right to Privacy, Surveillance and the Global Obligations of Corporations

DAVID BILCHITZ*

I. Introduction: The Technological Revolution and the Expansion of Corporate Power

The focus of discussions around the right to privacy traditionally has been on the state and the constraints in which it must operate to respect the private lives of citizens. Yet, recent technological changes relating to the internet and mobile telephones have increasingly led to the situation in which large amounts of personal information relating to individuals, pass through and are entrusted to, private corporations.[1] The very technological method through which the internet and mobile phones function always requires an intermediary in the communications (in contrast with direct personal communications between two people). That intermediary today is often a corporation of some kind which then potentially becomes privy to the content of a particular communication. In some cases, there are several intermediary corporations through which information passes in different jurisdictions: consider mobile short-messaging from one country to another which must pass through the networks of different providers. The existence of this technology and the intermediaries also enables states to gain unprecedented access to individual private communications.

The question that this paper seeks to address concerns specifically the duties of private corporations in respect of the right to privacy. It is important to recognise that the significant power that corporations have may be wielded for the

* This chapter is a shortened and modified version of an article published under the title D Bilchitz 'Privacy, Surveillance and the Duties of Corporations' (2016) *Journal of South African Law* 45–67. I am grateful to the editor and publisher for permission to reproduce segments of it here.
[1] For a description of this society of increasing surveillance, see NM Richards 'The Dangers of Surveillance' (2012) *Harvard Law Review* 1934, 1937–41.

corporation's own purposes (for instance, in monitoring the communications of its employees, or in mining data to assist its sales) or be harnessed for another entity's purposes (here, the focus will be on the state and the purposes of fighting crime and terrorism). If the right to privacy of individuals is to be protected, then we cannot anymore only think of the responsibility of the state. We need to develop an understanding of the obligations that private corporations also have in this regard.[2] This is particularly important in a globalised world where communications pass through the networks and servers of multiple corporations.

The specific question this chapter addresses is only one element of a broader challenge faced by the law relating to fundamental rights internationally—in domestic and international law—brought about by the increasing power of private sector actors to affect the interests underlying these rights.[3] There remains significant uncertainty as to the methodology for extending obligations under fundamental rights to corporations.[4] There are two routes through which such obligations can be imposed: fundamental rights can be recognised as imposing a set of direct obligations upon corporations; or they could be understood as imposing an indirect obligation on the state through its regulatory structures and laws to impose obligations upon corporations in respect of the right to privacy (this is commonly known in human rights law as the state's duty to protect). Whilst we may debate the merits of these two routes and whether there is any difference between them,[5] the result is the same: fundamental rights will have certain specific implications for corporations.

This chapter focuses on the direct route since it allows us to address squarely the implications we can derive from a fundamental right such as the right to privacy for the duties of corporations. In doing so, it draws on the analytical framework developed by the Constitutional Court of South Africa which has been confronted with expressly determining the direct application of human rights to corporate entities under certain circumstances. That framework, it shall be argued, provides

---

[2] Nothing in what is said here should be taken to absolve the state from its own obligations in relation to privacy. Individuals may also need to make some effort to protect their own privacy. At the same time, the power and importance of corporations in this area raises a live question as to the nature of their obligations in this regard which is the subject of this paper.

[3] There is a wide range of literature on this topic that has developed in recent years: see, for instance, A Clapham, *Human Rights Obligations of Non-State Actors* (Oxford, Oxford University Press, 2006); F Wettstein, *Multinational Corporations and Global Justice: Human Rights Obligations of a Quasi-governmental Institution* (Stanford, Stanford University Press, 2009) and D Kinley and J Tadaki, 'From Walk to Talk: the Emergence of Human Rights Responsibilities for Multi-national Corporations at International Law' (2004) 44 *Virginia Journal of International Law* 931.

[4] For the first detailed attempt to engage this question, see S Ratner 'Corporations and Human Rights: A Theory of Legal Responsibility' (2001) 111 *Yale Law Journal* 443, 496.

[5] See the argument in D Bilchitz, 'A Chasm between "Is" and "Ought"? A Critique of the Normative Foundations of the SRSG's Framework and Guiding Principles' in S Deva and D Bilchitz (eds), *Human Rights Obligations of Business: Beyond the Corporate Responsibility to Respect* (Cambridge, Cambridge University Press, 2014) 107–112 to the effect that the state's duty to protect logically implies certain direct obligations upon corporations.

a methodology for determining the relevant factors that can guide our understanding of the obligations of private sector entities. The goal of this paper is not though simply to make claims that are only of particular application in South African constitutional law, but to use its progressive constitutional framework to develop the analysis more broadly of how to extend the obligations underlying fundamental rights provision to corporations with a specific focus on what the right to privacy requires of corporations in the internet era. The aim is also not to consider particular legislative and common law rules enacted in South Africa or any other jurisdiction: indeed, this paper does not undertake any exhaustive analysis of existing law.[6] Instead, it seeks to examine the normative principles that flow from the right to privacy itself for determining the obligations of corporations in this regard: those principles, in turn, have implications for the specific legislative or common law measures that law-making bodies will impose. The approach adopted here is thus one that seeks to develop a set of principles for understanding the obligations of corporations that applies across the world and flows from the recognition of the right to privacy as a universal fundamental right.[7]

Part II of this chapter will focus on why the right to privacy should be found to place direct obligations upon corporations. It will utilise three factors developed by the Constitutional Court of South Africa in determining the general applicability of rights to private corporations as the basis for the argument: these include the underlying reasons for the protection of privacy, the potential impact of corporations on privacy and the role corporations play in society. This discussion will lay the foundation for Part III, which attempts to develop an understanding of the specific obligations flowing from the right to privacy and their implications for corporations. Given the attempt to develop universal principles that can be of use in determining corporate obligations, it draws on the well-known tri-partite international framework that recognises that fundamental rights impose obligations to respect, protect and fulfil fundamental rights. Throughout, this paper draws on a conceptualisation of corporations as entities that straddle the public/private divide which helps in understanding their role in the sphere of privacy. The focus of this discussion will be on the current challenges of ensuring a domain of privacy remains in the face of the possibilities of widespread surveillance of personal communications and transactions through internet and mobile communication technologies across sovereign borders. It is argued that, ultimately, corporations have an extensive range of obligations in relation to privacy which include

---

[6] In South Africa, there are a range of relevant laws including RICA and the Protection of Personal Information Act 4 of 2014. The common law also provided some protections for informational privacy. For an examination of the statutory and common law context in South Africa, see J Neethling 'Features of the Protection of Personal Information Bill, 2009 and the law of Delict' (2012) 75 *Journal of Contemporary Roman-Dutch Law* 241.

[7] The right to privacy is recognised in Article 17 of the International Covenant on Civil and Political Rights as well as in Article 8 of the European Convention on Human Rights and Article 11 of the Inter-American Convention on Human Rights.

obligations not impermissibly to invade privacy themselves, to protect individuals from invasion by third parties and states and, more radically, to assist in the creation of technology that enables individuals to realise their interest in private communications. It is also contended that they may only release information to states under strict conditions and may have a duty to resist the release of such information and to challenge an order to do so in courts or human rights bodies when their conformity with the requirements of the right to privacy is in doubt. This specific analysis it is hoped will demonstrate the importance of having a framework for determining how fundamental rights apply to private actors and how the conclusions of such a process can provide the basis for assessing the adequacy of existing legal frameworks across the world in this regard.

II. The Right to Privacy and Corporations: Justifying Direct Human Rights Obligations

Fundamental rights have traditionally been recognised as protecting individual interests against the overweening power of the state. With the growth in the power of private corporations to affect fundamental rights, however, there have been increasing calls for binding legal obligations to be imposed upon them in this regard, whether at international law or in the domestic sphere.[8] Yet, there remains significant uncertainty as to the methodology for extending fundamental rights obligations to the private sector and the exact scope and contour of their duties.

The South African Constitution[9] innovatively included a provision which extended the obligations in its Bill of Rights to corporate entities. Section 8(2) states that '[a] provision of the Bill of Rights bind a natural or juristic person if, and to the extent that, it is applicable taking into account the nature of the right and the nature of any duty imposed by the right.'[10] Section 8(4) also extended rights to corporate entities: '[a] juristic person is entitled to the rights in the Bill of Rights, to the extent required by nature of the rights and the nature of that juristic person.' As can be seen from these provisions, rights and duties may be considered to apply wholly, partially, or not at all to private entities. The Constitutional Court

---

[8] See, for instance, J Nolan, 'With Power Comes Responsibility: Human Rights and Corporate Accountability', (1991) 28 *University of New South Wales Law Journal* 581–613 and D Bilchitz, 'The Necessity for a Business and Human Rights Treaty' (2016) 2 *Business and Human Rights Journal* (forthcoming).

[9] Constitution of the Republic of South Africa Act 108 of 1996.

[10] There is some circularity in the way in which section 8(2) was drafted: for a critique and approach to interpreting it in the best light possible, see D Bilchitz, 'Corporate Law and the Constitution: Towards Binding Human Rights Responsibilities for Corporations' (2008) 125 *SALJ* 754, 775–76.

of South Africa has thus been faced with deciding when a right applies to a corporate entity and what its obligations are in this regard. The approach it has adopted is worth exploring in addressing the more general question raised above concerning how to capture the nature and scope of corporate obligations in relation to fundamental rights. Such an analysis may in turn assist at both the international law level and in other domestic jurisdictions with understanding how to approach this task. This paper engages specifically with the right to privacy and the general principles that should be adopted when understanding the obligations of corporations in this regard.

The starting point for such an analysis must be *Khumalo v Holomisa*,[11] where the constitutional court was faced with a defamation claim between two sets of private parties (one of which was a major media publishing house and the other a well-known politician). The South African common law of defamation required a plaintiff to allege and prove that a defamatory statement was made; it did not require the plaintiff to allege or prove that such a statement was false. Once it had been proved that a defamatory statement was made, the burden of proof shifted to the defendants to show that the publication of the statement was justifiable on one of the grounds recognised in law (such as it was true and in the public benefit, or represented a fair comment). The media publishing house in this case claimed that the failure of the law to require a plaintiff to prove the falsity of a defamatory statement insufficiently protected the right to free speech of the press. Seeing that the state was not a party to this case, the Constitutional Court framed the case as requiring a consideration of whether the right to freedom of expression could be applied directly between two private parties.[12]

In addressing this question, the judgment can be understood to refer to three factors which were important in deciding whether a right should be be 'applicable' to private parties. First, it mentioned that a court needed to consider 'the intensity of the right'[13] which appears to mean its importance within the constitutional order and perhaps the reasons for its protection. Secondly, the court would investigate the potential invasion of the right by persons other than the state. Finally, the court considered the nature of the parties before it and whether the right has a particular significance for them. The role of a private party within the broader society could also be considered. Since the case concerned the media and freedom of expression was vital to its operation, the right was held to be directly applicable to the private parties in that case.

---

[11] 2002 (5) SA 401 (CC).

[12] This framing may be questioned: given that the common law was being impugned, in effect, the constitutional challenge was to law that was applied by state institutions and, so essentially involved determining the requirements of free speech for the law of the state. Of course, the law was meant to regulate the relationship between private parties. This may be better classified as a type of 'indirect horizontal application': for a detailed engagement with this case and the problems with its reasoning, see S Woolman, 'Application' in S Woolman *et al* (eds) *Constitutional Law of South Africa* (Cape Town, Jutas, 2006).

[13] ibid para 33. See also I Currie and J De Waal, *The Bill of Rights Handbook* (Cape Town, Jutas 2013) 48 who suggest that this phrase is opaque but probably relates to the 'scope of the right'.

Abstracting from the particular context of this case, the factors outlined by the South African Constitutional Court provide a useful rubric through which to examine the implications that the right to privacy has for the obligations of private corporations at a more global level. This paper will continue to utilise the statements of the Constitutional Court, in particular where its doctrines and arguments have more universal application.

A. The Intensity and Importance of the Right to Privacy

The first factor outlined by the court requires a consideration of the underlying reasons for the protection of a particular right and why it has a particular importance in the international community and a polity such as the South African constitutional democracy. Some understanding thereof is of course necessary if we are to comprehend the reasons for why corporate entities should have obligations in this regard. There is of course much philosophical argument and dispute as to the exact reasons and rationale for the protection of privacy.[14] For the purposes of this paper, it will focus briefly on the approach of the South African constitutional court towards this question which offers a useful summary of some key rationales.[15]

The right to privacy is expressly protected in the South African constitution as follows:

'Privacy—Everyone has the right to privacy, which includes the right not to have—

(a) their person or home searched;
(b) their property searched;
(c) their possessions seized;
(d) the privacy of their communications infringed.'[16]

The rationale for the protections of privacy is given particular poignance against the backdrop of South African history where, as the court pointed out in a recent judgment, the police would often arrive without warning at the homes of individuals and subject them to frequent invasive searches without warrants.[17] The raw, visceral historical context of privacy violations in South Africa leads the court

---

[14] See, for instance, JJ Thomson, 'The Right to Privacy' (1975) 4 *Philosophy and Public Affairs* 295–314; AF Westin, *Privacy and Freedom* (The Bodley Head, 1970); WA Parent, 'Privacy, morality and the law' (1983) 12 *Philosophy and Public Affairs* 269–88; D Feldman, 'Secrecy, dignity and autonomy? Views of privacy as a civil liberty' (1994) 47 *Current Legal Problems* 41; AD Moore, 'Defining privacy' (2008) 39 *Journal of Social Philosophy* 411–28.

[15] For an overview of the constitutional law relating to the right to privacy and its impact on the common law, see D McQuoid-Mason, 'Privacy' in S Woolman *et al* (eds) *Constitutional Law of South Africa* (Cape Town, Jutas, 2006).

[16] Section 15 of the South African Constitution.

[17] *Gaertner v Minister of Finance* 2014 1 SA 442 (CC) para 1.

to an understanding of its jurisprudential foundations. Ackermann J in the early case of *Bernstein v Bester*, recognises privacy as being necessary to protect an individual's autonomous identity.[18] In *NM v Smith*, O'Regan J (dissenting) clearly recognises the importance of protecting a personal space in which we can pursue our own goals and from which we can choose to exclude the community.[19] In the *Hyundai* case, Justice Langa roots the protection of privacy in the notion of human dignity.[20] A further related rationale seeks to protect the freedom of the individual against the over-weening and arbitrary exercise of coercive power by the state. This rationale also connects privacy with the very maintenance of a sense of personal security on the part of individuals.[21]

Whilst recognising the importance of privacy, the courts in South Africa have always stressed that the intensity of the protected interest varies with the context in which an individual finds themselves. Thus, in *Bernstein*, Ackermann contends that we cannot consider individuals as islands unto themselves: individuals interact socially and communally and thus their autonomy cannot be abstracted from the communal context within which they operate.[22] This leads to the development of the court's graded approach towards privacy rights: 'Privacy is acknowledged in the truly personal realm, but as a person moves into communal relations and activities such as business and social interaction, the scope of personal space shrinks accordingly'.[23] The approach leads to a continuum of protection whereby stronger protections for privacy are afforded within the home and weaker protections as the individual moves into more public contexts. In the *Hyundai* case, Langa affirms this graded approach but clarifies that the right does extend—albeit in weakened form—also to the protection of individuals in more public spaces too.[24] Whilst the exact doctrines may differ in various jurisdictions, these justifications and arguments relating to the protection of the right to privacy are not only of application in the South African context but would apply universally.

B. The Potential Invasion of the Right

The corporate structure is the dominant business entity in the world today. The ability of corporations to have an impact upon the right to privacy of individuals in relation to personal information can be helpfully divided into two different areas. The first relates to the possibilities for violations of the rights of those

---

[18] *Bernstein v Bester* 1996 2 SA 751 (CC) para 65.

[19] *NM v Smith* 2007 5 SA 250 (CC) para 30.

[20] *Investigating Directorate: Serious Economic Offences v Hyundai Motor Distributors* 2001 1 SA 545 (CC) para 18.

[21] *Mistry v Interim Medical and Dental Council of South Africa* 1998 4 SA 1127 (CC) para 25.

[22] *Bernstein* (n 8) para 66–67.

[23] *Bernstein* (n 8) para 67.

[24] *Hyundai* (n 20) para 16.

who are a 'part' of the corporate structure itself and, in particular, its employees.[25] Countless individuals are employed by corporations and their waking hours are dominated by their work. They communicate via telephones, and computers that are provided by their workplaces. No doubt, given the large amount of time that individuals spend working, they also conduct personal transactions on work computers and phones. Corporate structures often have the ability to monitor everything that goes through their servers or to garner information from the work computers of employees: they can in this way also acquire large amounts of personal information about their employees. Whilst individuals may have a lesser expectation of privacy at work, as we have seen, the constitutional court of South Africa has maintained that the protections of the right do not disappear completely in the workplace.

The second area in which corporations have a large potential to invade the privacy of individuals is in respect of the services they provide to their customers. Most individuals today possess mobile phones, ordinarily bought or leased from corporations that have the ability to track the phone-calls made and data used. Individuals increasingly pay an internet service provider (ISP) to enable them to gain access to the internet. All data usage must go through the ISP's servers which, in turn, provides another opportunity for these companies to monitor their users' daily transactions. Banks similarly require the provision of private information to open accounts, as do retailers who can track every transaction that occurs on their systems.[26] All these very recent technological changes create the possibility of wide-spread monitoring and surveillance of individual communications and behaviour.

These changes in the modern world raise important questions concerning the nature and reasonableness of expectations of privacy. Can individuals claim not to know that they connect to the internet via an ISP which can track their behaviour? Yet, at the same time individual usage of the internet often takes place in the inner sanctum of the home to which the highest forms of privacy protection are accorded. The advent of computing and mobile technologies has allowed the most intimate of spaces to become potentially publicly accessible.[27] Clearly, the individual interests in autonomous identity, control over personal information, freedom and dignity do not disappear simply as a result of technological advances. As we have seen, these developments have given rise to a situation across the world where it is not only the state that may intrude on these important interests but private corporations too. As Richards writes, '[a]ny solutions to the problem of surveillance must thus take into account private surveillance as well as public'.[28]

[25] This category should not in the author's view be limited to employees and could involve shareholders for instance too.
[26] BJ Gould, 'Privacy, identity and security' in BJ Gould and L Lazarus (eds), *Security and Human Rights* (Oxford, Hart, 2010) 53 refers to this as our 'digital trails that may contain a wealth of personal information'.
[27] Gould ibid 65.
[28] Richards (n 1) 1958.

This potential for the invasion of the most intimate spaces of individuals as well as the extent of the daily transactions they conduct in the more public spaces of work and retail outlets provides a strong reason for the need to try and articulate principles that govern corporate obligations in this regard.

C. The Role of Corporations in Society and Privacy

The potential for corporate invasions upon the right to privacy also touches centrally upon the role that corporations play today in society. Corporations are the dominant business entity for a reason: the form itself offers significant legal benefits in that it is regarded as a separate legal person from those who own it or control it.[29] That separate legal personality in turn has two key legal implications: first, it creates a form of limited liability, in that shareholders only stand to lose their capital investment in the company if it goes insolvent and their personal assets are generally shielded from the fate of the company;[30] and secondly, it has perpetual succession, meaning that the company continues to exist irrespective of changes in its underlying ownership.

These features of the corporate form point to a complex purpose underlying its creation.[31] From the perspective of legislators who must decide to bring the corporate structure into existence, it is necessary to have a case for why society as a whole benefits from the creation of such an entity. Traditional reasons include the fact that the corporate form encourages risk-taking and innovation which are likely to help improve the lot of everyone in society over the longer term. These reasons cannot, however, involve a trampling on the rights of individuals which would undermine any social benefits to be achieved by the creation of a corporation. At the same time, this very reasoning rests upon the idea that the corporate form is a means through which individuals can pursue their individual interests in advancing their economic goals in life. From the perspective of individuals, the entity is a better means of realising their own business interests; legislators hope to harness this individual self-interest for achieving wider social benefits. The social purpose of a corporate structure places certain constraints on the achievement of individual self-interest: an obligation not to harm fundamental rights and to play a positive role in the fulfilment thereof is a crucial consequence that flows from this dual nature of the corporation.

---

[29] H Hansmann and R Kraakman, 'What is Corporate Law?' in R Kraakman et al (eds), *The Anatomy of Corporate Law: a Comparative and Functional Approach*, 1st edn (Oxford, Oxford University Press, 2004) 7.

[30] HS Cilliers et al, *Entrepreneurial Law* (Cape Town, Jutas 2000) 66.

[31] The author draws here from D Bilchitz, 'Do Corporations Have Positive Fundamental Rights Obligations?' (2010) 125 *Theoria* 1, 9–10 in which he articulates what he terms the dual perspectives from which we must view the corporate entity.

The fact that corporations affect the personal lives of individuals on a daily basis also provides a case for extending some of the protections offered by fundamental rights to them. Indeed, the Constitutional Court of South Africa has recognised that certain rights such as privacy must be extended to corporate entities: the reasons it has given for doing so, however, relate to the express purpose of protecting natural persons whose entitlements are primary.[32] If police can simply enter into corporate offices at will, they would violate the rights to privacy of individual employees, directors, customers and shareholders with a stake in the corporation. Recognition that corporations may benefit from the right to privacy does not automatically entail they have obligations flowing from that right. However, the rationale provided by the Constitutional Court of South Africa works both ways: since the interests of natural persons are primary and corporations have a large amount of power to affect these interests, it is necessary that societies recognise that corporations have obligations in this regard. A primary focus on the entitlements of natural persons and the manner in which they are affected by corporations provides a case for both the extension of rights protections to corporations as well as a recognition of their obligations.

III. Specifying the Obligations of Corporations: Privacy And Surveillance

This paper has thus far utilised the framework provided by the Constitutional Court of South Africa to provide a strong case for why the right to privacy should have implications for corporations. It now turns to consider in more detail, corporate obligations flowing from such rights.[33] The preliminary question that arises is one of methodology. As has been mentioned, it will not focus on existing legislation and common law in South Africa or elsewhere: since fundamental rights are amongst the strongest and most basic norms in any legal system—international or domestic—an understanding of their content must guide specific legal rules that develop rather than the other way round. It is thus necessary to have an independent normative basis for determining the content and implications of these rights that does not—in a circular manner—simply reproduce the existing status

---

[32] Hyundai (n 20) para 18 and *First National Bank of SA Ltd t/a Wesbank v Commissioner, South African Revenue Service; First National Bank of SA Ltd t/a Wesbank v Minister of Finance* 2002 (4) SA 768 (CC) para 45.

[33] Surprisingly, limited detailed attention has been given to how to extend particular human rights obligation to corporations. An example of a document that attempts to grapple with some of these issues in relation to the right to health is the *Human Rights Guidelines for Pharmaceutical Companies in Relation to Access to Medicines* UN Doc A/63/263 (11 August, 2008) available at www.business-human-rights.org/un-intl-orgs/un-intergovernmental-orgs/un/un-special-rapporteur-on-right-to-health.

quo:[34] the approach developed below thus will be rooted in normative principles relating to the right to privacy that have been developed in various jurisdictions around the world as well as a globally accepted framework for analysing fundamental rights obligations.

What is the basis upon which we can determine the concrete obligations that corporations have with respect to the right to privacy? Clearly, there is no need to begin with a tabula rasa. Much of the constitutional case law constructing the right to privacy though has developed in the context of state obligations. How do we translate the principles articulated in this context into ones relating to corporations? Steven Ratner suggests that, in attempting to articulate a theory of corporate responsibility, one can move '*down* from state responsibility and *up* from individual responsibility'.[35] This methodology draws on an understanding of the corporation that is consistent with the approach argued for here, whereby it is conceptualised as an entity that is neither wholly public nor private. Yet, whilst this method of working out corporate obligations is a useful way of proceeding, it also has its limitations, in that corporations—given their distinctive nature—may have a set of sui generis obligations which are neither held by the state nor individuals. Bearing this in mind, in determining corporate obligations it is useful to proceed engaging with the following key factors, some of which flow from the Constitutional Court of South Africa framework discussed above.

The first key question relates to understanding the basis for the protection of the privacy rights of individuals. This analysis enables one to focus upon what the interests of individuals are which require protection when considering the obligations of corporations. The second key question relates to the potential invasions people may complain of on the part of corporations. The third question relates to the need to ensure effective protection for the right which may itself help condition certain types of duties. The fourth question relates to the fairness of recognising that any duty falls upon a corporation. To do so, requires a conception of the character of the corporation as an entity and what the impact of any such duty will be upon the entity. Considerations of equity may also require limiting the scope of obligations to the field in which the corporation has an impact.[36] The fifth important question concerns the relationship between the corporation and the state in relation to a possible infringement. The closer the relationship between the corporation and the state, the greater the likelihood that duties more akin to those of the state will apply to the corporation.[37]

---

[34] It is also required as mentioned above by an analysis of the application provisions in the constitution: see N Friedman, 'The Common Law and the Constitution: Revisiting Constitutionality' (2014) 30 *South African Journal on Human Rights* 66–74.

[35] Ratner (n 4) 496 provides a very impressive analysis of the methodology of developing corporate obligations in relation to fundamental rights. The author accepts the point that we need not begin with a blank slate and draws on some of the key insights from his work with modifications that he believes are necessary.

[36] Ratner (n 4) 506–11.

[37] Ratner (n 4) 497–506.

The right to privacy has also traditionally been understood as a 'negative' right of individuals to be free from intrusion into their private space. Henry Shue famously challenged the understanding that particular rights only give rise to one particular form of obligation (negative or positive). Instead, he has argued that 'the complete fulfilment of each kind of right involves the performance of multiple kinds of duties'.[38] Each fundamental right, he claims, contains three correlative duties: duties to avoid depriving individuals of a right, duties to protect individuals from deprivation by third parties, and duties to aid the deprived to realise their right. In international human rights law, these duties have become known as the duty to respect, protect, and fulfil respectively. This framework is now generally employed in order to capture the obligations of the state with respect to fundamental rights in some of the General Comments of the United Nations treaty committees.[39] Given the attempt to understand the broad normative principles that enable us to determine the concrete obligations of corporations with respect to the right to privacy, it makes sense to utilise these three broad categories of obligations and to consider what is required of corporations in relation to each of them (in light of the methodology outlined above). Clearly, the right to privacy will have multiple concrete applications in a wide-range of contexts: the focus of this paper will involve understanding these obligations in the context of communications and the potential for surveillance.

A. The Duty to Respect

The duty to respect involves the key 'negative' obligation on an agent to avoid harm to the rights of individuals. This is the primary 'responsibility' that has been recognised currently at the international law level as having application to corporations in the United Nations Guiding Principles on Business and Human Rights.[40] Yet, as expressed in that document, it is a general duty whose concrete implications need to be developed and understood in relation to specific rights. What does this obligation require of corporations in relation to whether or not they may monitor information they can gain access to?

In answering this question, it is useful to consider the South African case of *NM v Smith*[41] which dealt with a claim for damages concerning the disclosure in a book of information about the HIV status of the applicants without their consent.

---

[38] Shue *Basic Rights* (Princeton, Princeton University Press, 1980) 52.

[39] See, for instance, General Comment no 12 on the Right to Adequate Food available at www.refworld.org/docid/4538838c11.html.

[40] This document is available at www.business-humanrights.org/en/un-guiding-principles. The word responsibility is in inverted commas, as this document does not recognise binding legal obligations upon corporations in that regard. For criticism of that position, see Bilchitz (n 5) 109–23.

[41] See (n 19) above.

The common law had traditionally required a clear intention wrongfully to disclose private information in order to found liability. Whilst a majority of the court found that this standard had been met, two minority judgments found that it had not and considered the need to develop the common law to allow for the *negligent* disclosure of private information. Such an approach had already been adopted in relation to media defendants in defamation actions which required the media to show that it had been reasonable in publishing certain material.[42] O'Regan J argued that it was appropriate to develop the common law in light of the obligations that flowed from the right to privacy to allow for damages where there had been negligent disclosures by the media given the power they wielded in relation to the private sphere of individuals. She stated the following:

> 'The nature of obligations imposed however is merely a requirement that the media establish that the publication is reasonable in the circumstances or that it is not negligent. Such obligations require the media to consider the constitutional rights at play and be persuaded that publication is nevertheless appropriate. The effect on the media, therefore, is to require them to act in an objectively appropriate fashion. In determining whether they have so acted, a court will bear in mind the particular constraints under which the media operate and will not impose a counsel of perfection in circumstances where it would not be realistic. The effect of such a rule would be to require editors and journalists to act with due care and respect for the right to privacy, prior to publishing material that infringes that right.'[43]

This heightened standard required of the media is helpful in a broader way in articulating the duties of corporations in respect of the right to privacy. The power of media outlets is similar to that of corporations in the technology and mobile-phone sector. Requiring corporations to avoid negligent disclosure of private information would place a duty of care upon them which requires them to take steps to guard against foreseeable harms.[44] This legal articulation of negligence connects well with the responsibility of due diligence recognised in the Guiding Principles on Business and Human Rights. This document requires businesses to conduct an assessment of the impact their operations may have on privacy rights, 'integrating and acting upon the findings, tracking responses and communicating how the impacts are addressed'.[45] This idea implies that businesses first have a duty to consider the possible impacts they may have on the privacy rights of individuals. The fact that there is an impact, however, does not determine that there is an obligation to desist from interfering with the privacy of an individual: it will all depend upon whether there is an impermissible violation that occurs through the negligent action of the corporation. To determine that,

---

[42] This approach was developed in the case of *National Media v Bogoshi* 1998 (4) SA 1196 (SCA) and approved by the Constitutional Court in *Khumalo* (n 14) above.

[43] *NM v Smith* (n 19) para 178.

[44] *Kruger v Coetzee* 1966 2 SA 428 (A) at 430E.

[45] Guiding Principle 17 (n 40).

it is necessary to consider the various facets of corporate engagement with the informational privacy of those with whom they interact.

i. Direct Corporate Duties

It is helpful to start with a simple case. In the course of its day-to-day operations, corporations may well have control over much personal information of employees: for human resource purposes, the corporation may require information about the phone number and address of an employee. This might be necessary to contact an individual or serve legal documents upon them. It would thus seem unreasonable to withhold such information from a corporation and its holding thereof would not infringe privacy rights. An employee though also has a reasonable expectation that such information is kept confidential and is not transmitted elsewhere unwittingly.

The more difficult cases relate to the fact that many corporations provide employees with computers and/or allow them to connect with their internet network. The question then arises as to whether the corporation has a right to any or all information contained on such a machine or transmitted through its network: may it also monitor or intercept any communications going through its network?

Traditional notions of property might be taken to suggest that if a computer is the property of a corporation, it is entitled to anything that is contained on the machine. The reality, however, is that a computer has become not only the basic modality through which individuals work but also one through which they conduct personal communications and daily transactions. Many individuals lack the resources to acquire a personal computer in addition to a work computer; moreover, it becomes inconvenient and inefficient continually to shift between different machines. The nature of computing is also changing: with the advent of cloud computing, increasingly individuals upload both personal and work-related information on to clouds which can be accessed on multiple machines. The workplace has also changed: corporations benefit from the fact that individuals are mobile and able to work in multiple locations both at the office and at home. These shifts increasingly mean that there is no clear boundary between personal information on a computer and that which relates to work. Moreover, a personal computer creates a sense of its being in the 'private' domain of an individual who interacts directly with it rather than something that is essentially 'public' in nature. These reasons, in my view, provide strong grounds for individuals to claim that they have a significant and legitimate expectation of privacy on their personal computers and mobile communications that has become objectively reasonable in the light of technological shifts and developments.

It thus seems wrong to adopt an approach that, in a wholesale manner, suggests everything on a corporate computer or network is 'public'. At the same time, the converse also seems difficult to assert: corporations may have a legitimate expectation that they are entitled to have access to and monitor the work performed by employees. They may also be concerned that their networks could be used for illegal activities such as the downloading of child pornography which would implicate them in such crimes. The graded approach outlined by the South African constitutional court to privacy appears to be particularly apposite in attempting to strike a balance between personal privacy on a computer and the legitimate rights of an employer. Thus, an employer should, in the author's view, be prohibited from interfering or gaining access to information that relates to the personal 'intimate' sphere of an individual's life; it may, however, monitor and gain access to information directly relating to the work of employees or that may violate any criminal laws.[46] Work folders should be clearly labelled as such and the presumption on all other data should be that it lies within the private sphere of an employee. It may be asked how a corporation could determine that criminal laws are violated without gaining access to the private information of an employee? The jurisprudence that has developed relating to the state can be useful in this regard and apply, with the necessary changes, to corporations. In other words, reasonable grounds can be required for any surveillance of the private information of an employee and a warrant required for any such interference.

An important question arises in this context as to whether an individual can consent to the release of their information. Traditionally, in relation to privacy, one of the key elements involves the individual's right to control information relating to them;[47] presumably, if they consent to such information being released, that is a decision that lies within their control. At the same time, it is necessary to have regard to the fact that consent does not take place within a vacuum and that power relations may alter the reality of such consent. Thus, if a person's prospective employer presents them with a contract which requires them to consent to the monitoring of all their information on their personal computer and which goes through the corporate server, the individual may have little choice but to sign that provision if they want the job. Recognising that jobs are, in most countries, in short supply, means that the individual's bargaining power is usually extremely limited. As such, general contractual provisions which appear to involve individual consent to the release of information are often effectively coerced. In such a context, human rights law should refuse to accept that one can waive the protections afforded by the right to privacy on the basis of such unequal power bargains.

Thus, a rather uncompromising position should be enforced whereby corporations have a clear obligation not to monitor or attempt to acquire personal information from individuals that is unrelated to their work. If they acquire such information, it should be destroyed and not disclosed to anyone else. In relation to information relating to the employee's work or corporate operations, it is the

---

[46] Practically, it would not be permissible to have access to the content of these machines and communications to decide what is permissible or not. Such a distinction would therefore require particular policies to be put in place (thus requiring employees to put all work in particular folders which the corporation can have access to) as well as specific filters which can stop illegal activities.

[47] *NM v Smith* (n 19) para 44.

duty of the corporation to inform individuals that they may monitor communications in this regard. Being informed provides the individual employee with a clear understanding of the expectations they can have of the company and its surveillance of their work-related activities. It also allows them to understand the possibility that technology could also enable unauthorised access to personal information on such computers and thus allows them to choose not to use work machines for certain purposes. Being informed also helps to minimise any sense that their personal integrity has been violated as may have occurred if such a programme of surveillance were to be done secretly.

ii. *Corporate Duties to Customers*

As has already been indicated above, one of the possible areas for the invasion of the right to privacy lies in the relationship between customers who purchase internet and mobile phone services from corporations. Take the example of the Internet Service Provider (ISP): most middle class people today sign up to a contract with a corporation which allows them to have access to the internet at home. Whilst in the personal sphere of their homes, individuals surf the net and conduct transactions all of which have to go through the network and servers of the ISPs. The ISPs consequently have vast potential to monitor and garner information from this most intimate core of people's lives.

It seems to me that the graded approach outlined by the South African constitutional court, once again, would require corporations to accord a very high level of protection to the information transmitted across its servers and networks which emerge from the homes of individuals. There is no real legitimate business interest as to why corporations may gain access to that information. Moreover, once again, the issue of consent raises its head as the ISPs may place a clause in any contract with a customer allowing them to monitor and gain access to the information transmitted across their networks. Since individuals have no choice but to rely on ISPs to connect to the internet which has become an important domain for the exercise of personal autonomy, once again, such corporations have the significant power to compel individuals to sign the contracts they devise. As such, it should not in general be regarded as possible for an individual to consent to the monitoring and surveillance of their activities by ISPs. Individuals may of course choose to make any personal information publicly available in their own time but not under contractual duress. Mobile phone operators should be regarded similarly given the way in which mobile phones today have become ubiquitous and an integral part of the personal domain of individuals. Both sets of corporations should have significant duties not to interfere with or seek to gain access to information of individuals within their private domain. The failure to do so will be a prima facie infringement of privacy rights: such an infringement may be held to be justifiable under certain circumstances which will be discussed in relation to the limitation of rights below.

B. The Duty to Protect

The duty to protect involves an obligation that is assumed not simply in relation to one's own conduct but that of other actors. Thus, the state is traditionally not only required to refrain from infringing rights itself: it is also required to ensure that other actors do not imperil the interests protected by fundamental rights. Thus, in *Velasquez Rodriguez v Honduras*,[48] this duty was articulated as follows:

> 'The State has a legal duty to take reasonable steps to prevent human rights violations and to use the means at its disposal to carry out a serious investigation of violations committed within its jurisdiction, to identify those responsible, to impose the appropriate punishment and to ensure the victim adequate compensation'.[49]

The very origins of the state itself in various philosophical theories, suggest that its role is, at least partially, to keep the peace and prevent the violation of rights of one individual by another.[50] It also has at its disposal various institutions such as the police and prosecuting authority which enable it to realise this function. This relationship between the duty to protect and the very nature of the state itself raises the question as to whether such a duty has any application in the context of corporations and the privacy of personal information.

To answer this question, it is necessary to refer to the empirical reality of the power that corporations wield more generally and in the technological realm in particular. Corporations today operate within elaborate networks of suppliers, contractors or subsidiaries. As such, these relationships raise the possibility that a corporation may not in and of itself violate a right but participate or aid in the violation thereof by another party. Recognition of these realities, has led to the development of the legal notion of 'complicity': corporations may not themselves harm rights but be complicit with others in doing so.[51] Difficult questions arise as to the scope and extent of complicity: as the UN Guiding Principles on Business and Human Rights point out, it has a wider 'moral' meaning—that involves benefiting from an abuse and being silent in the face of it—and a narrower legal meaning which focuses on whether the corporation has provided knowing practical assistance or encouragement which has a substantial effect on the perpetration of a

---

[48] *Velasquez Rodriguez v Honduras* 1988 Inter-American Court of Human Rights (judgment of 29 July 1988) paras 172 and 174 available at www1.umn.edu/humanrts/iachr/b_11_12d.htm.

[49] ibid para 174.

[50] See, for instance, Hobbes *Leviathan*, ed R Tuck (Cambridge, Cambridge University Press, 1996) Chapter 17 and Locke *Two Treatises of Government*, ed P Laslett (Cambridge, Cambridge University Press, 1988) Second Treatise Chapter IX.

[51] For an excellent attempt to define the contours of the legal notion of complicity, see the report by the International Commission of Jurists Expert Panel on Corporate Complicity (2008) available at www.icj.org/report-of-the-international-commission-of-jurists-expert-legal-panel-on-corporate-complicity-in-international-crimes/.

violation.[52] Whatever the exact ambit of complicity, it has been recognised widely that a corporation must take steps not only in relation to its own conduct but also in relation to others too with whom it has various relationships. Thus, the Guiding Principles on Business and Human Rights, for instance, recognise that the due diligence which a company must perform requires considering not only its own operations but the impact on rights which may 'be directly linked to its operations, products or services through its business relationships'.[53] To do so may require it effectively to regulate the behaviour of other parties with whom it has these relationships.

i. Corporate Duty to Protect and the State

Focusing now on the sphere of the privacy of personal information, corporations may of course have very close relationships with the state. In order to operate in a sphere like internet or mobile communications, specific regulatory approvals are required. Moreover, specific legislation often governs this area. A difficult issue arises here where the state attempts to use corporate entities as a method of monitoring private citizens. It is important that corporations recognise that they have a duty to protect the information of private individuals even against state interference and that this duty flows from the human right to privacy. They must thus assert their independence in relation to the state and resist becoming simply a part of state monitoring machinery. This duty arises from the fact that corporations assume control of personal information that they would never ordinarily have and may undermine the very core of an individual's intimate sphere. In a sense, corporations in this sphere in many ways exercise a level of power that is akin to that of the state with its power to monitor significant aspects of individuals' lives. Consequently, these powerful private entities are required to assume obligations to protect individuals against the invasion of their very intimate core. At the same time, corporations may be under a duty to disclose information to the state under particular circumstances envisaged in legislation and where a justifiable limitation of the right may take place (such as to protect individuals from terrorist activity). The duties of corporations in this regard will be discussed in more detail when discussing permissible limitations on the right to privacy in section D below.

ii. Corporate Duty to Protect and Other Private Actors

Corporations will in a similar vein have a duty to protect the personal information of individuals against intrusion by third parties. This may place an onerous

---

[52] Guiding Principle 17 Commentary (n 40). See also I Tofalo Overt And Hidden Accomplices: Transnational Corporations' Range of Complicity for Human-Rights Violations' in O de Schutter (ed) *Transnational Corporations and Human Rights* (Oxford, Hart, 2006) 335–339ff.

[53] Guiding Principle 17 (n 40).

set of positive obligations upon entities operating in this sphere to ensure the security of the communication networks established against invasion by third parties. Increasingly, providing effective security against hacking is becoming a very difficult task. Moreover, corporations may also have duties to help prevent aiding or abetting violations of the right to privacy of individuals even where a third party is the primary cause of such an infringement.

A fascinating recent case that involves the duty to protect, arose in relation to the question of whether a corporation that runs a search engine (Google) has a duty to assist an individual to have such information effectively hidden from public searches. The particular case related to a newspaper report containing detrimental information about the financial solvency of an individual that emanated from 1998. The applicant, a Mr Gonzalez, claimed that this information had no bearing on his current financial status; yet, every time a search was conducted on the internet, this information came up on the search engine which could be prejudicial to his current financial interests. The newspaper website which had initially uploaded the article refused to take it down. The individual then approached the courts, claiming that the newspaper should be forced to do so but also that Google, as a search engine, had a duty to prevent this information from being revealed when his name was searched. The case eventually reached the European Court of Justice which ruled in favour of Mr Gonzalez based upon a directive of the European Commission.[54] It found that Google, as the search engine, enabled this information about the individual continually to be highlighted and thus it contributed to a serious violation of Mr Gonzalez's right to privacy. Since, there was no legitimate reason for this information to remain publicly accessible, Google had a duty to prevent this information from being found and thus effectively the individual had a right to this information being withheld.[55]

Importantly, for our purposes here, Google was not the originator of the information about Mr Gonzalez but rather was responsible for a search engine which enabled such information to be found. Search engines are though powerful tools which render information accessible to individuals: as such, Google was under a duty not to help disseminate information placed on the internet by a third party. The case can thus be seen as an example of a duty on Google to take reasonable steps to prevent itself from being complicit in the violation of rights that is perpetrated by a third party.

C. Duty to Fulfil

The right to privacy has traditionally been understood to involve largely a negative right of an individual not to have the privacy of their communications

---

[54] *Google Spain v Agencia Espanola de Proteccion de Datos* (European Court of Justice, 2014) available at www.eur-lex.europa.eu/legal-content/EN/TXT/?uri=CELEX:62012CJ0131.

[55] *Google Spain* (n 51) paras 98–99.

(or home) infringed.[56] Yet, the Constitutional Court of South Africa has interest-ingly understood the right to involve a positive dimension too which may, in itself, place significant positive obligations upon other social actors.

Philosophically speaking, the right not to interfere or violate the personal, inti-mate domain of an individual suggests an interest that human beings have that is of importance in protecting the very integrity of that sphere. Recognising this point, Justice O'Regan writes in the *NM* case, that:

> 'We value privacy for this reason at least—that the constitutional conception of being a human being asserts and seeks to foster the possibility of human beings choosing how to live their lives within the overall framework of a broader community. The protection of this autonomy, which flows from our recognition of individual human worth, presup-poses personal space within which to live this life.'[57]

That understanding of privacy has, for example, led the court to recognise the need for a domain 'of private intimacy and autonomy which allows us to establish and nurture human relationships without interference from the outside commu-nity'.[58] It used this understanding to decriminalise a prohibition on consensual same-sex sexual conduct. The justices thus point to the fact that this right might be taken to be wider than a shield against state (or private sector) interference but actually require certain positive obligations to be performed to ensure that such a private sphere exists and is accorded adequate protection.[59]

Applying this thinking to modern communications entails that the state may have an obligation to help develop an infrastructure through which individuals are entitled to communicate and realise their personal projects without a concern that they will be interfered with. Such a communication's infrastructure could be achieved through setting up the regulatory structure and enabling the concrete technological set-up of networks to be developed. The government may also be under a duty to ensure that these services are provided to individuals, particularly those that cannot afford them. In many countries around the world, however, the actual provision of technological services such as internet or mobile communica-tions is left to the private sector. Importantly, if such a communications infrastruc-ture is regarded as part of the positive obligations to realise the right to privacy, then private corporations are key actors in enabling such a space to be developed. The fact that they choose to operate in a sphere that is deeply connected to a

---

[56] See section 14 of the South African Constitution and General Comment 17 on the Right to Pri-vacy available at http://www.refworld.org/docid/453883f922.html.

[57] *NM v Smith* (n 19) para 131.

[58] *National Coalition of Gay and Lesbian Equality v Minister of Justice* 1999 (1) SA 6 (CC) para 32.

[59] More concretely, such points have implications, for instance, for the right to housing as the home is the exemplar of the private sphere. The South African Housing Act 107 of 1997, for instance, in giv-ing effect to the constitutional right to have access to adequate housing outlines the goal of realising progressively for every South African 'permanent residential structures with secure tenure, ensuring internal and external privacy and providing adequate protection against the elements.' The very defini-tion of an adequate house thus requires the government to take into account privacy.

fundamental right, places certain positive obligations upon them. The reasoning here can be analogised to a situation in which corporations take on the provision of a health service: the fact that such an entity chooses to operate in a sphere relating to fundamental rights (for profit) places particular positive obligations upon them.

Similar reasoning was recently employed by the Constitutional Court of South Africa in a case dealing with the right to social security (section 27 of the South African constitution). A private company which was responsible for paying out social security grants to millions of people was held to have become an operational arm of the state and to have assumed constitutional obligations.[60] Whilst the classification of Cash Paymaster as an organ of state may be questioned, this judgment does suggest an important principle: that where a private company wishes to make money through assuming obligations in terms of a fundamental right, it must understand that it undertakes certain constitutional obligations which may condition how it operates. The modern communication infrastructure today can, it is argued, be understood to be an expression of the positive obligation to realise the right to privacy (and perhaps other rights as well such as freedom of expression): to provide a space in which individuals can express their autonomy as well as forge and develop their personal relationships. As such, the right to privacy places positive obligations on corporations to develop and design their networks in such a way that enables them to realise and facilitate the important interests of individuals in a personal sphere free from surveillance. These obligations may include a requirement to render such services affordable and to develop joint programmes—with government support—to grant access to these services to the indigent. The positive obligations of corporations in this sector would, of course, not require that they become loss-making entities, which would entail losing a key distinctive feature of being a private sector entity.

D. Limitations on the Right to Privacy

This chapter has thus far explored the possible content of corporate duties with respect to privacy and the monitoring of personal communications. The key test will relate to whether the individual has a reasonable expectation of privacy. The notion of 'reasonableness' here needs to be developed further as it contains in itself the possibility of limiting an individual's subjective expectation of privacy. It also builds into the very interpretation of the entitlement some conception as to when the interests it protects can legitimately be limited.

In section IIB, it was argued that employees may not in fact be able to invoke the protection of the right to privacy in relation to certain work-related matters as

---

[60] *AllPay Consolidated Investment Holdings v Chief Executive Officer of the South African Social Security Agency* 2014 4 SA 179 (CC) ('Allpay Remedy') para 56.

they lack an objectively reasonable expectation of privacy in that regard. The right itself thus cannot in and of itself be seen to prohibit all interferences with private communications.[61] In testing the reasonableness of an expectation, however, it is suggested that some of the factors traditionally used in determining whether a right can be limited will be relevant including—in particular—a proportionality enquiry. That would require determining whether there was any legitimate purpose for interfering with a subjective expectation of privacy, the relationship between the interfering means adopted and the purpose, whether there is an alternative that interferes less with the subjective expectation yet still achieves the purpose and a balancing of the interests of the individual in privacy and the company in question.

Corporations, it is contended, may also have a duty to test the constitutionality of any law which enables the state specifically to request certain personal information from a corporation about a private individual.[62] As we saw in section IIIB, a corporation has a prima facie duty to protect the privacy of individual communications. At the same time, it will be required to obey the provisions of a law which authorises the release of such information. Such laws may exist for pressing public purposes such as national security and to prevent terror attacks. In giving effect to its duty to protect, it is suggested that the corporation must make a judgment about the following two questions. First, it must be satisfied that the request by the state does in fact conform to the requirements of the law and the authorisations it permits; if it does not, the corporation may refuse to hand over the information in question. Secondly, it must be satisfied that the provisions of the authorising law itself are likely to be found to be in conformity with the constitution and the bill of rights. That will require a corporation to make an independent judgment that the provisions of the law relate to a legitimate purpose and are suitable, necessary and proportionate.[63] In giving effect to its duty to protect, a corporation (and the directors in charge of it) may thus be required to resist handing over information to the state if it considers it likely that to do so would violate rights unjustifiably. Individuals might be able to sue the corporations or its directors if it fails to do so. Naturally, if a corporation refuses to hand over information to the state, it would have to approach a court to determine whether its independent assessment

---

[61] A statute, however, could ban such interferences and only allow them in specific instances (RICA, in fact, generally bans interceptions but allows them in some of the circumstances suggested) but the point here is that this does not flow automatically from the right itself.

[62] In South Africa, such a law exists and is known as the RICA.

[63] The corporation could of course have regard to international developments in human rights law such as the case of *Digital Rights Ireland v Minister for Communications, Minerals and Natural Resources* (European Court of Justice, 2014) available at www.curia.europa.eu/juris/document/document.jsf?docid=150642&doclang=EN which found provisions allowing wide, drag-net surveillance not to be a proportionate limitation of the right to privacy.

is correct. There may thus be a duty to litigate in circumstances in which a corporation suspects that an unjustifiable limitation of a right will take place.

This last point connects with the very nature of corporations that was discussed above. It may be tempting to treat the corporate entity as simply an extension of the state apparatus for purposes of monitoring and communications when, for instance, the state is busy trying to fight crime and terrorism. Yet, to do so elides the distinctive nature of corporations which, as argued above, have both a private and a public dimension. Their public dimension means that they have duties to act in the public interest and in conformity with the law; yet, they also have a 'private' dimension and a capacity to act autonomously. That very ability means that they cannot simply be required to 'obey' the orders of a superior in the public sphere: they have duties to evaluate themselves—exercising their independent judgment—whether or not any request by the state meets the requirements of the right to privacy. If they have a strong suspicion that it does not, they cannot simply disobey but have a duty to test their view in court. Such a duty to exercise independent judgment will ensure vigilance in the private sector against excessive interferences by the state and help protect the rights of individuals. It might also lead to publicity and transparency over requests by the government for personal information. If corporations, for instance, in the USA had tried to test requests by the NSA for information, the programme of mass surveillance would have been revealed and its constitutionality tested in the courts. This is in fact desirable in a democracy and requires the exercise of vigilance by both the private and public sectors alike.

IV. Conclusion

The approach that has been adopted in this chapter has attempted to consider the difficult matter of how a human right traditionally litigated against the state applies to a private corporation. This is question of relevance today not only within the realm of particular jurisdictions but across the borders of states. Indeed, telecommunications and the internet span the globe: as such, a company based in a foreign state may end up having significant control over the personal information of individuals in a different state. The analysis in this chapter has not been focused on the laws of particular jurisdictions: it has rather sought to extract general normative principles derived from the internationally recognised fundamental right to privacy which can help determine the obligations of corporations across the world. The discussion conducted here is a first step in attempting to outline standards that apply irrespective of the location of the corporation and in relation to individuals who may lie within different jurisdictions. The problem, of course, is that there is a lack of enforcement mechanisms at present to give effect to such transnational, universal obligations. Initiatives such as the negotiation of a new treaty on business and human rights may well help plug such gaps and should therefore be welcomed in ensuring universal protection for privacy.[64]

   In this chapter, I have attempted to give expression to a conception of the corporation as a body that is neither wholly public nor wholly private and straddles the boundary between the two. Individual human lives are lived too between the 'private' spaces in which we operate and the public realm. Technology has brought us many positive boons in our lives but also the potential to render every sphere of human life 'public'. If we value privacy, then it is necessary to erect some boundaries between the private 'intimate sphere' and what is 'public'. Since corporations are the intermediaries through which this process occurs in the modern world, they are a crucial link in the chain in ensuring these boundaries are maintained. As such, attending to their obligations is not just an interesting intellectual project but a practical necessity if we wish to preserve the foundational entitlement to privacy.

---

[64] For a general case for such a treaty, see D Bilchitz 'The Necessity for a Business and Human Rights Treaty' (2016) 1 *Business and Human Rights Journal* 203–227.

Part IV

Perspective of NGOs and Oversight Authorities

8

Mass Surveillance and Oversight

HILDE BOS-OLLERMANN

I. Introduction

In 2013, Edward Snowden revealed that in their core task of collecting communications, intelligence and security services had been using all available digital methods on a hitherto unthinkable scale. A few years later, with the increased unrest in the Middle East, terrorist attacks in Europe itself, and many European jihadists travelling to fight with the extremist Islamic State in Syria and Iraq, the West seems to have grown more accepting of the pro-active methods of the intelligence community. Snowden has not led to a radical change in mass surveillance methods. After the initial shock came realism; the public wants its defenders of national security to be effective.

But the revelations have created awareness of the need for transparency regarding intelligence services' use of special powers and methods. And there is a renewed sense of the relevance of safeguards and oversight mechanisms. This paper aims to address these issues. What is required of oversight bodies to be effective in this digital era?[1] What view should one take of mass surveillance in the first place? What minimum safeguards are required? What are the obstacles confronting those tasked to oversee the intelligence services in the post-Snowden age?

In this chapter it is argued that there are new opportunities for oversight to be seized. In practice, it turns out to be possible to enhance its quality and effectiveness. Focus should be on smart oversight procedures, proactive reporting and new perspectives on international issues. This way, independent and strong oversight bodies can provide the public with an understanding of a proper balance between national security and privacy protection.

---

[1] The generic term oversight bodies is used here for the many different types of institutions overseeing intelligence services: parliamentary, judicial as well as expert accountability mechanisms. Such external oversight is to be distinguished from internal or executive control. The term oversight in this article is used primarily in the context of oversight of the lawfulness of the activities of the intelligence and security services and does not include oversight of efficacy.

II. Mass Surveillance: What's in a Word?

As always in fundamental discussions, clarity about terminology is vital. Since Edward Snowden's leaks, terms like 'metadata', 'untargeted interception' and 'mass surveillance' have become common parlance. However, since these terms are not always defined in regulation, they are being used in different ways, and they are often used loosely or inaccurately.[2] On the one hand, some journalists, activists and politicians for example say that Snowden's revelations prove that mass surveillance is ubiquitous. Those responsible for intelligence and security services, on the other hand, as well as some national oversight bodies, claim the opposite with similar conviction.

A. Mass

The word 'mass' in mass surveillance stands for 'untargeted', meaning not directed at a specific identified person. In mass surveillance, it is no longer the single telephone wire of the suspected terrorist that is tapped. The intelligence services seek to intercept entire cables or large web applications that process many millions of communications. This results in so called 'bulk collection', in which the agency gathers a lot of information about a lot of people, without individualised suspicion of wrongdoing directed at specific individuals.

But there is a continuum between interception that is targeted at an individual and interception that is not targeted at all. Intelligence and security services use various filters and techniques to focus their interception. What if, for the sake of identifying jihadists travelling from the Netherlands and Syria and vice versa, all communication between these countries is being intercepted? Is this non-targeted interception? Or is the focus on two particular countries sufficiently connected to a particular terrorist threat that it might be deemed targeted interception? What about interception aimed at a particular community or town? Does it make sense to draw distinctions between different degrees of bulk collection? A useful definition for making the distinction in this grey area is the definition for bulk collection used by the cybersecurity experts of the US National Research Council. The Council states that 'If a significant portion of the data collected is not associated with current targets, it is bulk collection.'[3] But that leaves a fairly wide range of intelligence conduct, some much more sweeping than others.

---

[2] European Commission for Democracy through Law (Venice Commission), 'Update of the 2007 report on the Democratic Oversight of the Security Services and report on the Democratic Oversight of Signals Intelligence Agencies', CDL-AD(2015)006, published 7 April 2015, 13–15.

[3] US National Research Council, 'Bulk Collection of Signals Intelligence: Technical Options', January 2015, 3, http://www.nap.edu/catalog.php?record_id=19414.

B. Surveillance

The term 'surveillance' proves to be even more difficult to define. Does it mean (1) mere interception or (2) interception plus storage, or (3) interception, storage and analysis?

These three definitions refer in fact to consecutive stages in the intelligence process. While governments have begun to acknowledge that they are engaged in bulk collection, they assert that mere collection does not constitute surveillance.[4] Civil society is naturally suspicious about any access intelligence services have to the data of thousands if not millions of innocent individuals. Once data has been collected, it is in the hands of the services to decide what to store and analyse. The working methods in the intelligence process are often secret, so it is understandable that from the perspective of civil society it is a small step from interception to surveillance.[5] These steps or stages and their impact on privacy will are discussed in the section on 'Safeguards in the Various Stages of Mass Surveillance' (IV.B).

C. Debating Mass Surveillance

A few years ago, most of this terminology was understood only by a small number of scholars and professionals. When the Dutch Review Committee for the Intelligence and Security Services (CTIVD) published a report in 2011 on the use of Sigint by the military intelligence and security service,[6] it proved to be almost too complex to be discussed in the media and Parliament. Nowadays, a broad range of journalists, bloggers, parliamentarians and even the man in the street, are participating in the debate about mass surveillance.

This debate is rapidly becoming blurry, not only because of the opposite views of governments and civil society but also because the debate suffers from differences in the use of terminology and 'exaggerated rhetoric', as the UK Independent Reviewer of Terrorism Legislation has called it.[7] This underlines the need to be as precise as possible: are we talking about targeted or non-targeted collection of data, do we scrutinise the mere interception or also the storage and analysis of this

---

[4] This perspective can be illustrated by the judgment on 5 December 2014 of the UK Investigatory Powers Tribunal in the *Liberty* case. The Tribunal found that GCHQ did indeed intercept substantial volumes of information on a statutory basis, but it subsequently applied a selection process to identify a smaller volume of data for analysis. The unselected intercepted material was deleted. The Tribunal concluded that the UK services were not seeking mass or bulk surveillance, Investigatory Powers Tribunal, 5 December 2014, *Liberty v GCHQ*, IPT/30/77/H, http://www.ipt-uk.com/section.aspx?pageid=8 at para 72.

[5] See for example the Human Rights Watch and ACLU report, 'With Liberty to Monitor All How Large-Scale US Surveillance is Harming Journalism, Law, and American Democracy', July 2014, https://www.hrw.org/sites/default/files/reports/usnsa0714_ForUPload_0.pdf./.

[6] CTIVD, Report nr. 28, 'The use of Sigint by DISS' 2011, http://www.ctivd.nl/?English.

[7] UK Independent Reviewer of Terrorism Legislation, David Anderson QC, 'A question of trust. Report of the investigatory powers review', June 2015, 245.

data. This is not only important in order to have more focused debates, but also to better understand the laws and procedures regulating the activities of the intelligence services.

III. The Necessity of Mass Surveillance

At the threshold, one must first ask whether mass surveillance is really a necessity. Do the intelligence and security services *have* to collect bulk data in order to be effective? How much information should these services have available for analysis? How important is it for them to be able to review past communications? Past events might become relevant to the present, for example, if a new target is identified and tracking his past activities might give indications about his future plans. But does 'just in case' constitute a necessity?

Reviewing the US National Security Agency's programme of bulk collection metadata on Americans' phone calls, the US Privacy and Civil Liberties Oversight Board (PCLOB) in its January 2014 report, found no examples where the programme had led to the disruption of a specific terrorist plot.[8] It stated that any programme that entails such high cost to the privacy of so many persons, requires a strong showing of efficacy. It therefore seriously questioned the necessity of bulk data collection. President Obama then required intelligence agencies to examine whether there was a way to obtain the communications of terrorism suspects without collection of metadata in such bulk, and instead leave the metadata in the possession of the phone companies that created it in the first place. In January 2015, cyber security experts from the US National Academy of Sciences concluded that they had not found smarter software techniques to replace bulk data collection.[9] They did not go into the question of whether reducing the collection of bulk data would result in too great a loss of effectiveness. In June 2015, however, Congress enacted the USA Freedom Act, which, among other things, ended bulk collection of metadata, and left that information in the hands of the phone companies, accessible by the security services only when they could show that they have reasonable suspicion that a particular phone number is connected to a suspected terrorist. A final answer to the question about the legitimacy of bulk collection in the US has yet to be found, but for the time being, Congress and the executive have agreed to end at least *domestic* bulk collection. (The USA Freedom Act was silent as to the bulk collection of foreign data and communications).

[8] Privacy and Civil Liberties Oversight Board, 'Report on the Telephone Records Programme Conducted under Section 215 of the USA PATRIOT Act and on the Operations of the Foreign Intelligence Surveillance Court', 23 January 2014, https://www.pclob.gov/library.html, 11.
[9] US National Research Council, 'Bulk Collection of Signals Intelligence: Technical Options', January 2015, http://www.nap.edu/catalog.php?record_id=19414, Conclusion 1.

In Europe, empirical research into the effectiveness of bulk collection is even more rare. The LIBE Committee of the European Parliament commissioned a multi-disciplinary study. For this purpose the researchers chose several technologies of mass surveillance on the basis of the Snowden revelations and 'educated guesses', and subjected them to technical assessment. The conclusion was that mass internet monitoring fares poorly in comparison with traditional surveillance techniques. It is difficult to verify this conclusion, since both the programmes and techniques that are used by European intelligence and security services, and their actual effectiveness remain classified.[10] In the UK however, the GCHQ did present some examples to the UK Independent Reviewer of Terrorism Legislation to prove that bulk surveillance is an effective tool.[11]

In general, it can be concluded that there is presently a lack of objective and insightful information about the effectiveness of bulk collection. This makes it difficult to judge its necessity. The reality is that many intelligence and security services already have a statutory power to collect bulk communication, and sometimes are even looking to extend these powers.[12] This makes it all the more relevant to press for information. Governments should give insight into the situations in which mass surveillance proves to be necessary to protect national security. But even then, views on effectiveness are subject to development and will never be final and universal. Concrete safeguards and accountability will be needed to keep the necessity of mass surveillance in concrete situations subject to ongoing assessment.

IV. What are the Minimum Safeguards that should be in Place?

The debate not only is complicated by the absence of a conclusive answer as to the necessity of bulk collection, but also by the knowledge that in many European countries a statutory basis already exists for the collection of bulk data. Especially in these times when threats to national security are becoming very concrete, it might not prove effective to uncompromisingly advocate against any form of mass surveillance. Even though one may have serious doubts, a pragmatic approach requires a focus on the safeguards instead.[13] Mass surveillance, whether

---

[10] SURVEILLE Paper Assessing Surveillance in the Context of Preventing a Terrorist Act, FP7-SEC-2011-284725, published on 29 May 2014.

[11] UK Independent Reviewer of Terrorism Legislation, David Anderson QC, 'A question of trust. Report of the investigatory powers review', June 2015, 269 and 337–38. This leads him to the conclusions that he has found no cause to recommend that bulk collection by GCHQ in its current form should cease.

[12] Eg, the UK, Germany, Sweden, the Netherlands.

[13] This discomfort and pragmatism regarding mass surveillance also appears from the 2014 report of the UN Special Rapporteur on the promotion and protection of human rights and fundamental

by interception, storage or use of communications, infringes on the privacy of the individuals concerned. And there are European and international standards that require adequate safeguards.

A. In Accordance with the Law: The Safeguard of Foreseeability

First and foremost, surveillance must be subject to a law that explicitly authorises and regulates the activities of the intelligence services. According to Article 8 of the European Convention on Human Rights and the relevant case law of the European Court for Human Rights (ECtHR), interference with privacy must be in accordance with the law. The law must enable the person concerned to foresee its consequences. Hence, legislation should be sufficiently clear so that individuals know when and how their privacy may be infringed upon, especially now that surveillance techniques are becoming more sophisticated and covert.[14]

The problem is that laws regulating the activities of the intelligence services tend to be rather brief and vague. Frequently, they give no information on how special powers, for instance the power of interception of communication, may be exercised in actual practice.[15] The reasoning is that terrorists and other targets should not become aware of detailed information on the capabilities and techniques of the services. This would enable them to adapt their conduct to avoid or minimise the risk that the services successfully deploy those capabilities and techniques against them.

In essence, this argument is valid; it should not be revealed when, how and against whom surveillance measures are being applied in practice. But the

---

freedoms while countering terrorism. He is not convinced of the necessity and proportionality of mass surveillance programmes, but focuses on making the safeguards as concrete as possible (Report, 23 September 2014, A/69/397, paras 51, 52).

[14] ECtHR 25 March 1983, *Silver and Others v United Kingdom* 5947/72, para 87; ECtHR 26 March 1987, *Leander v Sweden*, 9248/81, para 53; ECtHR, 29 June 2006, *Weber and Saravia v Germany* 5493/00, para 93; ECtHR 6 September 2006, *Segerstedt-Wiberg and others v Sweden*, 62332/00, para 76; ECtHR, 2 September 2010, *Uzun v Germany*, 35623/05, para 61; ECtHR, 21 June 2011, *Shimovo-los v Russia* 30194/09, para 68; See for an explanation about ECtHR case law in this regard CTIVD, report nr. 38, 'The processing of telecommunications data by GISS and DISS', 2014, http://www.ctivd.nl/?English, addendum legal framework for data processing, para II.2. The UN High Commissioner for Human Rights and the UN Special Rapporteur on the promotion and protection of human rights and fundamental freedoms while countering terrorism reach similar conclusions on the basis of Article 17 of the International Covenant on Civil and Political Rights, see Annual Report High Commissioner, 30 June 2014, A/HRC/27/37, para 25; Report Special Rapporteur, 23 September 2014, A/69/397, para 35–40.

[15] The UK legislation has frequently been criticised in this regard. Provisions on bulk interception warrants were seen as vague and ambiguous, see House of Lords and House of Commons Joint Committee, 'Report on the Draft Investigatory Powers Bill', published 11 February 2016, 87–90. For other examples of regulation of surveillance, see Fundamental Rights Agency, 'Surveillance by intelligence services: fundamental rights safeguards and remedies in the EU. Mapping Member States' legal frameworks', November 2015, para 1.3.

principle of foreseeability in line with ECtHR case law does require an answer to questions such as:

— Which behaviour legitimises the use of surveillance measures?
— What types of measures are available to the services?
— Which areas of private life will these measures infringe upon (communication, contacts, domestic sphere) and how severely will privacy be infringed?
— What regime applies to the interception and use of personal data?

There is no need to disclose the specific technical means used; it is the effect of such use, and the conditions, circumstances and scope of the infringements, that should be foreseeable.

B. Safeguards in the Various Stages of Mass Surveillance

Mass surveillance involves multiple interferences of privacy, related to the stages of: (1) interception/collection, (2) storage/removal/destruction and (3) usage/analysis of bulk communication. Therefore, privacy safeguards become increasingly concrete in these successive stages.[16]

i. Stage 1: Interception/Collection

Since privacy infringement starts with the collection of communication data, strong safeguards should be created for this stage in particular. The issue here is who decides that data may be collected. Should this be the executive power or an independent (judicial) body? Several international institutions, of which the ECtHR is by no means the least important, advocate the latter. Independent ex ante approval of interception is considered the strongest safeguard against abuse.[17] The obstacles and opportunities of ex ante independent approval are discussed later on in this chapter. In many European countries, however, it is the executive that decides. The ECtHR doesn't rule this out, although it does show a preference for independent ex ante assessment.[18]

Apart from who decides about the interception, safeguards should be incorporated into the approval decision-making process itself. To start with, there should be a proper statement of detailed and adequate reasons to serve as the basis for making a well-informed decision to approve or not to approve the interception.

---

[16] European Commission for Democracy through Law (Venice Commission), 'Update of the 2007 report on the Democratic Oversight of the Security Services and report on the Democratic Oversight of Signals Intelligence Agencies', CDL-AD(2015)006, published 7 April 2015, 25.

[17] ECtHR, 6 September 1978, *Klass v Germany*, 5029/71 para 55; UN Special Rapporteur on the promotion and protection of human rights and fundamental freedoms while countering terrorism (Report 23 September 2014, A/69/397, para 47).

[18] This follows from the ECtHR cases regarding the UK, where (at that time) the executive decided about the interception of communications, eg ECtHR, 18 May 2010, *Kennedy v UK*, 26839/05.

This statement should substantiate the necessity and proportionality of exercising the power as concretely as possible. It should explain why there were no other, less intrusive ways to acquire the desired information. 'States should be able to provide an evidence-based justification for this interference with the right to privacy', so the UN High Commissioner for Human Rights states.[19] In the case of bulk interception this is difficult, but should be attempted nonetheless by focusing the interception as much as possible on possible targets. Filters should be in place to limit the amount of intercepted bulk from the start. Services should be forced to narrow their attention as much as possible already at the interception stage, to select while they collect.[20] Nonetheless, the fact that untargeted interception is general by its very nature creates an inherent weakness of the safeguards in the interception phase. This underscores the need to create strong safeguards further down the intelligence process, too, and to regulate what can and should be done with the bulk information after it has been intercepted.

ii. Stage 2: Storage/Removal/Destruction

Once data has been collected, a procedure should be in place to safeguard that it is isolated and stored separately from other information which the service is processing. This way, the infringement on privacy can be kept as limited as possible. A clear boundary has to be created between the authority to intercept, and the authority to examine, analyse, or otherwise use the data. Legislation on removal and destruction of data should be as clear as possible. Preferably, it should state specific and short retention periods after which the data is to be destroyed.

iii. Stage 3: Usage/Analysis

The main interference with privacy occurs when the stored data is being accessed and used.[21] Hence, it is increasingly recommended to impose restrictions on how the collected data is examined and used—and by whom.[22] This requires identification of different forms of use, each governed by its own specific rules. Clear procedures should be put in place for each type of use, specifying the circumstances under which that specific use is permitted, for instance (automated) metadata analysis, profiling, access to communication content, or national or international exchange of (personal) data. Software should be developed to control the use of

---

[19] UN Special Rapporteur on the promotion and protection of human rights and fundamental freedoms while countering terrorism (Report 23 September 2014, A/69/397, p 5).

[20] B Jacobs, 'Select while you collect. Over de voorgestelde interceptiebevoegdheden voor inlichtingen- en veiligheidsdiensten'(2016) 4 *Nederlands Juristenblad* 256–61 (in Dutch).

[21] European Commission for Democracy through Law (Venice Commission), 'Update of the 2007 report on the Democratic Oversight of the Security Services and report on the Democratic Oversight of Signals Intelligence Agencies', CDL-AD(2015)006, published 7 April 2015, 15.

[22] US National Research Council, 'Bulk Collection of Signals Intelligence: Technical Options', January 2015, http://www.nap.edu/catalog.php?record_id=19414, Chapter 5.

collected data, so that queries can be restricted automatically and use of bulk data can be logged.

C. Oversight as a Final Safeguard

A final safeguard against abuse of mass surveillance is oversight of the intelligence services by an independent body that holds these services accountable. Accountability can take different forms: to Parliament, to the judiciary or to an expert body.[23] Although the ECtHR does have its preferences, for instance for judicial ex ante oversight, it does not impose a particular blueprint. It judges each system in each country on its own merits. Different institutions can have complementary oversight tasks, for example a parliamentary committee monitoring in an ex ante capacity, a communications commissioner with an ex post role and a special tribunal mandated to handle complaints.[24] As described, the various stages of mass surveillance also require different forms of oversight. It hence seems valuable to have different institutions complement each other and form a patchwork of safeguards that cover the most important elements of the work of the intelligence- and security services.

V. Obstacles and Opportunities for Oversight of Mass Surveillance

The oversight of intelligence and security services is full of obstacles, especially where mass surveillance activities are concerned. But with each obstacle comes an opportunity.

A. Oversight Quality

i. *Obstacles: Specialisation, Means and Mandate*

a. No Specialised Oversight

It often turns out to be too difficult for general oversight bodies, such as a data protection authority or Parliament in general, to adequately keep intelligence

---

[23] See for more background on these different forms of accountability the European Commission for Democracy through Law (Venice Commission), 'Report on the Democratic Oversight of the Security Services', CDL-AD(2007)016, published 11 June 2007.
[24] In *Klass v Germany* (5029/71, 6 September 1978) the ECtHR considered the German system with a parliamentary committee conducting both ex ante oversight and an ex post complaint procedure in line with the Convention), as it also did with respect to the UK system with a Commissioner

and security services accountable. The character of surveillance today demands a degree of specialisation if oversight is to be meaningful. A great number of developed countries however, do not have specialised oversight for intelligence and security services.[25] The oversight bodies that do exist are still relatively young; 10, 20 or maybe 30 years old. Intelligence oversight seems to be part of one of the later stages of constitutional or democratic development. It can be seen around the globe that this obstacle is being turned into an opportunity; countries are developing oversight, and increasingly learn from each other while doing so.[26]

b. Limited Means

Even if a specialised oversight mechanism is in place—for instance a special parliamentary committee—lack of capacity can be a serious obstacle. Mass surveillance activities do not only take place in secret, they are also highly complex and technical. How can mass surveillance be effectively monitored by parliamentarians who have their hands full dealing with a variety of national politics issues? Or how can a single judge assess all the interception applications of an intelligence service if it is only a small part of his daily job in court? It requires time and expertise to understand mass surveillance techniques and the underlying operational circumstances and to verify the national security claims of the intelligence services. Limited means can turn any specialised oversight body into a paper tiger.

Of course, oversight bodies should be lean and mean. No extensive bureaucracies that repeat all the work of the intelligence services themselves. The challenge is to find the appropriate size and capacity todeliver quality work.

c. Mandate

A limited mandate can be an obstacle to effective monitoring, especially when it restricts the oversight body's access to information. In that situation an oversight body is in no position to meaningfully assess the lawfulness of mass surveillance activities.

But a very broad mandate can also be problematic. For example, if the oversight extends to comprise ex ante oversight of all interception powers. Ex ante oversight may be conducted by a judge (in most European countries this is the case in law enforcement), by an independent committee of experts (eg in Belgium) or a committee of parliament (eg in Germany). Such a mandate pre-supposes a check of the merits of the case and of the necessity and proportionality of the interception. This form of ex ante oversight is often regarded as the most important safeguard

---

conducting ex post oversight and a special tribunal that handles complaints in *Kennedy v UK* (26839/05, 18 May 2010).

[25] Fundamental Rights Agency, 'Surveillance by intelligence services: fundamental rights safeguards and remedies in the EU. Mapping Member States' legal frameworks', November 2015, paragraph 2.3, figure 4 provides an overview of specialised oversight bodies across the EU.

[26] See for example DCAF democratic oversight development projects in the southern and eastern parts of Europe and the Middle East, www.dcaf.ch.

against abuse of interception powers.[27] Expectations for effective privacy protection are set high. And the procedure sounds solid: if the independent body refuses permission, the privacy infringement will not take place. However, for the procedure to work the ex ante oversight must be more than symbolic. In practice one must ask how well-informed the oversight body is, and how thorough and objective its assessments are. With hundreds of interception operations taking place every year, and especially when they involve intercepting bulk data, judging the merits and assessing the proportionality and necessity of an operation is a very complex task.[28]

ii. Opportunity: Smart Oversight Procedures

These obstacles—lack of specialised oversight, lack of capacity or mandate and an abundance of oversight tasks—simultaneously present opportunities to raise the quality level so that the oversight of mass surveillance can be made effective. The question is how. An answer can be found in what can be called smart oversight procedures. These include the following elements:

a. Legal Knowledge

Oversight bodies should be experts on privacy regulation and data protection. They should have the necessary legal knowledge to determine what is proportionate and necessary in mass surveillance and they should be experts in striking a well-reasoned balance between privacy and national security.

b. Knowledge of the Intelligence and Security Services

Oversight bodies should also know the internal procedures, modus operandi and day to day struggles of intelligence services inside out. They have to know all about priority setting, threat assessment, available methods and the expertise of the intelligence services. While keeping an appropriate distance, they have to become intimately acquainted with the services. They should be able to have a fully informed discussion with the services about, for example, how proportionate concrete bulk interception is, and whether or not national security requires storage of the bulk data.

c. Seeking Information Proactively, Instead of Waiting to be Informed

Oversight bodies have to seek information themselves, instead of waiting to be informed. They should have direct access to information and to the ICT systems

---

[27] ECtHR 6 September 1978, *Klass v Germany*, 5029/71 para 55, UN Special Rapporteur on the promotion and protection of human rights and fundamental freedoms while countering terrorism, (Report 23 September 2014, A/69/397), para 47.

[28] But this form of independent ex ante oversight seems to be popular nonetheless, see, eg, the UK Investigatory Powers Bill, as introduced to Parliament on 1 March 2016, Chapter 4.

that collect and process information. In the case of mass surveillance this also means direct access to both the information collected and the internal decision-making processes regarding that information. This way, they are not dependent upon what the intelligence services choose to reveal (in either briefings or documents). The oversight body itself should choose what it wants to learn about, and should acquire this information independently.

d. Understanding Modern Technology

The expertise that is required to understand how mass surveillance works in practice is not easily acquired. Services themselves struggle to attract the smartest ICT specialists and so should the oversight bodies. An oversight body should not be dependent on the service for an explanation about how systems work. It should have staff that know how to find their way, how to ask the difficult questions, how to see through misleading answers. The oversight body should have the expertise to evaluate the ICT applications the services use to process bulk data.

e. Causing Smart Software to be Put into Place

Finally, overseeing mass surveillance requires more than handwork. Smart ICT applications should not only serve the intelligence process but its oversight as well. A large part of the information that is relevant for the oversight body, such as the effectiveness of interception and how bulk data has been handled, can also be acquired through automated processes. According to the cybersecurity experts of the US National Academy of Science, more powerful automation could improve the precision, robustness, efficiency and transparency of the controls.[29] This can reduce the burden of controls on not only analysts but also oversight bodies.

These smart procedures pre-suppose a sound foundation in the law of the mandate and capacities of the oversight body. The national law should leave no doubt about the tasks and means of oversight, and sufficient capacity should be provided in order to realise these statutory goals.

B. Transparent Oversight

i. Obstacle: Everything is Secret

One of the challenges for oversight bodies is that they must by necessity conduct much of their investigations and work in secret. This can be explained by the tight legal provisions on secrecy and also by the fact that the oversight body itself is not in a position to express its views on the legitimacy of secrecy. Just like the work

---

[29] US National Research Council, 'Bulk Collection of Signals Intelligence: Technical Options', January 2015, http://www.nap.edu/catalog.php?record_id=19414, Chapter 5, conclusion 3.2.

of the intelligence services, the work of their overseers is shrouded in a culture of secrecy. To a degree, this is valid. It can be unavoidable to conduct a policy of neither confirming nor denying. The work of intelligence and security services will become impossible if they are forced to disclose when and how they have used special methods in every individual case. And if the aim is to have intelligence services that are smarter and quicker than the enemies of the state, their working methods have to be enveloped in a certain degree of mysteriousness. But this has its limitations, as explained above. Accountability requires a degree of transparency.

ii. Opportunity: Public Reporting

Oversight bodies should publicly report on their findings. In doing so, they should be as open as possible. In their reports, they should provide clarity about:

— The legal framework for the work of the services, including how the principles of necessity and proportionality should be interpreted in practice;
— How the legal framework is applied by the services, which internal procedures are in place, (eg regarding the isolation of and access to intercepted data, or regarding the retention periods after which irrelevant data must be removed) and whether these procedures and their application in actual practice provide sufficient safeguards.
— How intensively special methods are used;
— When and how the services have overstepped the boundaries set by national law and international human rights law. Individual cases can be anonymised, but still require explanation.

All this may seem controversial, and it may take some creativity, but it is possible. To give an example regarding mass surveillance, in 2014 the Dutch Oversight Committee published two reports regarding the General Intelligence and Security Service (GISS). In these reports it described:

— The Dutch legal framework for hacking operations, including the requirement that by law these operations had to be targeted and proportionate;
— The lack of established internal procedures at GISS to ensure that the hacking of web forums is done within the parameters of this framework;
— The increase of the activities of GISS in this area;
— The unlawful hacking of several web forums. These web forums were of such a general nature that hacking them and thereby intercepting these web forums in their entirety was not proportionate. The interception should have been limited to relevant communications.[30]

These reports enabled Parliament to debate about both law and practice and question the responsible minister about these findings.

---

[30] CTIVD, report number 39, 'Activities of GISS on social media', 2014, http://www.ctivd.nl/?English.

Public reporting inherently means discussion between the oversight bodies and the services of the responsible ministers. And if it is the executive that ultimately decides about disclosure, as is the case in many countries, this can pose a considerable challenge.

But if accountability and oversight are to serve their function, public reporting cannot be optional. Oversight provides a retrospective constraint on the executive, which reduces reasons for scepticism and a lack of trust.[31] When oversight bodies keep their findings secret or speak in riddles, the consequence is that society and international organisations will prefer to lend their ear to whistleblowers and investigative journalists.[32]

C. The Internationalisation of Oversight

i. *Obstacle: Limitations to National Oversight*

Intelligence services are increasingly working in an international environment where they organise bilateral and multilateral operations and exchange information, also in bulk.[33] The competence of national oversight bodies is limited, however, to the information about such co-operation that is available at the national services. And even access to this information may be further restricted. On the basis of the 'third party rule' or the principle of 'originator control', many national oversight bodies have no access to telexes and other information received from abroad. And in any case, they can investigate only one side of the co-operation, for example whether their own national intelligence disseminated the data lawfully. What foreign services do with this data remains unknown. The expression 'accountability deficit' has already been coined for this obstacle which from the human rights perspective is a deficit that is hardly acceptable.[34]

---

[31] MP Colaresi, *Democracy Declassified. The Secrecy Dilemma in National Security* (Oxford, Oxford University Press, 2014), 10 and 145, UK Independent Reviewer of Terrorism Legislation, David Anderson Q.C., *A question of trust. Report of the Investigatory Powers Review, June 2015,* 245.

[32] J van Buuren, 'From Oversight to Undersight: the Internationalisation of Intelligence' (2013) 24 *Security and Human Rights* 250–52. Some European studies rely heavily on the Snowden revelations, without taking the reports of oversight bodies into account. See for example EU LIBE Committee, 'National programmes for mass surveillance of personal data in EU Member States and their compatibility with EU Law', study October 2013, www.europarl.europa.eu/studies; Council of Europe Parliamentary Assembly, Committee on Legal Affairs and Human Rights, 'Report on Mass Surveillance', AS/Jur (2015) 01.

[33] I Leigh, 'Accountability and intelligence cooperation. Framing the issue', in H Born, I Leigh and A Wills (eds), *International Intelligence Cooperation and Accountability* (London, Routledge, 2011), 3–17.

[34] European Commission for Democracy through Law (Venice Commission), 'Report on the Democratic Oversight of the Security Services', CDL-AD(2007)016, published 11 June 2007, 26; H Born, 'International Intelligence Cooperation: the Need for Networking accountability', speech at the NATO Parliamentary Assembly, 6 October 2007, available at www.dcaf.ch; UN Special Rapporteur on the promotion and protection of human rights and fundamental freedoms while countering terrorism (Report 4 February 2009, A/HRC/10/3) p 17; I Leigh, 'Accountability and intelligence cooperation. Framing the issue' in H Born, I Leigh and A Wills (eds), *International Intelligence Cooperation and*

ii. Opportunity: Exploring International Oversight Opportunities

The road to overcome this obstacle is not easy to find. The creation of an international 'intelligence codex' has been suggested, laying down mutually acceptable rules. An international oversight body should then be established to oversee
international intelligence co-operation.[35] Logical as this may seem, in the world
of national security it is a non-starter. Intelligence co-operation itself is a complex
process, taking place under strict conditions and dictated by national considerations. Eager as some international institutions may be to create an international
oversight body, it is not to be expected that national states will be willing to relin-
quish this most delicate part of their sovereignty.[36] When further exploring this
opportunity, one must realise that it might take decades to get even the strongest
allies any closer to a form of international oversight of intelligence co-operation.

Another, more feasible option might be to strengthen relations between national
oversight bodies.[37] Oversight bodies now meet both bilaterally and multilaterally,
for example, during conferences. On these occasions they exchange information
on working methods, challenges and findings. The goal of these meetings is to
learn from each other. But it could be taken a step further. For example, national
oversight bodies could discuss their year plannings, identifying relevant cross-
border oversight issues. Then they could select a topic which they would both like
to investigate, each within its own jurisdiction. For example, how is mass interception used to track down jihadis who want to fight or have fought in Syria? Or, what
role does intelligence co-operation play in tracking down these jihadis? What are
the principles for the exchange of personal data and are these taken into account
by the various intelligence services? After having identified a topic, oversight bodies could fine tune the planning and setup of their investigations. And each should
then seek to publish its findings, so that common lessons can be drawn from comparing the different public reports. All this could be done without compromising
state secrets. This option may seem too cautious, but could be the start of a strong

Accountability (London, Routledge, 2011) 8, EU LIBE Committee, 'Working document on Democratic
oversight of Member State intelligence services and of EU intelligence bodies', 21 December 2013;
Annual Report 2014–15 of the Dutch Review Committee on the Intelligence and Security Services, 35,
www.ctivd.nl/english.

[35] Council of Europe Parliamentary Assembly, Committee on Legal Affairs and Human Rights,
'Report on Mass Surveillance', AS/Jur (2015) 01, 30, EU LIBE Committee, 'Working document on Dem-
ocratic oversight of Member State intelligence services and of EU intelligence bodies', 21 December
2013. Before the Snowden revelations, academics already explored and advocated this opportunity;
R Aldrich, 'International intelligence cooperation in practice', in H Born, I Leigh and A Wills (eds),
International Intelligence Cooperation and Accountability (London, Routledge, 2011), 37.

[36] European Commission for Democracy through Law (Venice Commission), 'Report on the Democratic Oversight of the Security Services', CDL-AD(2007)016, published 11 June 2007, 17.

[37] See also the Annual Report 2014–15 and 2015 of the Dutch Review Committee on the Intelligence
and Security Services, www.ctivd.nl/english. The incentives for intelligence oversight co-operation as
well as the different ways for his co-operation to take shape are explored in B de Jonge, 'Closing the gap

network of likeminded oversight bodies, creating common standards and contributing to international transparency and debate.[38]

VI. Concluding Remarks

If the first person to inform the public of the activities of intelligence and security services is a whistleblower, something is wrong with the oversight mechanisms. Today more than ever, oversight of intelligence and security services has to be put into the position to provide stability and objectivity in a debate that is too often driven by scandals and secrets.

Oversight bodies can't perform their tasks in silence, or stay under the radar. They have an autonomous responsibility to make sure that accountability takes place in public. Not only should oversight bodies be able to be open about their findings, they should also be transparent about their own working methods. Are they really applying smart oversight procedures, or are they merely functioning as rubber stamps?

In order to be effective in the area of mass surveillance, oversight bodies must innovate, acquire technical expertise, and further professionalise their working methods. The internationalisation of intelligence should also have its effect on national oversight. Building an international network of oversight bodies that seek co-operation where possible requires some creativity, but it might prove to be the most valuable step forward.

Seizing the opportunities for adequate and transparent oversight is not optional. Credibility of both the intelligence and security services and of accountability mechanisms rely on it.

between debate and reality: Cooperation between intelligence oversight bodies' (2013) 24 *Security and Human Rights* 253–63.

[38] H Born, 'International Intelligence Cooperation: the Need for Networking accountability', speech at the NATO Parliamentary Assembly, 6 October 2007, available at www.dcaf.ch; Annual Report 2014–15 and 2015 of the Dutch Review Committee on the Intelligence and Security Services, 36, www.ctivd.nl/english; H Born, I Leigh and A Wills, 'Making international intelligence cooperation accountable', Geneva 2015, 156–59.

9

In re EPIC and the Role of NGOs and Experts in Surveillance Cases

MARC ROTENBERG[1]

In June 2013, The Guardian published the first of several documents obtained by Edward Snowden from the National Security Agency. The first document released was a previously secret order issued by the US Federal Intelligence Surveillance Court that required the Verizon telephone company to disclose the telephone records of its customers to the NSA every 90 days. The breadth of the order was unparalleled and raised immediately the question how civil liberties organisations, such as the Electronic Privacy Information Center ('EPIC'), should proceed. This article explores EPIC's litigation strategy in that matter and, more broadly, the various strategies that civil liberties organisations and experts pursue in cases that raise new challenges to privacy in trans-national relations. Organisations such as EPIC are exploring a wide range of new litigation opportunities, made possible in part, by the willingness of courts to consider the views and expertise of third parties, often described as 'intervenors' or 'amicus curiae'.

The Electronic Privacy Information Center was established in 1994 to focus public attention on emerging privacy and civil liberties issues, following the successful campaign to stop the NSA proposal for key escrow encryption, known as 'the Clipper Chip'.[2] EPIC was established with the support of legal scholars and technical experts, who shared a common interest in developing practical strategies to respond to the challenges posed by new surveillance techniques. The organisation has operated for more than 20 years as an independent non-profit organisation, pursuing a wide range of policy activities, including support for new legal frameworks, technological innovation, and international coalitions.

---

[1] EPIC Senior Counsel Alan Butler, EPIC International Law Counsel Fanny Hidvegi, and EPIC IPIOP clerk Stephen Stanwood assisted in the preparation of this article.

[2] See Rotenberg, 'EPIC: The First Twenty Years' in Rotenberg, Horwitz, and Scott (eds), *Privacy in the Modern Age: The Search for Solution 1–3* (The New Press, 2015).

An organisation such as EPIC may pursue litigation in several different ways. First, it may represent specific clients who allege violations of law or their constitutional rights. The ACLU brought such a suit on behalf of a coalition of journalists following the passage of the FISA Amendments Act of 2008, arguing that the Director of National Intelligence violated the First and Fourth Amendment by authorising the collection of their international communications. In *Clapper v Amnesty International USA*,[3] the US Supreme Court ruled that the plaintiffs lacked standing to bring their case because they could not demonstrate that their communications had in fact been intercepted by the NSA pursuant to the revised FISA provisions.[4]

A civil liberties organisation may also sue on its own behalf for violations of the organisation's legal or constitutional rights. EPIC frequently sues United States agencies for violations of the Freedom of Information Act, most recently bringing suit against the Department of Justice for failure to release the EU-US 'Umbrella Agreement'.[5] In that case, the DOJ withheld from the public the text of the agreement entered into by US and EU agencies concerning the transfer of personal data between countries for law enforcement purposes.[6] Obtaining the contents of this agreement from the DOJ is critical for political accountability. Congress adopted the 'Judicial Redress Act',[7] a bill that is a core component of the Umbrella Agreement, with little knowledge of the actual agreement.[8] Subsequent to passage, EPIC did obtain the text of the agreement but the agency's delay had effectively frustrated meaningful public participation in the debate.[9]

EPIC has also brought cases in its own name, outside the open government realm, in such matters as a challenge to the deployment of airport body scanners in US airports and the failure of the FAA to issue privacy rules prior to the deployment of drones in the United States.[10] In the body scanner case, the US Court of Appeals for the DC Circuit ruled that the US Department of Homeland Security violated the Administrative Procedure Act when it failed to conduct a rulemaking and accept public comments prior to deploying body scanners in US airports.[11] The agency was ordered to undertake rulemaking. The backscatter X-ray devices

[3] 133 S Ct 1138 (2013). See also EPIC, 'Clapper v Amnesty Int'l USA' (2013) www.epic.org/amicus/fisa/clapper/.

[4] ibid. at 1155.

[5] 'EPIC Sues for Release of Secret EU-US "Umbrella Agreement"' (4 November 2015), www.epic.org/2015/11/epic-sues-for-release-of-secre.html.

[6] EPIC, 'EPIC v DOJ—Umbrella Agreement' (2015) www.epic.org/foia/eu-us-data-transfer/.

[7] HR 1428, 14th Cong (2015).

[8] Tim Ryan, 'EPIC Wants Info on US Data Sharing Deal', Courthouse News Service, 5 November 2016, available at www.courthousenews.com/2015/11/05/privacy-group-wants-info-on-u-s-data-sharing-deal.htm.

[9] Tim Cushing, 'DOJ Agrees to Hand Over Document to EPIC' (2016) *Techdirt* (29 January), available at www.techdirt.co /blog/?tag=umbrella+agreement.

[10] *EPIC v DHS* 653 F2d 1 (DC Cir 2011). See also EPIC, 'EPIC v DHS (Suspension of Body Scanner Program)' (2015) www.epic.org/privacy/body_scanners/epic_v_dhs_suspension_of_body.html. *EPIC v FAA* No 15-1075 (filed 4 May 2015 DC Cir) See also EPIC, 'EPIC v FAA -Challenging the FAA's Failure to Establish Drone Privacy Rules' www.epic.org/privacy/litigation/apa/faa/drones/.

[11] ibid at 8.

were subsequently removed from US airports and replaced by the less revealing millimetre wave devices.[12]

An organisation may also provide a brief in support of a matter currently pending in a court as either amicus or intervenor depending on the extent of the decision's potential impact on the organisation.[13] Over the years, EPIC has participated as amicus curiae in many cases concerning emerging privacy and civil liberties issues. For example, in 2015, EPIC filed a brief in support of consumers who sued Spokeo for violating the Fair Credit Reporting Act by publishing inaccurate information about them and failing to follow the legal procedures required to ensure accuracy.[14] In another case before the US Supreme Court, EPIC filed a brief in *Utah v Strieff*, concerning whether evidence obtained from a government database following an unlawful stop should be admissible.[15]

Recent developments raise the possibility that US organisations could also participate in proceedings before courts in the European Union where the organisation has expertise that may help a court resolve a pending matter.[16] This article examines ways in which organisations such as EPIC, participate in these matters.

I. *In Re EPIC*

The public release of the Verizon order provided an opportunity for EPIC to bring a direct legal challenge to the NSA domestic surveillance programme.[17] Due to the fact that EPIC's claim also concerned the authority of the Foreign Intelligence Surveillance Court (FISC), a court of specialised jurisdiction, a key question was how best to challenge the Court order.[18] A related question concerned the substance of the argument: whether to raise a broad constitutional claim, or a narrow argument based on statute. EPIC adopted a narrow challenge as to the legal basis to challenge the FISC's determination, and not a broader constitutional challenge. In the end, that strategy paved the way for the US Congress to enact legislation to end the bulk collection of domestic telephone records.

---

[12] Michael Grabell, 'TSA Removes X-Ray Body Scanners From Major Airports' (2012) *ProPublica* (19 October) https://www.propublica.org/article/tsa-removes-x-ray-body-scanners-from-major-airports.

[13] In US law, an intervenor participates as 'a matter of right'. Fed RCiv Pro Rule 24. An amicus participates as a 'friend of the court'. Fed R Civ Pro Rule 37.

[14] EPIC, 'Spokeo v Robins' (2015) https://www.epic.org/amicus/spokeo/.

[15] EPIC, 'Utah v Strieff' (2015) https://www.epic.org/amicus/strieff/.

[16] See, eg, EPIC, 'EPIC Seeks to Intervene in Privacy Case Before European Court of Human Rights' https://epic.org/2016/01/epic-seeks-to-intervene-in-pri.html ('EPIC has asked the European Court of Human Rights for permission to submit an amicus brief in a case concerning mass surveillance').

[17] See EPIC, 'In re EPIC—NSA Telephone Records Surveillance' (2015), www.epic.org/privacy/nsa/in-re-epic/.

[18] After extensive consultation and research, EPIC determined that the FISC ruling could only be challenged directly to the US Supreme Court with a Petition for Writ of Mandamus. EPIC's conclusion followed from the statute that established the FISC, the Foreign Intelligence Surveillance Act itself,

At the core of EPIC's argument was the simple claim that the FISC lacked the authority under Section 215 of the USA Patriot Act to compel the production of all telephone records concerning solely domestic communications. EPIC prepared an extensive petition to the US Supreme Court arguing: (1) that the FISC exceeded its statutory authority; (2) that EPIC had standing as a Verizon subscriber to bring the claim; and (3) that no court other than the US Supreme Court had jurisdiction to review the FISC decision.[19] Part of EPIC's litigation strategy was to gather legal scholars, technology experts and notable members of Congress, who enacted the FISA, in support of the EPIC petition. In the end, four groups filed amicus briefs in support of EPIC's petition. The amici included experts in national security law and federal court jurisdiction, as well as former members of the Church Committee, whose investigation of intelligence abuses in the 1970s prompted enactment of the Foreign Intelligence Surveillance Act, including former Vice President Walter Mondale.

During the pendency of *In re EPIC*, Judge Claire V Eagen of the Surveillance Court wrote the first opinion justifying the telephone record collection programme. That opinion was then approved for rapid declassification by the Director of National Intelligence.[20] The Eagen opinion was then cited by the Solicitor General in its brief to the Supreme Court in opposition to the EPIC petition.[21]

The Supreme Court ultimately denied EPIC's petition and never reached the claims on the merits.[22] But several other cases were filed in federal court challenging the telephone records collection programme on Fourth Amendment grounds.[23] More significantly, the EPIC case helped launch a debate in the US Congress about the scope of NSA surveillance within the United States, and specifically the use of the section 215 authority. In the Fall of 2013, while the EPIC petition was still pending before the US Supreme Court, Senator Patrick Leahy, the longest-serving US senator, and Congressman Jim Sensenbrenner, the original co-author of the 2001 Patriot Act, introduced the USA Freedom Act.[24] As Senator Leahy explained:

'The government surveillance programs conducted under the Foreign Surveillance Intelligence Act are far broader than the American people previously understood. It is time for

---

which precluded intervention by non-parties and did not provide the Foreign Intelligence Surveillance Court of Review with general appellate authority over the FISC. EPIC could not seek review in federal district court because those courts also lack appellate jurisdiction over the FISC. Unlike these other courts, the Supreme Court has inherent constitutional authority to oversee all federal courts.

[19] See generally Petition for Writ of Mandamus and Prohibition, or a Writ of Certiorari, *In re EPIC*, 134 S Ct 638 (2013) available at www.epic.org/privacy/nsa/in-re-epic/EPIC-FISC-Mandamus-Petition.pdf.

[20] *In re FBI* No BR 13–109, 2013 WL 5741573 (Foreign Int Ct Rev 29 Aug 2013).

[21] Brief of the US, *In re EPIC*, 134 S Ct 638 (2013).

[22] *In re EPIC* 134 S Ct 638 (2013).

[23] See *Smith v Obama* 24 F Supp 3d 1005 (D Idaho 2014); *ACLU v Clapper* 959 F Supp 2d 724 (SDNY 2013); *Klayman v Obama* 951 F Supp 2d 1 (DDC 2013). See also EPIC, 'Smith v Obama' (2015), www.epic.org/amicus/fisa/215/smith/.

[24] Dan Roberts, 'Congressional duo launch NSA overhaul bill and urge "meaningful reform": Patrick Leahy and Jim Sensenbrenner introduce USA Freedom Act to curtail spying and "restore confidence in

serious and meaningful reforms so we can restore confidence in our intelligence community. Modest transparency and oversight provisions are not enough. We need real reform,
which is why I join today with Congressman Sensenbrenner, and bipartisan coalitions in
both the Senate and House, to introduce the USA FREEDOM Act.'[25]

In June 2015, the USA Freedom Act passed the US Senate 67–32, and was later
signed by the President into law. The USA Freedom Act was the first legislative
response to the disclosure of the NSA bulk collection of telephone metadata,
which the FISC believed section 215 of the Patriot Act permitted.[26]

The central aim of the USA Freedom Act was to reverse the FISC interpretation
of section 215, which had provided the basis for the Verizon order. This was the
focus of *In re EPIC* and the amicus effort. The strategic decision to focus on the
narrow statutory claims provided the basis for the Congress to revise the statute.

A. The Role of Amicus

The most effective amicus is one that presents new information to a court. Such
briefs typically rely on expert reports and studies that help inform a court's understanding of the context and circumstances of the case and do not simply echo the
arguments of one of the parties.[27]

This strategy, sometimes described as the 'Brandeis Brief', follows from a brief
that Louis Brandeis prepared for the US Supreme Court in *Muller v Oregon*, concerning a state law regarding the number of hours women were allowed to work.[28]

---

our intelligence"' (2013) The Guardian (29 October), available at www.theguardian.com/world/2013/
oct/29/nsa-overhaul-bill-legislation-usa-freedom-act.

[25] Senator Patrick Leahy, 'Leahy & Sensenbrenner Join To Introduce USA FREE-
DOM Act: Legislation Ends Dragnet Collection Of Phone Data & Adds Meaningful Oversight Of Surveillance Programs', 29 October 2013, available at www.leahy.senate.gov/press/
leahy-and-sensenbrenner-join-to-introduce-usa-freedom-act.

[26] Mike Debonis, 'Congress turns away from post-9/11 law, retooling U.S. surveillance powers'
(2016) *The Washington Post* (2 June), available at www.washingtonpost.com/politics/senate-moves-
ahead-with-retooling-of-us-surveillance-powers/2015/06/02/28f5e1ce-092d-11e5-a7ad-b430fc1d-
3f5c_story.html. See also David Cole, 'Reining in the NSA' (2016) *New York Review of Books* (2 June),
available at www.nybooks.com/daily/2015/06/02/nsa-surveillance-congress-sunset/.

[27] Expert reports are typically independent, objective, and prepared by leading experts unrelated to
the matter under consideration. In the United States, the National Academies of Science has published
several reports that are useful in cases concerning privacy and technology. See, eg, Committee on DNA
Technology in Forensic Science of the National Academy of Science, 'DNA Technology in Forensic
Science' (1992) 122 *National Academy Press* ('In principle, retention of DNA samples creates an opportunity for misuses—ie, for later testing to determine personal information. In general, the committee
discourages the retention of DNA samples.') cited in EPIC amicus brief, *US v Kincaide* No 02–50380
(9th Cir 2002). The Department of Justice also publishes many reports that may be useful for cases
concerning criminal justice. See, eg, Bureau of Justice Statistics, 'Improving Access to and Integrity
of Criminal History Records', (July 2005) *NCJ* 200581, cited in EPIC amicus brief, US *v Herring* No
07–513 (US 2009). and then in *US v Herring* 555 US 135 ___ (Ginsburg, J, dissenting). Reports that are
prepared specifically in the context of litigation are likely to carry less weight with the courts as the bias
of the report becomes readily apparent.

[28] 208 US 412 (1908).

At the time, there was a significant doctrinal split in American law about the authority of the state to regulate private employment contracts. Brandeis, at the time a leading public advocate, chose to gather evidence of the social and health impact of long working hours and unsafe working conditions. This was contrary to a lawyer's typical intuition to state legal claims and rely on prior legal authority. The argument was intended to educate as much as it was to persuade as to why a court should reach a certain result in a pending matter.

Over many years, EPIC has followed a similar strategy across a wide range of privacy and civil cases that have arisen in US courts. For example, in *Herring v United States*,[29] a case challenging the validity of an arrest made on the basis of inaccurate criminal justice records, EPIC argued that 'government and commercial databases are filled with errors' and are increasingly exempt from 'important privacy and accuracy requirements'.[30] Justice Ginsburg filed a dissenting opinion in *Herring* on behalf of four Justices, citing to EPIC's amicus brief for the conclusion that 'Police today can access databases that include not only the updated National Crime Information Center (NCIC), but also terrorist watchlists, the Federal Government's employee eligibility system, and various commercial databases'.[31]

Similarly, in *Maryland v King*,[32] a case challenging the warrantless collection of DNA samples from arrestees, EPIC argued that as the federal DNA database 'has expanded, so too has the collection of this particularly sensitive personal information', and outlined the findings of the Presidential Commission for the Study of Bioethics, which 'warned about the collection of whole genome sequence data by law enforcement agencies and urged the adoption of a consistent floor for privacy protection'.[33]

More recently EPIC filed an amicus brief, joined by 24 technical experts and legal scholars, in *Riley v California*,[34] a case concerning the warrantless inspection of an individual's cell phone incident to an arrest. EPIC argued that 'Modern cell phone technology provides access to an extraordinary amount of personal data' including 'sensitive and intimate information' and that the inspection of a cell phone would expose files 'stored both on the phone and on remote servers that are accessible from the phone'.[35] EPIC provided extensive detail about the

[29] 555 US 135 (2009). See also EPIC, '*Herring v US*' (2015), www.epic.org/privacy/herring/.

[30] Brief Of Amici Curiae EPIC, Privacy And Civil Rights Organisations, And Legal Scholars And Technical Experts In Support Of Petitioner, *Herring v United States* 555 US 135 (2009) 6, available at www.epic.org/privacy/herring/07-513tsac_epic.pdf.

[31] *Herring v United States* 555 US 135, 155 (2009) (Ginsburg, J, dissenting).

[32] 133 S Ct 1 (2012). See also EPIC, '*Maryland v King*' (2015) www.epic.org/amicus/dna-act/maryland/.

[33] Brief Of Amici Curiae EPIC And Twenty-Six Technical Experts And Legal Scholars In Support Of Respondent, *Maryland v King*, 133 S Ct 1 (2012), available at www.epic.org/amicus/dna-act/maryland/EPIC-Amicus-Brief.pdf.

[34] 134 S Ct 2473 (2014). See also EPIC, '*Riley v California*' (2015), www.epic.org/amicus/cell-phone/riley.

[35] Brief Of Amicus Curiae EPIC And Twenty-Four Technical Experts And Legal Scholars In Support Of Petitioner at 3–4, *Riley v California* 134 S Ct 2473 (2014), available at www.epic.org/amicus/cell-phone/riley/EPIC-Amicus-Brief.pdf.

personal data collected on cellphones, citing technical reports, news articles, and expert opinion. These factual propositions were essentially non-controvertible, presented not as legal argument but as empirical data relevant to the court's consideration of the dispute. The court unanimously ruled that the warrant-less inspection of a cell phone incident to arrest violated the Fourth Amend-ment. Chief Justice Roberts opinion for the court cited directly to EPIC's amicus brief.[36]

In another case, *Clapper v Amnesty International USA*,[37] EPIC filed an amicus brief in support of the plaintiffs with two discrete goals. First, EPIC argued that the plaintiffs' claim that their international communications had been inter-cepted under the revised FISA provision was likely because 'the NSA's SIGINT capabilities and past practices support a reasonable belief that the communica-tions of United States persons will be intercepted'. EPIC further explained that 'the NSA has an almost boundless capacity to intercept private communica-tions, including those of U.S. persons' and 'current technologies developed by intelligence contractors and other agencies show that the government is capable of the type of broad signal collection' that the plaintiffs had alleged in their complaint.[38]

These arguments turned out to be prescient, as the documents disclosed by Mr Snowden made clear that the NSA was sweeping up international communica-tions on a massive scale. The arguments presented in EPIC's brief also caught the attention of Justice Breyer, who wrote in a dissenting opinion on behalf of four Justices:

'The Government does not deny that it has both the motive and the capacity to listen to communications of the kind described by plaintiffs. Nor does it describe any system for avoiding the interception of an electronic communication that happens to include a party who is an American lawyer, journalist, or human rights worker. One can, of course, always imagine some special circumstance that negates a virtual likelihood, no matter how strong. But the same is true about most, if not all, ordinary inferences about future events. Perhaps, despite pouring rain, the streets will remain dry (due to the presence of a special chemical). But ordinarily a party that seeks to defeat a strong natural inference must bear the burden of showing that some such special circumstance exists. And no one has suggested any such special circumstance here.'

EPIC's amicus brief in *Clapper* also served a second purpose: to signal to the court and the Congress the growing concern about the lack of transparency in the reporting on the NSA surveillance activity. Prior to the filing of the amicus brief in *Clapper*, EPIC had testified before the House Judiciary Committee in opposition to the renewal of the FISA Amendments Act. At the hearing in 2012, prior to the

---

[36] See *Riley v California* 134 S Ct 2473 (2014), 2490–94.

[37] 133 S Ct 1138 (2013). See also EPIC, '*Clapper v Amnesty International USA*' (2015).

[38] Brief Of Amici Curiae EPIC, Thirty-Two Technical Experts And Legal Scholars, And Eight Privacy And Transparency Organisations In Support Of Respondents at i, *Clapper v Amnesty International USA*, 133 S Ct 1138 (2013), available at www.epic.org/amicus/fisa/clapper/EPIC-Amicus-Brief.pdf.

Snowden disclosures, EPIC had warned that the revised FISA provisions 'gran[t] broad surveillance authority with little to no public oversight'.[39]

The second part of the EPIC amicus brief in *Clapper* advanced this argument. EPIC explained to the court 'without adequate public reporting, respondents' apprehension that NSA intercepts the communications of U.S. persons is reasonable'. EPIC noted that the Federal Wiretap Act adopted in 1968 provides for public reporting that details the number of persons affected by interception. In contrast, the FISA Amendments Act provides for no public reporting and minimal oversight of collection on a mass scale. EPIC stated that increased public reporting and oversight would enable meaningful review and an evaluation of costs and benefits.[40]

EPIC did not simply argue that the concern about unlawful surveillance was well founded; EPIC also argued that this concern followed from the government's failure to establish adequate reporting requirements, a legislative goal that EPIC was simultaneously pursuing in Congress. This important transparency issue later became the focus of NSA surveillance reform efforts following the disclosures by Mr. Snowden.

In *City of Los Angeles v Patel*,[41] 36 members of the EPIC Advisory Board joined an amicus in support of the proposition that warrantless searches of hotel records are unconstitutional because they would impinge on the freedom of political and religious organisations to gather without being subject to police inspection.[42]

EPIC's Advisory Board, comprised of leading technical experts and legal scholars, actively participate in the preparation of EPIC's amicus briefs. In this regard, the briefs not only provide research to complement the party's arguments, they also provide the credibility and support of relevant experts.

i. Effectiveness of Amici

Research on the impact of amicus briefs in the United States suggest that non-ideological organisations are more likely to influence a court's view of a matter than briefs submitted by organisations that are strongly associated with a political view.[43] Data also plays an increasingly important role in the consideration of amicus briefs.[44] For these reasons, the participation of scientific and technical

---

[39] Hearing on the FISA Amendments Act of 2008: Before the Subcomm. on Crime, Terrorism, and Homeland Sec. of the H. Comm. on the Judiciary (2012) (testimony and statement of Marc Rotenberg, Executive Director, EPIC).

[40] Brief Of Amici Curiae EPIC at i, *Clapper v Amnesty International USA*, 133 S Ct 1138 (2013).

[41] 135 S Ct 400 (2014). See also EPIC, '*City of Los Angeles v Patel*' (2015), www.epic.org/amicus/patel/.

[42] Brief Of Amici Curiae EPIC And Thirty-Six Technical Experts And Legal Scholars In Support Of Respondents, *City of Los Angeles v Patel*, 135 S Ct 400 (2014), available at www.epic.org/amicus/patel/EPIC-Amicus-Brief.pdf.

[43] See generally Joseph D Kearney and Thomas W Merrill, 'The Influence of Amicus Curiae Briefs on the Supreme Court' (2000) 148 University of Pennsylvania Law Review 743–855.

[44] See Adam Liptak, 'Seeking Facts, Justices Settle for What Briefs Tell Them' (2014) New York Times (1 September) at A10, available at www.nytimes.com/2014/09/02/us/politics/the-dubious-sources-of-some-supreme-court-facts.html.

organisations, as well as individual scientific and technical experts is more likely to influence a court's decision. At the same time, some litigants will adopt a strategy of multiple amici participants from a variety of political perspectives with the hope that this will diminish the political association of any one brief.

II. Opportunities in US Courts

There are few restrictions on the filing of amicus briefs in US appellate courts. Typically any group or individual may file a brief with the consent of the parties or by leave of the court, so long as that brief complies with the court's other procedural rules.[45] Most state appellate courts have similar rules and procedures for filing amicus briefs. Federal district courts do not have formal rules, but they do have inherent authority to accept amicus filings and occasionally they request such participation.[46]

Not all courts are equally welcoming of amicus briefs. For example, the US Courts of Appeals for the DC Circuit typically limits amicus briefs to one per party. The practical consequence is that potential amici seeking to file in the DC Circuit must collaborate on a single brief that reflects their collective views. For example, EPIC and other public interest groups filed a joint brief in the DC Circuit in a significant Freedom of Information Act case, *CREW v FEC*,[47] arguing that an adverse ruling 'closes the courthouse doors to countless FOIA requesters, diminishing government transparency and agency accountability'.[48]

As a general matter, it is wise for amici to co-ordinate their filing even in jurisdictions where there are no limitations on the numbers of briefs. One obvious reason to co-ordinate filings is to ensure that no redundant or conflicting arguments are presented. Another reason is to identify issues and constituencies that should be incorporated in the overall amicus strategy.

III. Opportunities for Amici in the ECtHR and the CJEU

This section explores opportunities for NGO and expert participation at the European Court of Justice and the European Court of Human Rights.

---

[45] See Fed R App P 28.

[46] 'From time to time, the Supreme Judicial Court solicits amicus ("friend of the court") briefs or memoranda from parties not directly involved in a case, but that may have an interest or opinion about a case pending before the court.' Massachusetts Court System, "Amicus Announcements", www.mass. gov/courts/case-legal-res/case-information/amicus-announcements/.

[47] 711 F3d 180 (DC Cir 2013).

[48] Brief Of Amici Curiae Public Citizen, Electronic Frontier Foundation, EPIC, OMB Watch, Openthegovernment.Org And Project On Government Oversight (POGO) In Support Of Plaintiff-Appellant

A. European Court of Human Rights

The European Court of Human Rights (ECtHR) has increasingly become an important source of influential decisions on surveillance and data protection law. The ECtHR has established that the protection of personal data is fundamentally important to an individual's right to respect for privacy and family life.[49] The court has also found that legal safeguards must be in place to supervise the activities of clandestine surveillance agencies.[50] These safeguards must provide adequate and effective guarantees against abuse.[51]

Disputes in the European Court of Human Rights involve a Member State that is signatory to the European Convention on Human Rights (ECHR). The Member States are described as 'Contracting Parties'. Forty-five of the 46 Contracting Parties to Convention 108 are Member States of the Council of Europe. Uruguay, the first non-European country, acceded in August 2013.[52]

Rule 44 of the ECtHR permits the participation of third party interveners in matters before the Court. Contracting parties are given 12 weeks following notification to express interest in submitting written comments or to take place in a hearing. Rule 44 also anticipates that the Council of Europe Commissioner for Human Rights will submit written comments or take part in the hearing. Rule 44(2) further states the President of the Chamber may grant leave to 'any person concerned who is not the applicant, to submit written comments or, in exceptional cases, to take part in a hearing'.[53]

The Rule sets out additional factors to be considered by third party interveners. For example, there is an obligation to co-operate fully with the Court and there are sanctions for the failure to comply with an order of the Court.[54] Participants are also admonished to 'participate effectively' in the proceedings and to avoid 'inappropriate submissions'.[55] If an individual fails to pursue an application, the Chamber may strike the application out of the Court's list under Rule 43.[56] The ECtHR has accepted third-party interventions by several US non-profits, including Amnesty International, the Columbia Law School Human Rights Clinic and the Open Society Justice Initiative.[57] According to one commentator:

> '[t]here is no prescribed form, no fee… and no need to seek the consent of the parties. The only requirements are that the request must be "duly reasoned" and made in one

at 3, *CREW v FEC*, 711 F3d 180 (DC Cir 2013), available at www.citizen.org/documents/CREW-v-FEC-Amicus-Brief.pdf.

[49] Cases 30562/04 and 30566/04 *S and Marper v the United Kingdom* [GC], at 41 (4 December 2008).

[50] Case 58243/00 *Liberty and Others v the United Kingdom*, at 62 (1 July 2008).

[51] Case 35623/05 *Uzun v Germany* at 63 (2 September 2010).

[52] FRA (2014) at 17.

[53] Rules of Court (2014), available at www.echr.coe.int/Documents/Rules_Court_ENG.pdf.

[54] Rule 44(A)—Duty to Co-operate with the Court; Rule 44(B) Failure to Comply with an order of the Court.

[55] Rule 44(C)—Failure to participate effectively; Rule 44(D)—Inappropriate submissions by a party.

[56] Rule 44(E)—Failure to pursue an application.

[57] European Court of Human Rights, 'Judgments and decisions' (2012) available at www.echr.coe.int/Pages/home.aspx?p=caselaw.

of the official languages of the Court: French or English. The usual approach of NGOs in the UK is simply to fax a letter requesting leave to the Registry of the Court, setting out the relevant case, the NGO's interest and a brief outline of the proposed intervention.'[58]

Communications containing requests for leave can be made to the Registrar any time within 12 weeks after the ECtHR has offered notice to the appropriate national government that it is considering the case.[59]

Leave to make written comments as a third party intervenor is 'almost always granted, subject to the standard conditions that the submissions will not exceed ten pages and that the intervener will not seek to address either the facts or the merits of the case'.[60] Once leave is granted, the Registrar will communicate further instructions on how to get the written comments before the Court. Once there, all parties to the case have a chance to submit 'observations' in response to the comments and if a party chooses to do so, the intervener can submit another round of comments in response to that party.[61]

B. The Court of Justice of the European Union

With the adoption of the Lisbon Treaty, much of the recent focus in EU surveillance law has shifted from the Court in Strasbourg to the Court in Luxembourg. The Court of Justice of the European Union (CJEU) has issued important decisions on such matters as the EU Data Retention Directive and the obligation of commercial search engines to remove links to information that is no longer relevant.

The provisions for participation by amici before the CJEU are narrower than before the European Court of Human Rights. According to Article 40 of the rules of the Court:

> 'The same right [to intervene] shall be open to the bodies, offices and agencies of the Union and to any other person which can establish an interest in the result of a case submitted to the Court. Natural or legal persons shall not intervene in cases between Member States, between institutions of the Union or between Member States and institutions of the Union.'[62]

Despite this broad language ('any other person which can establish an interest'), interventions by non-profits at the CJEU 'are much less common than those before the European Court of Human Rights...mostly because of the extremely

---

[58] Eric Metcalfe, 'Third Party Interventions in the UK: A JUSTICE Report' (2009) 23. Available at www.justice.org.uk/data/files/resources/32/To-Assist-the-Court-26-October-2009.pdf.

[59] Elona Fani, 'Preparing a Case for the European Court of Human Rights' ISUFI and International Associates. Available at www.hg.org/article.asp?id=4832.

[60] Metcalfe, above at n 58.

[61] Fani, above at n 59.

[62] Protocol on the Statute of the Court of Justice, Article 40. European Union (28 June 2009).

restrictive approach the Court takes toward interventions in the public interest'.[63] As one commentator on EU law notes, the CJEU has consistently construed 'interest in the rest of the case' very narrowly, severely limiting organisations' standing to intervene:

> 'It is not sufficient for the intervener to be in a similar situation to one of the parties to the proceeding and for it to maintain on that ground that it has an indirect interest in the grounds of the decision. A person's interest... is insufficient if the operative part of the decision to be taken by the Court has no bearing on that party's legal position or economic status.'[64]

The CJEU addressed the standing (locus standi) issue for public interest organisations directly in *Greenpeace International v Commission*, where the Court reiterated that it had been 'consistently been held that an association formed for the protection of the collective interests of a category of persons could not be considered to be directly and individually concerned ... by a measure affecting the general interests of that category'.[65]

The only remaining avenue for intervention in a pending CJEU case is to 'be granted leave [to intervene] by the referring national court'.[66] National courts likely have more liberal intervention standards than the CJEU does, but the exact procedures for applying for leave to intervene will vary from court to court. National courts may also be resistant to foreign non-profits attempting to intervene in their cases.

C. Supreme Court of Canada

Non-profits typically intervene in Canadian Supreme Court proceedings once the Court has agreed to hear the case.[67] After the Court grants an appeal, the appellant and respondent file their 'factums', which are the equivalent of petitioner and respondent briefs before the United States Supreme Court. The Canadian Supreme Court Act's Rule 56 requires that parties who want to intervene must file a motion for intervention 'within four weeks after the filing of the appellant's factum'.[68]

---

[63] Metcalfe, above, n 58 at 24.

[64] Koen Lenaerts; Ignace Maselis; Kathleen Gutman, *EU Procedural Law* (Oxford, Oxford University Press, 2014) 829.

[65] *Stichting Greenpeace Council (Greenpeace International) and Others v Commission of the European Communities*. European Court Reports 1998 I-01651. http://goo.gl/Ha0yYf.

[66] Metcalfe, above n 58 at 25.

[67] Note that the phrase amicus curiae also exists in Canadian law but refers to a disinterested attorney usually appointed by the court rather than to a third-party advocating for a particular result. See generally Lloyd Duhaime, 'Amicus Curiae Legal Definition' Duhaime.org. www.duhaime.org/LegalDictionary/A/AmicusCuriae.aspx (last visited 24 February, 2015).

[68] Supreme Court Act (RSC, 1985, c S–26).

The SCC has historically been quite generous in granting intervener status. A study of motions interventions before the court between 2000–08 found that the SCC granted 1641 out of 1751 total motions (94%). That included 217 out of 249 (87%) motions from public interest groups, who were the second largest source of interventions after public Attorneys General.[69] After the SCC grants leave, interveners have eight weeks to file their 'factum' (brief) and 'book of authorities' (citation table). Rule 42 sets out the contents and structure of intervener factums.[70]

Once complete, intervener factums must also conform to strict requirements on printing and binding before they are filed with the court and served on other parties. Detailed information about the printing, print filing, electronic filing, and service requirements are available on the SCC website.[71]

IV. Current Matters

A. Safe Harbour Challenge (CJEU)

In 2013 the Irish Data Protection Supervisor (IDPS) formally declined to investigate Facebook for violations of user data protection rights following Mr Snowden's disclosure that the company had shared data about European Citizens with the US National Security Agency.[72] Following the announcement of the IDPS, privacy advocate Max Schrems brought a challenge in the Irish High Court and the court agreed to refer the case to the CJEU.[73] The CJEU subsequently granted several prominent intervenors leave to file briefs, including the European Data Protection Supervisor and several data protection authorities.[74]

The CJEU issued an opinion in the *Schrems* case in October 2015, finding that the trade arrangement (Safe Harbour) between the US and the EU was invalid

---

[69] Benjamin R, D Alarie and Andrew J Green, '*Interventions at the Supreme Court of Canada: Accuracy, Affiliation, and Acceptance*' 48.3/4 Osgoode Hall L. J. 381-410 (2010). http://digitalcommons.osgoode.yorku.ca/ohlj/vol48/iss3/1.

[70] Detailed instructions for service and filing documents at the Supreme Court of Canada are available at www.scc-csc.gc.ca/ar-lr/gl-ld2014-01-01-eng.aspx#J.

[71] Printing and binding information for the Supreme Court of Canada is available at www.scc-csc.gc.ca/ar-lr/gl-ld2014-01-01-eng.aspx#D1b.

[72] www.europe-v-facebook.org/hcj.pdf.

[73] www.europe-v-facebook.org/Order_ADJ.pdf.

[74] The EDPS was first permitted to intervene in the CJEU in two cases concerning the privacy of Passenger Name Record (PNR) data under the European Data Protection Directive (95/46). Press Release, 'PNR: EDPS first reaction to the Court of Justice judgment', European Data Protection Supervisor (30 May 2006), available at www.europa.eu/rapid/press-release_EDPS-06-8_en.htm?locale=en. Following the intervention of the EDPS on behalf of the European Parliament, the CJEU voted to annul the two PNR-sharing agreements between the Council of Europe and the United States. Press Release No 46/06, 'Judgment of the Court of Justice in Joined Cases C-317/04 and C-318/04', CJEU (30 May 2006), available at www.curia.europa.eu/jcms/upload/docs/application/pdf/2009-02/cp060046en.pdf.

because it failed to ensure the protection of fundamental rights under Articles 7, 8, and 47 of the European Charter of Fundamental Rights.[75] The Court also found that independent data protection agencies have the legal authority to enforce the rights set out in the Charter as against future decisions by the European Commission under Article 25(6) of the Data Protection Directive of 1995. The Court's opinion creates a strong presumption that any similar framework—a 'Safe Harbour 2.0'—will also be found invalid.

In fact, in early 2016, the United States Department of Commerce and the European Commission proposed a new arrangement, the so-called 'Privacy Shield', to replace Safe Harbour following the *Schrems* case.[76] The proposal was wildey criticised by consumer organisations in the European Union and the United States as failing to provide adequate protection for trans-border data flows as required by the opinion of the European Court of Justice.[77]

The concerns of the NGOs about the Privacy Shield were given legal force when the Article 29 Working Group, the committee of privacy officials responsible for assessing proposals to transfer personal data outside of the EU, rendered its opinion on the Privacy Shield in April 2016.[78] As the chair of the Working Party explained, 'there's still work to do. We need to ensure that protections of the Privacy Shield are indeed essentially equivalent to what is available in Europe'.[79]

Although the rules of the CJEU limit the opportunity to third party participation, the *Schrems* case provides a good example for the ability of data protection authorities to influence decisions of the CJEU. Working with these authorities could provide an additional opportunity for NGOs to influence the development of international law and safeguard fundamental rights.

[75] C-362/14 *Maximillian Schrems v Data Protection Commissioner* 2015 http://curia.europa.eu (6 October 2015), reprinted in Anita L Allen and Marc Rotenberg, *Privacy Law and Society* (West, 2016) 1452–84, available at www.privacylawandsociety.org.

[76] Mark Scott, 'U.S. and Europe in 'Safe Harbor' Data Deal, but Legal Fight May Await' (2016) *New York Times* (2 February) at B1, available at www.nytimes.com/2016/02/03/technology/us-europe-safe-harbor-data-deal.html;. See also EPIC, 'Privacy Shield: EU-US Data Transfer Agreement', www.epic.org/privacy/intl/privacy-shield/.

[77] 'The Transatlantic Consumer Dialogue (TACD) urges the European Commission not to adopt the Privacy Shield. This scheme does not adequately protect consumers' fundamental rights to privacy and data protection, as established in the EU Charter of Fundamental Rights and the 1995 Data Protection Directive, seen in the light of the European Court of Justice decision on Safe Harbour.' TACD, 'Resolution on the EU-US Privacy Shield Proposal', 7 April 2016, Document No: INFOSOC 54/16, www.tacd.org/wp-content/uploads/2016/04/TACD-Resolution_Privacy-Shield_April16l.pdf.

[78] Article 29 Working Party, 'Opinion 01/2016 on the EU-U.S. Privacy Shield draft adequacy decision', 13 April 2016, www.ec.europa.eu/justice/data-protection/article-29/documentation/opinion-recommendation/files/2016/wp238_en.pdf.

[79] Mark Scott, 'Europe's Privacy Watchdogs Call for Changes to U.S. Data-Transfer Deal', (2016) *New York Times* (13 April) at B2, available at www.nytimes.com/2016/04/14/technology/europe-us-data-privacy.html.

B. GCHQ Challenge

The Investigatory Powers Tribunal (IPT) recently rejected a challenge to the mass surveillance of UK citizens by the GCHQ in a case brought by UK privacy organisations. The groups argued, 'their private communications may have been monitored under GCHQ's electronic surveillance programme, Tempora. They also argued that information obtained through the Prism and Upstream programmes of the NSA may have been shared with British intelligence services, sidestepping protections provided by the UK legal system.[80]

Civil liberties organisations in both the EU and the United States are already working together on the challenge, participating as both parties and amici.[81] This trend is likely to continue as courts increasingly confront challenges brought about by advances in technology and systems of surveillance that put fundamental freedoms at risk.

V. Conclusion

Civil liberties organisations have a variety of strategies to pursue challenges to state surveillance. In addition to claims brought on behalf of clients or of the organisation, it may be wise to pursue amicus strategies that strengthen claims currently pending in courts. Such interventions should be undertaken in collaboration with the interested party, relevant experts, other organisations and comply with all procedural requirements necessary for participation. These strategies may become increasingly important as more disputes arise concerning the permissible scope of surveillance in a democratic society.

---

[80] *Guardian*, www.theguardian.com/uk-news/2014/dec/05/uk-mass-surveillance-laws-human-rights-tribunal-gchq.

[81] EPIC, 'European Court of Human Rights International Privacy *Liberty v GCHQ*. EPIC Seeks to Intervene in Privacy Case Before European Court of Human Rights', 22 January 2016, www.epic.org/2016/01/epic-seeks-to-intervene-in-pri.html.

Part V

Transatlantic Perspective

10

A Transatlantic Privacy Pact?: A Sceptical View

STEPHEN J SCHULHOFER*

Everywhere in the world, twentieth-century safeguards for privacy vis-à-vis the government were radically incomplete. But individuals nonetheless had many practical ways to shield private information.

The digital revolution has upended this structure. Government access to personal information and its ability to extract revealing personal details from them are exponentially simplified. Although these developments largely work to the advantage of State surveillance, law enforcement has its own needs for clarification, at the same time that citizens need new means of refuge from state scrutiny.

Prominent privacy and human-rights advocates urge that the answer to these problems lies in a multilateral agreement requiring states to adhere to uniform, privacy-sensitive standards, with no discrimination between their own nationals and those of other countries.[1] An international movement of privacy activists is promoting a 'Snowden Treaty' to achieve a similar objective.[2]

As a substantive matter, it is surely right to consider the problem from the perspective of universal human rights. Yet as an institutional matter, the turn to an international agreement will sideline the courts, disempower legislative bodies and privacy advocates, defuse commercial pressure for strong privacy safeguards, and create a dynamic controlled almost exclusively by the executive and its national security establishment.

I do not want the fox to design this henhouse. This essay explains why that would happen in a multilateral process and why its consequences for worldwide privacy are not attractive. On the contrary, national sovereignty should continue to frame the search for solutions.

---

* The author is grateful for the helpful comments of Eyal Benvenisti, David Cole, Federico Fabbrini, Ryan Goodman, Chris Sprigman, Richard Stewart, and for assistance with foreign-law sources from Annmarie Zell.

[1] See, eg, Ian Brown, Morton H Halperin, et al, *Towards Multilateral Standards for Surveillance Reform* (Oxford Internet Institute Discussion Paper, January 2015), available at www.papers.ssrn.com/sol3/papers.cfm?abstract_id=2551164; David Cole and Federico Fabbrini, 'Reciprocal Privacy? Towards a Transatlantic Agreement', in (Federico Fabbrini & Vicki Jackson eds), *Constitutionalism Across Border in the Struggle against Terrorism* (Cheltenham: Edward Elgar Publishing 2016).

[2] The group's website is available at www.snowdentreaty.org/.

Part I describes privacy protection in the pre-digital world and explains how the digital era has eroded many practical safeguards. Part II summarises recent proposals for restoring a more privacy-protective environment by means of international agreements. The remainder of the paper argues that these well-intentioned proposals are unlikely to accomplish their objective.

Although the ultimate concern is for privacy and democracy worldwide, Part III opens the analysis parochially, by arguing that a multilateral approach would be bad for Americans. Part IV argues that international agreements would be bad for privacy and democracy in the rest of the World as well, because American commitments to national security oversight can exert a stronger upward pull on global norms than can the terms of any foreseeable international agreement. Paradoxically, the jurisdictional competition that usually precipitates a 'race to the bottom' is more likely, in this context, to prompt a 'race to the top'.

This author takes no pride in supporting an approach that bears an uncomfortable resemblance to celebratory 'American exceptionalism'. That concept has a well-deserved reputation for moral insensitivity and catastrophic consequences. In the setting of the global privacy dilemma, however, the normally powerful attractions of international co-operation and universal conceptions of human rights present distinct dangers. The effort to find international common ground in this area should not be encouraged but instead cautiously opposed.

I. Spheres of Privacy—Before and After the Digital Transformation

In the pre-digital era, individuals who sought shelter from government spying had many means of self-protection. The information age radically alters this equation. Digital files concerning a person's health, finances, travel, and consumption are not—and rarely can be—stored entirely within the physical home. Instead they are now lodged in the data banks of internet service providers (ISPs), hospitals, and merchants or simply in 'the cloud'. Although cloud storage occurs somewhere here on Earth, users may not know its location and have little physical ability to shield their stored records from outside scrutiny.

At the same time, government access to such records is incomparably faster, cheaper and more comprehensive. Information in digital form also permits almost limitless, cheap, permanent storage. Digital data can be probed for links and patterns that are invisible when corresponding information is held in hard copies.

These developments also destabilise legal safeguards because data moves over capricious routes to its destination and because its place of private-sector storage may not even be known. So the protections of domestic law and jurisdictional principle erode. Information can be accessed from locations that bear little relationship to the nationality of the persons affected or the physical site of pertinent data. Police and intelligence agents can therefore search in another country without ever setting foot in it and (arguably) without meeting the privacy safeguards or legal-assistance procedures of the other country. Since the US, the EU and most other nations do not extend their privacy protections to foreign nationals abroad, the privacy safeguards of the searching country and those of the nation where the search occurs may both fall by the wayside.

Edward Snowden documented the consequences. Although NSA's vast metadata collection programme has been held illegal under US law,[3] its warrantless spying on EU citizens in Europe appears to be lawful as a matter of US law. And conversely EU Member States can legally spy on Americans who are in the US. That loophole is compounded by mutual assistance and incidental collection. Each nation can acquire information on its citizens by co-operating with foreign intelligence services and can collect such information itself by targeting communications of foreign nationals in contact with its citizens and suspects of unknown nationality who turn out to be its citizens. From all these directions, the sheltered spaces for private life face unprecedented threats, to the considerable advantage of governments who are keen to spy.

Law enforcement and the intelligence community face new challenges as well. Global communication multiplies the capacity of extremist groups to recruit and support sympathisers; new weapons enable isolated individuals to cause great harm; new vulnerabilities result from the cyber-dependent character of contemporary commercial, financial and military infrastructure. Uncertainty about governing law can chill private-sector co-operation and cast doubt on the ability to use acquired information in court.

Governments thus have valid needs to gain a legal imprimatur for their newly powerful surveillance modalities. At the same time citizens need new ways to preserve zones of private life sheltered from government intrusion. Effective limitations on surveillance power and effective forms of oversight are more essential than ever.

II. Emerging Proposals for Reform

A number of scholars and advocates seek to address some of these problems through a multilateral accord requiring signatory nations to adhere to shared principles, uniform standards or at least minimum standards for internet surveillance. David Cole and Federico Fabbrini envision a transatlantic compact, in which the United States and EU members would accept common privacy

---

[3] *ACLU v Clapper* 785 F.3d 787 (2d Cir. 2015). See also US Privacy and Civil Liberties Oversight Board, Report on the Telephone Records Program Conducted under Section 215 of the USA Patriot Act and on the Operations of the Foreign Intelligence Surveillance Court 10–11 (23 Jan 2014).

safeguards in counter-terrorism investigations and commit themselves to respecting common or reciprocal minimum standards for their own and each other's
nationals.[4] Ian Brown, Morton Halperin and their collaborators propose an even
more ambitious framework—an international agreement uniting a broad cohort
of co-operating states (possibly including non-democratic states).[5] It would
establish 'a high ceiling rather than a low floor for human rights protection',[6]
including tough threshold requirements for interception and access to stored
data, 'minimisation' to ensure that acquired data is used only for its intended
purpose and robust oversight.[7]

An international framework of this sort would assure legitimacy for justified
intelligence-gathering while plugging the loopholes that currently invite exploitation and abuse. A 'privacy-conscious' international framework,[8] referred to here as
PCIF, would strengthen human-rights norms, while also meeting the needs of ISPs
and data storage services whose business inevitably transcends national borders.
It would also preserve the social, political and economic benefits that people the
World over have reaped from the unobstructed global internet. Supporters of the
PCIF approach include knowledgeable scholars and advocates with a long track-
record of good judgment and demonstrated commitment to civil liberties.[9]

Nonetheless, the next two sections show that privacy will be better protected,
for Americans and the World at large, if we resist the lure of a privacy-conscious
international framework.

III. Implications for Americans

A comparison of the privacy safeguards available to Americans under current law
to those that would apply in a PCIF regime faces three hurdles. First, American
law is unclear and in flux. Second, the same is true for other nations that might
be candidates for inclusion in an international treaty. Third, the outcome of any
multilateral negotiation is inevitably speculative.

Despite this complexity, two generalisations are broadly accurate and sufficient
to move the discussion forward. First, in the domain of national security and safeguards against surveillance by the government, American law—for all its flaws—is
more detailed and more protective of privacy than its current counterparts any-
where else in the world.[10] This point should not be misread as self-congratulatory

---

[4] Cole and Fabbrini, n 1 above.
[5] Brown, Halperin, et al, n 1 above.
[6] ibid, pp 3–4.
[7] See ibid, pp 25–32.
[8] Brown, Halperin, n 1 above, p 29.
[9] See notes 1–3 and 7–9 above.
[10] For discussion of the French and UK regimes, which are detailed but much more permissive, see text at nn 19–40 below.

American egoism. The infrastructure and resources dedicated to surveillance by the American intelligence community dwarf those to be found elsewhere, and accordingly the need for limitation and oversight is many times more pressing in the American case. In addition, Americans face considerable exposure to government surveillance in practice—as indeed the Snowden revelations document— even when safeguards provided by law are theoretically robust.

Second, emerging reforms are unlikely to alter this basic picture: national security surveillance will continue to be regulated more tightly under American law than elsewhere.

This section briefly documents these two benchmarks. The next section then considers the prospects for an international agreement that harmonises divergent national regimes.

A. Surveillance under Current American Law

Outside the national security domain, American surveillance law features four important safeguards: (1) individualised judicial approval ex ante; (2) probable cause for threshold authority to intercept communications; (3) proportionality (absence of less intrusive means) and (4) equal treatment of US citizens and foreign nationals present within the US.[11]

In national security matters, two additional points are salient: (5) For domestic national security concerns, identical requirements apply, with no relaxation of the restrictions governing ordinary criminal investigation.[12] (6) Finally, even when national security has an international dimension, similar safeguards apply to surveillance targeting Americans and resident foreigners. Specifically, for 'US persons' (American citizens and permanent residents), electronic surveillance for national security purposes must be authorised in advance by a judicial warrant based on probable cause to believe that the target is (or 'may be') committing a foreign intelligence crime. At least in theory, US persons enjoy these protections against interception at sites within the US—the servers and switching facilities of American telecom companies—even when they themselves are outside US borders.[13] Non-US persons enjoy broadly similar safeguards—ex ante judicial authorisation and a particularised (though more relaxed) conception of probable cause, but only when they are in US territory.[14]

American legal protection of privacy nonetheless suffers from significant short-comings. Apart from its limited safeguards against *commercial* use of private data, American law also displays four notable weaknesses in protecting against *government* surveillance. First, it imposes few *use restrictions* on intelligence once

---

[11] See 18 USC at 2510 onwards.
[12] *United States v United States District Court (Keith)* 407 US 297 (1972).
[13] FISA Amendments Act of 2008, 50 USC at 1881a onwards. Section 703 (2008).
[14] Foreign Intelligence Surveillance Act of 1978, 50 USC at 1801 onwards. (1978).

it is gathered.[15] Second, it affords diminished protection for metadata and other *information held by third parties*. This is an especially large loophole, as there is currently no constitutional restraint on the government's authority to obtain information from third parties without a warrant or any individualised suspicion. And in the information era, third parties hold a virtually complete digital record of our electronic communications, web searches and location at all times. To be sure, government access to third-party data is cabined by a dense web of US statutory restrictions. These are roughly comparable to constitutional requirements with respect to email in transit, but for all other data held by third parties, the statutory restrictions are pallid in comparison to the constitutional requirement of probable cause.[16]

The third weakness of US law is that surveillance effectuated abroad and surveillance targeting foreigners outside American territory are subject only to loose programmatic oversight.[17] Finally, through the magic of incidental collection, foreign-targeted surveillance allows NSA to intercept, retain and use voluminous quantities of communications content of Americans in contact with targeted non-US persons. Intelligence collected 'incidentally' in this way is subject to 'minimisation' safeguards, but these safeguards are not robust because they permit such intelligence to be turned over to law enforcement and other government agencies and used against US persons in a variety of loosely defined circumstances.[18] Even with these limitations, however, American law governing national security surveillance is quite specific and restrictive.

B. Surveillance Law Elsewhere

For present purposes, commentary here focuses on just two jurisdictions—France, because it illustrates recent, particularly detailed legislation, and the UK, because it would be a leading participant in any multilateral negotiation among parties likely to share common values. The paper then turns to international human rights law as a competing or complementary source of privacy protection. A wider survey could profitably consider other Western nations where national security surveillance is restricted more or less tightly than in France and the UK, but detail of this sort would not change three basic conclusions:

---

[15] To be sure, American law, unlike that of most other countries, forbids the use in court of illegal intercepts and any of their proximate fruits. But the use restrictions on legally gathered intelligence are not stringent, and in foreign intelligence matters, they are largely secret to boot.

[16] Although strong safeguards protect email in transit, there is no exclusionary rule available to sanction violations. For email content in storage, weaker limits apply, and statutory limits on acquiring metadata, financial records, and the like are weaker still. See Stephen J. Schulhofer, *Rethinking the Patriot Act* (New York: Century Foundation Press 2005) 55–78.

[17] FISA Amendments Act of 2008, Section 702. See n 14 above,.

[18] See 'Minimization Procedures Used by the National Security Agency in Connection with Acquisitions of Foreign Intelligence Information Pursuant to Section 702 of the Foreign Intelligence Surveillance Act of 1978, as Amended', available at www.clearinghouse.net/detailDocument.php?id=79333.

1. There is wide variation among Western democracies on such fundamental issues as the required level of suspicion, the role of suspect-specific judicial approval ex ante, and the degree to which transparency and oversight are relaxed in the national security context.
2. International human rights law and institutions have limited capacity to reconcile national differences or impose strong minimum standards in national security matters; and
3. US safeguards against government surveillance, for all their shortcomings, are far more robust, even with respect to third-party data, than those now found or likely to emerge elsewhere.

i. France

In ordinary law enforcement, wiretapping must be authorised by a *juge d'instruction* (examining magistrate).[19] However the magistrate has wide discretion in deciding whom to tap, for how long, and the level of suspicion required. There is no requirement of probable cause or any written statement of the basis for issuing the wiretap order.[20] Crucially, the magistrate is not independent in the American sense. She is charged with investigating the offence and assembling the proofs; her role is not that of an American judge, who may issue a warrant only because she is not engaged in 'the often-competitive enterprise of ferreting out crime'.[21]

National security wiretaps are even less constrained. Under 1991 legislation, such surveillance required only the authorisation of the Prime Minister or his delegate, acting on the advice of an independent commission.[22] Such interception was lawful without regard to conditions like those applicable to criminal investigations. With no limits on modalities of surveillance or anything else, national security surveillance was in effect not governed by statute or case law at all.

Terrorist attacks in Paris in 2015 provided the opportunity to fill that vacuum. The new regime[23] maintains the Prime Minister's approval authority but replaces the independent Commission with a non-independent 'Commission for Control of Intelligence Methods' (CNCTR). The Prime Minister, who appoints the majority of its members, can disregard its advice,[24] and in any event the CNCTR is deemed to approve any surveillance order if it fails to give the Prime

---

[19] *Code de Procédure Pénale* (Code of Criminal Procedure), art 100 (France).

[20] ibid, arts 100 onwards.

[21] *Coolidge v New Hampshire* 403 US 443 (1971).

[22] See Franck Johannès, *Un Projet de Loi sur Mesure pour les Services Secrets* (A Draft Law Custom Made for the Security Services), (2015) LE MONDE, 21 March, p 11.

[23] *Loi 2015–912 du 24 Julliet 2015 relative au renseignement* (Law 2015–912 of 24 July 2015 relating to intelligence), JOURNAL OFFICIEL DE LA RÉPUBLIQUE FRANÇAISE [JO] [OFFICIAL GAZETTE OF FRANCE], 26 July 2015, p 12735 (Fr). (The final legislative vote occurred on 24 June; the official date of enactment is that on which the *Conseil constitutional* rendered its judgment upholding the law).

[24] Art 821–1.

Minister its advice within 72 hours.[25] The law 'limits' surveillance to seven capacious purposes,[26] authorises bulk collection of both metadata and content on the basis of algorithms that the security services deem useful, and permits storage of such intelligence for up to five years. Lastly, the law granted the Direction Générale de la Sécurité Extérieure (DGSE) virtually unrestricted licence to capture communications to and from France, by attaching 'black box' filters to undersea cables, a practice that DGRE reputedly had pursued for years without authority or acknowledgment.[27]

In July, the French *Conseil Constitutionnel* struck down the DGRE authority to place interception devices outside French territory, because that authority gave French nationals no safeguards at all.[28] In all other relevant respects, the *Conseil* upheld the statute.[29] Even for surveillance of French citizens within French territory, the new regime requires no particularised suspicion, no independent approval ex ante and no judicial oversight.

If challenged in the European Court of Human Rights, the French regime is by no means guaranteed to survive. But regardless of its future prospects, it makes clear that US commitments to probable cause and suspect-specific judicial review are by no means shared across all the Western democracies.

ii. The UK

Electronic surveillance in both criminal and national security investigation is governed primarily by the Regulation of Investigatory Powers Act 2000 (RIPA).[30] Interception of content requires a 'warrant' issued by a Secretary of State (one of the principal cabinet ministers) on application of a senior security-service or police official. The Secretary may issue the warrant only when 'he believes' such interception 'necessary … in the interests of national security, … preventing or detecting serious crime, [or] safeguarding the economic well-being of the United Kingdom'; and 'proportionate to what is sought to be achieved'.[31] The Secretary must limit

---

[25] Art 821–3, 2.

[26] Art 811–3, authorizing the intelligence services to use the specified means of surveillance to gather information for purposes of 'national defense, foreign policy, execution of international obligations, economic, industrial and scientific interests,' prevention of terrorism, prevention of 'collective violence posing a grave threat to public peace,' prevention of organised crime and delinquency, and prevention of the proliferation of weapons of mass destruction.

[27] Art 854–1.

[28] Conseil constitutionnel [CC] [Constitutional Court] décision No 2015–713 DC, 23 July 2015, JO 12751 (Fr).

[29] ibid.

[30] EII, 2000 Ch 23. RIPA is supplemented by the Data Retention and Investigatory Powers Act 2014 (DRIPA), which subjects all communications service providers to the data access provisions of RIPA. Also, the Telecommunitcations Act 1984, s 94, gives the security services broad authority, in the interests of national security, to issue certain orders to communications providers. The use of that authority has not hitherto been subject to oversight, but national-security surveillance apparently is conducted primarily (albeit not exclusively) under RIPA.

[31] ibid, ss 5–6. But economic well-being is not a sufficient justification when seeking information pertaining to persons who are within the British Isles. ibid, s 5(5).

the retention and use of intercepted material 'to the minimum that is necessary for the authorised purposes';[32] thereafter such material must be destroyed.

A domestic warrant must target identified persons or premises. But this limitation nonetheless permits 'thematic' warrants, which can target an association of persons, and in such cases the required specificity of selection terms and the strength of the association between persons who constitute such a group are not clearly defined.[33] In addition, looser pre-requisites apply to acquiring communications to and from abroad. But indiscriminate bulk collection is impermissible, and when external communications intercepted relate to someone present in the UK, they can be examined only for up to six months.[34] Even for domestic interception, however, RIPA requires no adversarial oversight, no judicial review ex ante or ex post, and no particularized suspicion, only an internal record of why each interception was necessary, proportionate, and sufficiently minimised. Authority to collect non-content data is even more flexible.[35]

Oversight takes two forms. An 'Interception of Communications Commissioner'—a sitting or former judge appointed by the Prime Minister—is given a role similar to that of an Inspector General in the US executive branch. He reports annually on interception and non-content acquisition practices. The Prime Minister must transmit the report to Parliament, but can redact material when he deems its release 'contrary to the public interest'.[36] Second, RIPA creates an Investigatory Powers Tribunal (IPT) with exclusive jurisdiction to hear complaints by any aggrieved person relating to alleged violations of RIPA or the European Convention on Human Rights.[37]

The Commissioner's oversight has been far from perfunctory. His office has audited after the fact more than half the interception warrants issued, passing independent (though confidential) judgment on necessity/proportionality, and issuing numerous recommendations, a large proportion of which have been accepted by the government.[38] The IPT operates more openly, and it can grant relief in individual cases. However British law drastically truncates its potential; it is near-impossible for a surveillance target to invoke its jurisdiction because RIPA makes it a crime for anyone having knowledge of the issuance of an interception warrant to fail 'to keep secret all matters' pertaining to it.[39]

---

[32] ibid, s 15(2).

[33] Report of the Interception of Communication Commissioner 6.73 (March 2015), HC 1113, available at www.iocco-uk.info.

[34] RIPA, ss 8(4), 16(3).

[35] ibid, ss 21–23.

[36] ibid, ss 57–58.

[37] ibid, ss 65–67. Legislation recently introduced in the UK and still pending at this writing could significantly modify the UK regime in respect to both surveillance powers and the regime of oversight. See text at n 49 below.

[38] See Statement by the Interception of Communications Commissioner's Office (12 March 2015), available at www.iocco-uk.info.

[39] RIPA, s 19. FISA warrants are secret too, but they must be disclosed if any evidentiary fruit of the surveillance is to be used in a criminal prosecution. In contrast, RIPA categorically forbids the use in court of intercept evidence but permits the use of such surveillance as leads to evidence which can

UK civil liberties groups did succeed in invoking ITP jurisdiction when Snowden revealed that NSA was transferring PRISM and UPSTREAM intercepts of those UK groups to GCHQ (its UK counterpart). The ITP held that transfers prior to the litigation had been illegal, but that subsequent transfers were not. The Tribunal reasoned that because GCHQ had kept secret the safeguards applicable to that material, the prior transfers lacked the transparency essential for surveillance 'according to law'. However, subsequent transfers raised a different issue because GCHQ had disclosed a safeguard during the litigation—namely, that NSA material was handled just like intercept intelligence acquired directly under RIPA. The content of that safeguard remained largely secret, but the Tribunal declared that the safeguards were substantively sufficient, and that transparency was now respected, because the safeguards had been 'signposted', even if their content had not been disclosed.[40]

The Tribunal's judgment, now on appeal to the European Court of Human Rights, may fail at least some requirements of European human rights law (see below). However, for the moment, the key point is that the UK, however close it may seem to US civil liberties traditions, remains light years apart in its approach to national-security surveillance.

iii. European/International Human Rights and the EU

The European Union is not only a government in its own right but also the site of actively developing international human rights law. For the latter, the principal authority is the Charter on Fundamental Rights (CFR), which binds EU members when implementing (or failing to implement) EU law. The EU is not a party to the European Convention on Human Rights (ECHR), but it has historically used the ECHR as a source of inspiration for its human rights jurisprudence. Both the CFR and the ECHR protect a right to private life but permit infringements to the extent 'necessary in a democratic society'.

European law, as developed by the European Commission and the two courts with jurisdiction to enforce the human rights treaties—the European Court of Human Rights (ECtHR) for the ECHR and the European Court of Justice (ECJ) for the CFR—has evolved into a strong privacy-protective regime, but with significant limitations. Broadly speaking, this body of law mirrors the American picture in two respects but differs in many others. Like the US, the EU protects foreign nationals in-country but not when they are outside EU borders. And both US and EU law insist that interference with privacy is permissible only when necessary and proportionate to the pursuit of legitimate purposes.

---

be used, with the proviso that there must be no disclosure of the 'circumstances from which its origin [from intercept evidence] may be inferred.' RIPA, s 17(1)(a).

[40] *Liberty (The National Council of Civil Liberties) & Others v Secretary of State for Foreign and Commonwealth Affairs & Others* [2015] UKIPTrib 13_77-H (Investigatory Powers Tribunal, 6 Feb 2015), available at http://www.ipt-uk.com/docs/Liberty_Ors_Judgment_6Feb15.pdf. See Ioanna Tourkochoriti, 'The Transatlantic Flow of Data and the National Security Exception in the European Data Privacy Regulation: In Search for Legal Protection Against Surveillance' (2014) 36 Univ Penn J Int Law 459.

Where the regimes differ, EU law is more protective in three related ways—it rejects the American third-party doctrine, imposes robust limits on retention and use of data held in the private sector, and recognises a 'right to be forgotten'.

Conversely, EU law is weaker than the American in three respects. First, while EU courts require oversight of surveillance powers, they do not require judicial oversight.[41] Instead, the ECtHR grants member states a wide 'margin of appreciation' and accepts that legislative or even internal executive oversight can be deemed independent of investigating authorities. Second, EU conceptions of necessity and proportionality do not require that surveillance focus on individuals rather than broad groups or that individualised suspicion attach to the surveillance target. Proportionality might generate such safeguards in some contexts (and thus preclude bulk collection), but they do not make probable cause a presumptive necessity.[42]

Third, EU surveillance and data-privacy jurisprudence does yet not resolve, in any detail, the ways in which national security should alter the dictates of necessity and proportionality. Thus, European human rights law currently has no counterpart to the detailed specificity of US FISA; its restrictions on national-security surveillance are at best speculative by comparison to those of the US.

The next section considers the extent to which these contrasts may change as the US and EU regimes evolve in the near future.

C. Forthcoming Changes

Emerging American developments suggest progress in the three areas where US law is weak—third-party transmission/storage, use restrictions and foreign nationals. The Second Circuit held NSA's bulk collection programme illegal on statutory grounds,[43] and one Supreme Court Justice has suggested the need to reconsider the third-party doctrine.[44] President Obama has limited the purposes for which data collected in bulk can be used and has extended to foreigners abroad (though in loop-hole ridden terms) the safeguards available to US persons when

---

[41] *Klass v Germany* 2 ECtHR 214 (ser A) (1978); *Kruslin v France* 176-A 12 ECtHR 547 (ser. A) (1990).

[42] See, eg, cases cited at n 41 above.

[43] *ACLU v Clapper* 785 F3d 787 (2d Cir 2015).

[44] See *United States v Jones* 132 S Ct 945, 957 (2012) (Sotomayor, J., concurring) (stating that 'it may be necessary to reconsider' the third-party doctrine). Several federal courts of appeal have addressed the third-party doctrine as it applies to law enforcement access to cell phone location data. The Eleventh Circuit, sitting en banc, applied a robust version of the third-party doctrine in holding that police could obtain 67 days of historical location data from the service provider without a warrant, relying on the fact that the records had been created by a private company for legitimate business purposes. *United States v Davis* 785 F3d 498 (11th Cir 2015). The Fifth Circuit has likewise held the Fourth Amendment inapplicable to such records. *In re Application of U.S. for Historical Cell Site Data* 724 F3d 600 (5th Cir 2013). In contrast, the Fourth Circuit has held that law enforcement must have a warrant issued on probable cause in order to obtain records of cell phone location data for any period exceeding 14 days. *United States v Graham* 796 F3d 332 (4th Cir (2015). To date, the Supreme Court has declined to reconcile these decisions, but it will likely have to do so in the near future.

information is acquired overseas.[45] Finally, for the first time in decades, Congress has forcefully pushed back.

The USA Freedom Act of 2015[46] prohibits the bulk collection of metadata and limits the authority to collect metadata selectively.[47] In addition, the statute enhances transparency and adversarial process in the Foreign Intelligence Surveillance Court, by requiring publication of important rulings and by establishing a cadre of security-cleared amicus curiae to argue legal issues of general significance.[48]

For US privacy advocates, much work remains to be done, particularly with regard to minimisation, limits on government access to third-party data, and the government's authority to collect communications content in surveillance targeting non-US persons who are outside US borders. As a result, US capabilities pose an undiminished threat to foreign nationals and (through incidental collection) to Americans. Even so, the USA Freedom Act represents a significant step forward.

At the time of writing, UK and other European laws governing national security surveillance continue to evolve, with important draft legislation introduced in Britain on 4 November 2015,[49] and the French emergency decree and other legislation currently contemplated in response to the Paris terrorist attacks of 13 November 2015. Despite pressure at the national levels to grant broader surveillance powers, emerging ECJ/ECtHR jurisprudence may impose new safeguards. Such safeguards, however, will certainly be no more restrictive than EU standards applicable *outside* the national security context. Thus, they will—at best—mirror ECJ/ECtHR jurisprudence with respect to ordinary law enforcement, emphasising the need for legislative definition of surveillance powers and requiring necessity, proportionality and oversight but with a substantial 'margin of appreciation'. There is as yet little evidence that the ECJ/ECtHR will insist on adversarial oversight, probable cause or case-specific judicial review.

Two recent ECJ decisions actively engage with substantive limitations. *Digital Rights Ireland*[50] involved a challenge to the 2006 EU Data Retention Directive

---

[45] Presidential Policy Directive/PPD-28, 'Signals Intelligence Activities' (17 Jan 2014) (hereinafter PPD-28). Section 4(a)(1) of the Directive specifies that '[p]ersonal information [concerning non-U.S. persons] shall be [retained and] disseminated only if the [retention and] dissemination of comparable information concerning U.S. persons would be permitted ....' But information concerning a non-US person often will intrinsically not to be 'comparable' to otherwise similar information concerning a US person.

[46] USA Freedom Act of 2015, PL 114–23 (2 June 2015).

[47] A mandate to produce 'call detail records' must be authorised by FISA court order issued on a showing that (1) the records are tied to a 'specific selection term'; (2) they are relevant to 'an authorized investigation...to protect against international terrorism'; and (3) there is 'reasonable, articulable suspicion that such specific selection term is associated with a foreign power engaged in international terrorism...or an agent of a foreign power engaged in international terrorism.' USA Freedom Act of 2015, s 101.

[48] ibid, ss 401–402.

[49] Draft Investigatory Powers Bill, 4 Nov 2015, available at www.gov.uk/government/publications/draft-investigatory-powers-bill.

[50] Joined cases C-293/12, C-594/12 *Digital Rights Ireland and Seitlinger and Others* (EU: C: 2014:238) available at http://curia.europa.eu/juris/document/document.jsf?text=&docid=150642&pageIndex=0&doclang=en&mode=lst&dir=&occ=first&part=1&cid=1308564.

(DRD), which required telecom providers to retain communications metadata for up to two years and to make such data available to law enforcement and security agencies of the national government. In April 2014 the ECJ held the DRD to violate the right to privacy protected by the CFR.

Several steps in the court's analysis are important. First, the ECJ, in marked contrast to US jurisprudence, held that the mere retention of such data in private sector hands, without consent, represented a significant interference with privacy – an interference compounded by the prospect that government agencies could obtain access to it. Second, the ECJ held that although the objective of the DRD (facilitating the fight against crime and terrorism) was legitimate, the DRD was disproportionate to this goal and thus not 'strictly necessary'.

Six features of the DRD contributed to that conclusion. (1) Data was retained without any 'evidence capable of suggesting that their conduct might have a link, even an indirect or remote one, with serious crime';[51] (2) The conditions for law enforcement or security-service access to the data were not specified; (3) There was no requirement of prior review 'by a court or by an independent administrative body';[52] (4) The retention period was not sufficiently discriminating because it did not distinguish between types of data or their potential usefulness; (5) The security of retained data was not sufficiently guaranteed; (6) Finally, DRD did not prevent retained data from being transferred abroad.

Digital Rights Ireland may contain the seeds of a robust European-law requirement of individualised suspicion and ex ante judicial review.[53] A much narrower reading seems plausible, however. The disproportionate character of the DRD is manifest in its indiscriminate features (neither individual suspicion nor even a remote link; neither judicial nor administrative review) and its failure to incorporate *any* of the six safeguards mentioned. Whether the court will insist that data-retention and data-access regimes respect a strong version of *all six* conditions, under all circumstances, is by no means settled.

In *Schrems v Data Protection Commissioner*,[54] decided in October 2015, the ECJ struck down an EU Commission 'safe harbour' decision that permitted European companies to transfer personal data from the EU to the US on the assumption that US law provided safeguards equivalent to those of EU law. The court pointed to several distinct flaws in the safe harbour provisions. In particular, those provisions authorised storage of transferred personal data in the US 'without any differentiation, limitation or exception being made in light of the objective pursued and

---

[51] ibid ¶ 58.

[52] ibid ¶ 62.

[53] See Federico Fabbrini, 'Human Rights in the Digital Age' (2015) 28 *Harvard Human Rights Journal* 65, 86 (concluding that the decision 'rules out anything short of individualized, court-approved requests by national security and law enforcement authorities to collect and use metadata … for specific searches.').

[54] Case C-362/14 *Maximillian Schrems v Data Protection Commissioner* judgment 6 October 2015 (not yet reported), available at http://curia.europa.eu/juris/document/document.jsf?text=&docid=169195&pageIndex=0&doclang=EN&mode=req&dir=&occ=first&part=1&cid=134472.

without an objective criterion ... for determining the limits of the access of the public authorities to the data and of its subsequent use'.[55]

Like *Digital Rights Ireland, Schrems* condemns common US practices that afford minimal protection to metadata held by third parties. At the same time, neither decision acknowledges the substantial safeguards that US law affords for communications content. Even with respect to metadata, neither decision addresses surveillance targeted specifically at national security threats. Though justly celebrated by privacy advocates, the recent ECJ decisions nonetheless rest primarily on the indiscriminate character of the permitted intrusions, which were necessarily disproportionate to information-gathering needs of widely varying importance. The ECJ has not yet come to grips with the international human rights of non-EU citizens or necessity/proportionality requirements in the national security context specifically.

Beyond any conclusions that can be drawn from parsing the jurisprudence, the prospects for a European solution to the global privacy dilemma are further clouded by the complex structure of the European institutions. The European Commission, the European Parliament and most recently the ECJ have been strong voices for privacy protection, but EU decision-making power is shared with (or predominantly allocated to) the EU Council (a body composed of member-state government ministers), which for more than three years has resisted Commission efforts to put EU privacy-protective legislation on a firmer footing. Moreover, both the Commission and the ECJ seem to lack jurisdictional competence with regard to national decisions in the law enforcement and national security domains. The ECtHR does have jurisdiction to review actions by individual states in those domains. However, it may have even less independent power than the ECJ, as implementation of its rulings largely depends on the willing support of the member state concerned. In sum, changes now on the European horizon are unlikely to meet justifiable needs to protect privacy in global communication.

One place to which privacy advocates have turned for help is the right to privacy enshrined in Article 17 of the International Covenant on Civil and Political Rights (ICCPR). Article 17 affords a plausible basis for insisting that internet surveillance satisfy strong threshold prerequisites, respect known limits on the retention and use of personal data, and be subject to independent oversight.[56]

Though not to be undervalued or discouraged, this effort will fall short for several reasons. First, the US government is notoriously inattentive to robust conceptions of human rights as understood in the international community, and the enforcement powers of the UN Human Rights Committee are not comparable to those of EU/ECHR law, as the former lie primarily in the domain of moral suasion. Moreover, the international law scholarship is often incomplete, because much of

---

[55] ibid.

[56] See, eg, Report of the Special Rapporteur on the Promotion and Protection of Human Rights and Fundamental Freedoms While Countering Terrorism (23 September 2014), available at http://www.un.org/en/ga/search/view_doc.asp?symbol=A/69/397.

it is framed in terms applicable to law enforcement generally, without taking on board the extra flexibility and secrecy that is arguably 'necessary in a democratic society' in the case of national security surveillance.[57] Above all, to the extent that human rights norms are informed by prevailing practice in the international community, a fair account of requirements applicable in the national security context would have to acknowledge that the level of protection commonly respected worldwide in this domain is quite minimal.

For these reasons, privacy advocates are right not to place all hopes on the broad jurisprudence of international human rights. Albeit for different (primarily universalist) reasons, they have sought a privacy-sensitive multilateral framework that signatory states would accept as binding. What, however, can be the expected shape of such an agreement, and where will it leave Americans and others once its provisions enter into force?

IV. The Dangers of Multilateralism

One obvious obstacle to an international agreement is the wide—probably unbridgeable—gulf between privacy commitments in the West and in many undemocratic governments. However, even within the framework of a narrower US-EU negotiation or one among Western democracies, the complexity of the issues and the diametric opposition between US and other Western approaches suggest that reaching common ground will be arduous and slow. A more fundamental concern is whether an international agreement is worth striving for. To be sure, the international perspective is normally more balanced and progressive than the one that dominates in the domestic American setting, a contrast that helps give 'American exceptionalism' its bad name. But the human rights advantages of internationalism are unlikely to be realised in a multilateral national-security negotiation. The concerns include the risk of regression to the mean, institutional dynamics and the merger of floor and ceiling.

A. Regression to the Mean

In an international negotiation, conferees are unlikely to accept on each issue the most privacy-protective features of any participant's national regime, and to set aside their own perceived needs for national-security intelligence. The norms emerging from any international negotiation will inevitably be situated somewhere between the most protective and least protective conceptions of the participants.

---

[57] See, eg, Convention for the Protection of Human Rights and Fundamental Freedoms, 4 November 1950, Art 8, 213 UNTS 221, 230.

The risks in a truly *global* negotiation are especially pronounced. Any broadly inclusive framework will include authoritarian regimes determined to preserve their freedom of action with regard to surveillance. Cole and Fabbrini are surely right that any agreement tolerably protective of privacy will have to be confined to a US-EU framework, with the possible addition of such Western democracies as Canada, Australia and New Zealand.

In a negotiation among Western democracies, where are the compromises likely to be struck? One way to foresee the likely outcome is to focus on the institutional dynamics that would shape multilateral negotiations.

B. Institutional Dynamics

The prospect of an international data-privacy agreement evokes memories of the process that produced the ICCPR and similar human-rights milestones. But responsibility for framing national-security surveillance principles will not be entrusted to human rights specialists. The dynamic will be quite different.

i. *The American Dimension*

Consider first the US side of the negotiating table. Who would lead the American team? The answer is unambiguous and, for privacy advocates, chilling. This will be a job for the national-security establishment—FBI, NSA, the Director of National Intelligence and the White House National Security Council. Presumably, a State Department official will round out the team, but the voices of civil liberties will be at the edges of discussion. Neither Congress nor the courts will control American negotiating priorities. And an executive agreement in the exercise of the President's Article II Commander-in-Chief powers could enter into force without legislative involvement or approval at all.

These pessimistic conclusions require some qualification. Since the President's Article II powers in this domain are shared with Congress,[58] international standards more permissive than FISA would have no effect without statutory endorsement. However, a global framework, once agreed upon, would trigger powerful pressure upon Congress, from commercial interests and from the national-security establishment, for new legislation to bring FISA requirements into conformity with the more permissive multilateral regime.

In any event, on many key points, FISA delegates responsibility to the Executive. These issues include targeting procedures, minimisation, and data retention/use restrictions for both domestic and foreign interception. A common international framework on these issues would not expressly conflict with FISA and therefore would enter into force without legislative approval. To be sure, Congress is already sidelined to a degree on these matters, but with an important

---

[58] *Hamdan v Rumsfeld* 548 US 557 (2006).

qualification: Both the FISA court and the congressional Intelligence Committees have oversight authority in these areas that they could lose if more porous standards were enshrined in an international agreement. (The next section explains why internationally agreed standards could override any judicial oversight that might otherwise be constitutionally mandated.)[59]

The upshot is that on the US side, a multilateral approach will give even greater primacy than usual to the national-security establishment and marginalise the strongest sources of pro-privacy leverage. At least from the selfish perspective of Americans concerned to protect their own privacy, there is strong reason to prefer a more parochial, go-it-alone strategy.

ii. The European Dimension

On the European side there are several parallels and one significant contrast to the American picture. Privacy-conscious voices are strong in the UK House of Commons, in the European Parliament and in the most relevant courts— the ECJ and the ECtHR. In contrast to America, however, a powerful executive body, the European Commission, has been a proactive advocate of data-privacy safeguards.

The problem for privacy protection on the European side, however, is the limited competency of the Commission relative to that of Member States, because in national-security and law-enforcement matters, the Commission's authority is circumscribed.[60] As a result, any US-EU negotiation would likely be dominated on the European side by Member-State governments—meaning the Interior Ministries and security services such as GCHQ and DGRE. These players would likely control the terms of any acceptable accord.

Absent an international agreement, would the European Parliament, the national parliaments and the ECJ/ECtHR exercise greater influence? Perhaps there would be little difference, given the power that the security services would exercise in either scenario. It seems likely, however, that EU institutions can achieve higher levels of privacy protection in a framework internal to the EU than they can realise in a multilateral negotiation dominated by Member State security services.

Indeed, a comparable dynamic has become an important feature of the broader international landscape, with the increasing 'fragmentation' of international norms. Since World War II, powerful states have repeatedly exploited specialised regulatory regimes and one-time multilateral negotiations on specialised topics to enhance their dominance.[61] Across multiple areas, such fragmentation has made co-ordination and influence more difficult for their opponents, and thus allowed

---

[59] See text at nn 69–72 below.

[60] See, eg, HM Government, 'Review of the Balance of Competences between the United Kingdom and the European Union' available at www.gcn.civilservice.gov.uk.

[61] Eyal Benvenisti and George Downs, 'The Emperor's New Clothes: Political Economy and the Fragmentation of International Law' (2007) 60 *Stanford Law Review* 595.

dominant states even more freedom of action.[62] This dynamic, which Benvenisti and Downs find over a wide range of international agreements,[63] provides reason for pessimism about the benefits of an international privacy accord. To be sure, applicable law will remain even more fragmented in the *absence* of an international accord. But as Benvenisti-Downs note:[64]

'powerful states...limit political coordination among weaker [interests] [by creating] detailed agreements in one-time multilateral settings....Such venues provide a less congenial setting for engaging in political coordination than does the ongoing legislative process that takes place within most states.'

Fragmentation also weakens the influence of international courts. Benvenisti-Downs observe:[65]

'Constitutionalism...gives [international tribunals] an incentive to identify the values and goals of less powerful [interests] in order to justify their decisions about what constitutes the values of the international community. [But specialized multinational agreements impair the] effort on the part of international tribunals to define the nature of these state obligations and the overarching principles of the international community from which they are derived....The cacophony of isolated functionally specific venues... permits powerful states to stave off the emergence of any [constitutionally based] obligation that they do not expressly impose on themselves...'

If an international compact governing electronic surveillance were to succumb to this prevalent dynamic, the consequences for privacy rights worldwide would be unfortunate.

C. The Merger of Floor and Ceiling

To the worry that a multilateral accord could dilute safeguards that would otherwise apply, one possible answer is that an international agreement cannot override minimum constitutional standards as enforced by US courts and the ECJ/ECtHR. This answer, however, is inaccurate for three reasons.

First, if such an agreement set only a floor of protection, it would defeat the very objective—inter-jurisdictional uniformity—that the multilateral accord aimed to produce in the first place. An accord providing only for minimum safeguards would not serve the goals of law enforcement, the security services, and the private-sector ISPs. The same difficulty stands in the way of a framework that limits cross-border surveillance, without diluting safeguards states must observe for

---

[62] ibid, pp 599, 607 (noting that '[fragmentation] increase[s] the transaction costs [of] the political coordination necessary [for opposing interests] to form a coalition that could more effectively bargain with their more powerful counterparts...[It allows] a hegemon or a group of powerful states to prevent weaker [parties] from cooperating in order to erode the hegemon's dominance.'

[63] Benvenisti and Downs, n 61 above.

[64] ibid, p 612.

[65] ibid, pp 630–31.

surveillance of their own citizens and surveillance within their own borders. Cole and Fabbrini see new cross-border restrictions, however modest, as an unequivocal gain, since current cross-border protections are essentially nil. They are surely right if the resulting regime—with different safeguards depending on the site of interception and the nationality of the target—proves sustainable. But commercial, law-enforcement and even civil-liberties interests would likely make such an arrangement sufficiently complex to trigger strong pressure (much like those that prompt PCIF proposals now) to align the two regimes—in this case by diluting the pre-existing 'domestic' rights. Unfortunately, therefore, we cannot assume that a process producing new cross-border safeguards will simply give us something better than nothing, rather than prompting an uncertain trade-off of currently strong domestic protections for improved international ones.

To be sure, American ISP executives until now have been forceful voices for data privacy. But that position may not be solely attributable to civil-liberties idealism; American ISPs have commercial imperatives to ensure that US privacy safeguards remain robust. Otherwise, the cloud-computing and data-storage business of privacy-conscious consumers will increasingly migrate to off-shore havens where governments establish privacy-sensitive regimes for the purpose of attracting such business—the cyber-equivalent of a Cayman Islands tax haven, but in the opposite direction: Inter-jurisdictional variation in tax rates triggers a race to the bottom, but variation in privacy safeguards will unleash different forces because the 'magic of the marketplace' will tend to draw business to places where data is most secure.

This commercial dynamic underscores one reason why international uniformity poses such an acute danger for privacy advocates. As long as surveillance standards vary across jurisdictions, US-based ISPs have a powerful reason to insure that US safeguards remain as good or better than those of other countries where a competitor could locate. But international or US-EU uniformity would defuse private-sector commercial needs to keep US domestic safeguards strong.[66] Although jurisdictional competition often triggers a 'race to the bottom', in international surveillance, jurisdictional competition can spur a 'race to the top'.[67]

Other factors would reinforce this dynamic. Many salient requirements under US law, though constitutionally inspired, have no firm constitutional pedigree. Under pressure for international uniformity, safeguards currently mandated

---

[66] Of course, any rogue nation seeking to become the Cayman Islands of Privacy would refuse to join a multilateral agreement imposing uniform standards. That risk of migration to non-signers is multiplied in the Cole-Fabbrini proposal for an accord limited to Anglo-American powers or the US and the EU Member States. But the ability of small nations to pursue a Cayman Islands strategy would be constrained by the need for a skilled workforce, cheap, reliable electricity, a cool climate (ruling out the Caribbean) and excellent connectivity not subject to firewalls that ISPs based in the major developed World might be able to deploy.

[67] Indeed Bilyana Petkova finds such a 'race to the top' on privacy safeguards more generally within the US federal system. Bilyana Petkova, 'Privacy and Federated Lawmaking in the European Union and the United States: Who is Defying the Status Quo?' (NYU, Jean Monnet Working Paper Series, 2015).

could be relaxed—for example, with respect to minimisation and foreign territory interception—without raising insurmountable constitutional objections.

Another factor that connects international uniformity to weaker safeguards is more surprising: Constitutional safeguards would not necessarily override more permissive international standards, because the constitutional minimum under US domestic law would migrate downward to reduce discrepancies between the two. This counter-intuitive dynamic is nonetheless possible—even likely—because of the peculiarities of the US 'administrative search' doctrine.

The US constitutional prerequisite for a lawful search ordinarily is probable cause and a warrant. But the 'administrative search' exception provides that when a search serves 'special needs distinct from the ordinary interest in law enforcement',[68] the constitutional requirement changes to 'reasonableness', assessed under the totality of the circumstances.[69] A surveillance for preventive intelligence-gathering, as distinct from one aimed primarily at gathering evidence for criminal prosecution, is a quintessential example of a 'special needs' search that must satisfy only this flexible 'reasonableness' standard.[70] As a result, a warrant and probable cause may or may not be constitutionally required, depending on the many considerations relevant to 'reasonableness'. The outer limits of executive power under this doctrine have not been tested, because US statutory law generally requires a warrant and probable cause even for national-security surveillance. But this picture could change if international negotiations prompted relaxation of US statutory requirements.

Although the Bush administration and the Foreign Intelligence Surveillance Court of Review repeatedly asserted a 'foreign-intelligence exception' to the warrant requirement,[71] this claim is surely extravagant. The Supreme Court has never approved under the administrative search rubric any warrantless search remotely equivalent in intrusiveness to ongoing electronic surveillance. Any such invasion of privacy could be deemed reasonable only on a strong showing of need, with judicial oversight relaxed only to the extent demonstrably necessary. Within this framework, something roughly similar to FISA becomes a Fourth Amendment imperative, particularly with respect to surveillance within US borders.

Enter an international agreement. In the administrative-search framework, a pre-existing Fourth Amendment requirement will override a more permissive regime of 'special needs' surveillance when the latter is unreasonable. A substantial relaxation of FISA's safeguards could well be deemed unnecessarily permissive and thus unconstitutional if adopted only to satisfy the demands of the US national-security establishment. However, in the context of an international

---

[68] See, eg, *New Jersey v TLO* 469 US 325, 351 (Blackmun, J, concurring).
[69] See generally Stephen J Schulhofer, *More Essential than Ever: The Fourth Amendment in the Twenty-First Century* 93-114 (New York: Oxford University Press 2012); Stephen J Schulhofer, 'On the Fourth Amendment Rights of the Law-Abiding Public' in Gerhard Casper and Dennis J Hutchinson (eds) *The Supreme Court Review* (1989, 87–163).
[70] See, eg, *MacWade v Kelly* 460 F3d 260 (2d Cir 2006).
[71] See, eg, *In re Sealed Case* 310 F3d 717 (For Intel Surv Ct Rev 2002).

accord motivated by the complexities of global data transmission and storage and by legitimate concerns for inter-jurisdictional uniformity, the constitutional calculus would change; reduced safeguards could conceivably pass muster.[72] For Europe, similar considerations presumably would be influential at the ECJ/ ECtHR, where the margin of appreciation makes this sort of flexibility even more likely.

The upshot is that an international negotiation could become a 'make my day' moment for Western security services. Far from propelling uniform, privacy-sensitive norms for US-EU citizens, such a framework would invite negotiators around the table to 'impose' on themselves a surveillance regime more permissive than any to which they would otherwise be subject. Given the structure of a mul- tilateral negotiation, a race to the regulatory bottom seems far more likely than migration toward the privacy-protective top.

In summary, the seemingly attractive prospect of a privacy-sensitive interna- tional agreement poses large risks for internet users throughout the world. The remaining question, however, is whether a go-it-alone strategy will offer greater hope or instead will simply leave undisturbed the loopholes that render so much of the American regulatory apparatus toothless, not only for citizens of other nations but for Americans themselves.

V. Embracing Sovereignty

Reform of American domestic legislation is most likely to succeed when it aims to tighten safeguards for US persons. This parochial perspective is unappealing, but it is not merely self-regarding; it is grounded in the concept of privacy itself.

Privacy serves roughly, two distinct objectives. One is to protect individual autonomy and enable personal growth. The other is to protect democracy by cre- ating sheltered spaces for investigative journalism, political association and dis- sent.[73] The former goal is jeopardised by surveillance from any direction, but the latter is most strongly implicated when citizens face surveillance by their own gov- ernment.[74] Bracketing for a moment the problem of inter-jurisdictional sharing of intelligence, US data-collection programmes pose a far greater risk of chilling political dissent within the US than of chilling political activity by Germans or Canadians critical of their own governments. Thus, it is not necessarily unjustified

---

[72] The above analysis does not encompass surveillance in ordinary law enforcement, which is ineli- gible for administrative-search treatment. See *City of Indianapolis v Edmond* 531 US 32 (2000).

[73] Schulhofer, n 69 above, pp 11–14, 179.

[74] To be sure (and worth more than a footnote), government surveillance of foreign nationals threatens democratic values when the intelligence product is used to chill or obstruct foreign journalists investigating that government's extraterritorial abuses. Surveillance by a nation like the US, which pro- jects its economic and military power worldwide, poses an especially acute danger in this regard.

to insist on especially effective safeguards when US intelligence agencies spy on Americans.[75]

This parochial point nonetheless implies a need to protect non-US persons, because the foreign-target loophole obliterates large chunks of the protection that the US government must guarantee its own citizens. Incidental collection (intelligence on Americans obtained by targeting persons of foreign or unknown nationality) is now virtually impossible to avoid. It can be mitigated by restricting the retention and use of US-person information, but such 'minimization' is at best only a band-aid. American self-interest should powerfully motivate efforts to plug the foreign-target loophole – a dynamic that Cole and Fabbrini may underestimate.[76]

Multilateral sharing poses similar risks. Threshold requirements should limit the ability of US agencies to accept from other countries information pertaining to Americans, and minimisation should ensure that such information is used only for narrow purposes. Measures like these would protect US citizens even in a World where other governments are free to spy on them at will. A vital remaining question, however, is whether US reforms giving privileged protection to Americans would bring non-Americans within their compass.

The leading reason to expect this to happen is less humanitarian than commercial. American ISPs have a compelling, multi-billion dollar interest in retaining the business of foreign customers. Foreign companies and individuals that get stronger privacy protection from service providers at home will hesitate to use less-protective US-based ISPs. Indeed, market forces have already created opportunities for cloud-computing and data-storage services to establish themselves outside the US.[77]

This threat to the revenue stream of US-based ISPs may have been a factor in President Obama's (frustratingly vague) declaration that NSA will extend to foreigners the same safeguards that it respects in its surveillance of Americans.[78] Conversely, of course, the non-citizen loophole represents a powerful *advantage* for NSA, one it will fight to keep. However, its opposition to non-citizen safeguards will be just as strong in PCIF negotiations, except that the latter context offers no offsetting push-back from the private sector, which loses much of its reason to support strong domestic privacy safeguards once assured that competitors in other countries cannot offer anything better.

---

[75] See Ryan Goodman, 'Should Foreign Nationals Get the Same Privacy Protections under NSA Surveillance—or Less (or More)?' (2014) *Just Security* (29 October).

[76] See Cole-Fabbrini at Ch 11 below.

[77] See Christopher Jon Sprigman and Jennifer Grannick, 'US Government Surveillance: Bad for Silicon Valley, Bad for Democracy Around the World', (2013) *The Atlantic* (June).

[78] See PPD–28, above n 45, s 4 ('*To the maximum extent feasible* consistent with the national security, these policies and procedures are to be applied equally to the personal information of all persons, regardless of nationality…Personal information shall be retained only if the retention of *comparable information* concerning U.S. persons would be permitted ….') (emphasis added).

A similar dynamic can fuel a relatively simple international solution—bilateral parity. Instead of seeking a comprehensive multilateral framework, any nation could negotiate a bilateral agreement with any other, each party merely committing to extend to citizens of the other, whatever safeguards it observes in surveilling its own citizens.[79] The non-discrimination component creates built-in equity and since this approach does not require either party to adjust its substantive surveillance principles, it can produce agreement without the difficult negotiations needed to find common ground in an area where traditions and practices vary widely even among the democracies.[80]

In so far as predictions can be made in this complex and politically fraught area, it seems that solutions at the national level, supplemented when appropriate by bilateral parity commitments, can address the global threat to privacy more quickly, with greater hope of adequate substantive content, than can a search for a uniform PCIF.

VI. Conclusion

A robust right to privacy is essential for personal growth and democratic politics. Yet that right is jeopardized by the globalisation of communication, the jurisdictional uncertainties that surround the physical situs of data in transmission or storage and the virtually universal refusal of governments to extend privacy protection to non-citizens abroad. Ideally, an international accord would set uniform or at least minimum standards to protect this essential human right. But the politics, economics and institutional dynamics that would shape such an agreement suggest that an international accord would heavily favour security-service preferences and would likely weaken privacy protections worldwide. Paradoxically, global privacy is likely to be better protected if domestic surveillance laws, especially those of the United States, are left to evolve on their own terms, without resort to a comprehensive multilateral framework.

---

[79] It could be argued that *Schrems* forecloses this solution, to the extent that it held that the privacy protections available under US law (even for US citizens) are insufficient to meet European standards. This reading of *Schrems* however, assumes that the disproportionality analysis underlying the ECJ decision in *Schrems* would not require qualification in the context of surveillance and data access for national security purposes. This author considers it unlikely that future ECJ jurisprudence will read *Schrems* so broadly.

[80] Cf the approach to fair trial procedure reflected in the Geneva Conventions. They establish no common framework for war-crimes trials; they simply require each signatory to extend to soldiers of the other the same safeguards it observes in trying its own personnel. See Geneva Convention Relative to the Treatment of Prisoners of War (12 August 1949) arts 102, 106, 108.

11

Transatlantic Negotiations for Transatlantic Rights: Why an EU-US Agreement is the Best Option for Protecting Privacy Against Cross-border Surveillance

DAVID COLE AND FEDERICO FABBRINI

'Europeans, like Americans, cherish your privacy. And many are skeptical about governments collecting and sharing information, for good reason. ... We care about Europeans' privacy, not just Americans' privacy.'

US President Barack Obama, Speech, Hanover, 25 April 2016

I. Introduction

National borders have become increasingly irrelevant in the digital age.[1] Data flies across national borders and back without hindrance, without a visa, and often without knowledge on the part of the individual who created the data. Information backed up on 'the cloud' is often stored in countries far from the originating source. These facts, coupled with the ability of computers to collect, retain, and analyse massive amounts of digital information, offer security services unprecedented opportunities to spy on large numbers of people far beyond their own borders. By scooping up information in foreign countries, or collecting foreign communications as they pass through their own country, security services can gain access to a great deal of communications. And as these developments are relatively recent, the laws that protect privacy have not kept pace.

---

[1] See Report of the United Nations High Commissioner for Human Rights on The Right to Privacy in the Digital Age, 30 June 2014, A/HRC/27/37.

These concerns seemed relatively speculative until June 2013, when Edward Snowden disclosed that the US National Security Agency (NSA) had been conducting dragnet electronic surveillance of private communications worldwide. One of the most troubling aspects of the gap between law and technology underscored by Snowden's disclosures is that domestic and transnational legal regimes generally offer little or no protection from surveillance conducted by foreign nations.[2] US citizens have little or no legal protection from surveillance conducted against them by European or other nations, and Europeans have little or no legal protection from surveillance conducted against them by US agencies. As documented by official public reports, the NSA exploited that loophole in unprecedented fashion, collecting hundreds of millions of 'foreign' electronic communications.[3] Given the ease of sharing information, this end-run around privacy protections could undermine any real security with respect to online privacy.

To address this lacuna, in earlier work we made the case for a transatlantic privacy compact between the EU and the US as a way to protect privacy rights against cross-border surveillance.[4] As we argued, the EU and the US are closer in terms of existing privacy protections than is conventionally claimed. Both systems protect privacy in their respective internal domestic spheres as a matter of constitutional and statutory law, but make exceptions for national security and law enforcement surveillance. And neither system places any meaningful limits on what its intelligence agencies can do to the privacy of non-citizens overseas. Given this state of affairs, we proposed that the EU and the US should consider a compact extending a minimal level of privacy to each other's citizens on a reciprocal basis. This might simply involve a commitment not to discriminate on the basis of citizenship, that is, to extend to foreign nationals the same protections from surveillance that the US and the EU extend to their own citizens. Or it might entail mutual agreement on specific minimum privacy safeguards that EU citizens and residents should enjoy vis-a-vis US surveillance, and vice versa.

To support this view, we advanced four related arguments. First, a transatlantic privacy compact is an indispensable instrument to prevent circumvention of key constitutional guarantee through transnational state action. Second, a precedent for this sort of agreement already exists, in the 'five eyes agreement' by which the US, UK, Australia, Canada and New Zealand extend certain privacy protections to each other's nationals. Third, a transatlantic compact could foster trust between the EU and the US, at a time when cooperation is most needed to face common

---

[2] See D Cole and F Fabbrini, 'Bridging the Transatlantic Divide? The United States, the European Union and the Protection of Privacy Across Borders' (2016) 14 *International Journal of Constitutional Law* 220 and D Cole and F Fabbrini, 'Reciprocal Privacy: Towards a Transatlantic Agreement', in F Fabbrini and V Jackson (eds), *Constitutionalism Across Borders in the Struggle Against Terrorism* (Elgar 2016) 169.

[3] See European Parliament Resolution of 12 March 2014 on the US NSA surveillance programme, surveillance bodies in various Member States and their impact on EU citizens' fundamental rights and on transatlantic co-operation in Justice and Home Affairs, P7_TA(2014)0230.

[4] Cole and Fabbrini (n 2).

threats. Fourth, increasing transatlantic privacy protections is crucial to support growing interconnections between the EU and the US, including in the field of trade.

Our colleague and friend Stephen Schulhofer has offered a powerful argument against a multi-national privacy compact.[5] Schulhofer argues that privacy protections are more likely to be secured in domestic fora, and within the US in particular, and cautions that any effort to conclude a legally binding transnational agreement on the protection of privacy may backfire. According to Schulhofer, 'the politics, economics and institutional dynamics that would shape such an agreement suggest that an international accord would heavily favor security-service preferences and would likely weaken privacy protections worldwide'.[6] In his view, representatives from the security services would dominate negotiations, states would be unlikely to agree to anything that requires them to improve their own privacy protections, thus guaranteeing only a very minimal level of protection and such an agreement might then exert downward pressure on existing domestic privacy protections on both sides of the Atlantic. Moreover, he argues, market forces may themselves push in favour of privacy, as corporations and nations compete for the business that strong privacy protections may entice. 'Paradoxically,' Schulhofer concludes, 'global privacy is likely to be better protected if domestic surveillance laws, especially those of the United States, are left to evolve on their own terms, without resort to a comprehensive multilateral framework.'[7]

We share Schulhofer's scepticism about the feasibility of pursuing a *global* treaty on privacy, given the widely divergent privacy commitments of the world's nations. Our proposal is to begin with a *transatlantic* agreement between the US and the EU, given the substantial similarities these systems have in terms of respect for democracy, privacy, and the rule of law. Even in the more specific context of EU-US relations, Schulhofer's cautions are well-taken. An agreement drawn up by security officials without meaningful input from privacy proponents risks being a step backward, and it is conceivable that diluted domestic protections might follow in its wake. But as we will show, the incentives and dynamics that worry Schulhofer are not inevitable, and on balance, we think that the benefits of a transnational compact outweigh the risks. This is especially the case with respect to cross-border surveillance, from which domestic law on both sides of the Atlantic provides no meaningful protection, and therefore cannot be made worse by transnational agreement. Schulhofer's concerns militate in favour of proceeding with attention to the potential downside risks, but should not foreclose the attempt. Moreover, the cross-border spying loophole is unlikely to be closed through purely

---

[5] See S Schulhofer, Ch 10 in this volume and S Schulhofer, 'An International Right to Privacy? Be Careful What You Wish For' (2016) 14 *International Journal of Constitutional Law* 238.

[6] Schulhofer, Ch 10 in this volume, 195.

[7] Ibid.

domestic initiatives. Most countries will be unwilling to limit their own powers without a reciprocal commitment from others.

In addition, and perhaps most importantly, domestic law development and transnational agreements are not mutually exclusive, and can be mutually rein-forcing. That is, domestic privacy rules may provide the impetus for transatlantic agreements, and in so doing may mitigate the risks Schulhofer cites. Indeed, as we will show, recent developments provide an example of just such a dynamic: in the EU, the European Court of Justice (ECJ) expanded domestic privacy protections,[8] invalidating an existing transatlantic privacy pact allowing private corporations to transfer data from the EU to the US. This in turn prompted the negotiation of a new transatlantic agreement that, by necessity, affords greater privacy protec-tions, including against access by national security agencies, to transferred data. Thus, domestic and transatlantic processes may work together to produce privacy protections that either one on their own would be unlikely or unable to effectuate.

Part II responds to Schulhofer's critique of a transnational approach. While we concede that, at least in the US, security officials are likely to play a role in negotia-tions, this is true with respect to any rules developed at the domestic level as well, and therefore is not a reason to favour the domestic over the transatlantic track. The answer to this concern in both settings is active civil society engagement and advo-cacy. We see no reason to believe that the problem of security official involvement is categorically worse at the transatlantic level. Nor do we believe a 'regression to the mean' is inevitable, as Schulhofer suggests.[9] Rather, the content of an agreement is likely to depend on the strength of demands for privacy made by civil society organ-isations and the public at large. International agreements have proved a force for the elevation of domestic human rights protections in the past, and there is no inherent reason that they cannot continue to serve that function. Finally, while Schulhofer is right that market forces may support privacy protections in some respects, they can also cut the other way. Internet service providers have built their business mod-els on the exploitation of customers' private information, and thus are not always going to be strong advocates for privacy. We are not confident that leaving privacy to market forces is an acceptable option, and maintain that direct engagement by states, corporations, and civil society is both necessary and desirable.

Part III moves beyond the binary character of the debate thus far, and sug-gests that domestic law development and transatlantic compacts are not mutually exclusive, but can work together to advance privacy. As a recent example we point to the October 2015 *Schrems* decision of the ECJ and its aftermath.[10] The decision, based on privacy rules internal to the EU, has prompted the renegotiation of a transatlantic agreement allowing private corporations to transfer customer data

---

[8] See F Fabbrini, 'The EU Charter of Fundamental Rights and the Right to Data Privacy: The ECJ as a Human Rights Court' in S De Vries et al (eds), *The EU Charter of Fundamental Rights as a Binding Instrument* (Hart 2015) 261.
[9] Schulhofer (n 5) 187.
[10] Case C-362/14 *Schrems* ECLI:EU:C:2015:650.

from the EU to the US.[11] In this instance, as Schulhofer predicted, a 'domestic' legal development is principally responsible for the advance in privacy rights, but it could not have been effectuated without a transatlantic compact. That compact, negotiated in the shadow of the ECJ *Schrems* decision and the scrutiny of European data protection watchdogs, promises improved privacy protections for EU residents' data when it is transferred to the US. In this instance, domestic and transatlantic processes worked together to advance privacy. In the end, privacy's protection in a world in which borders are increasingly irrelevant will likely rest not on exclusively domestic developments, nor solely on transnational or international agreements, but on the interplay between them.

II. The Advantages and Necessity of a Transatlantic Compact

Privacy is vulnerable to transnational infringement in ways that were unimaginable just a decade ago.[12] This fact of life of the modern digital era means that if we are to safeguard privacy effectively, its guarantees must not stop at the border's edge. But transnational protections are unlikely to arise without transnational negotiations. Rights are a function of political will, and the relevant political actors, when it comes to transnational privacy, are by definition beyond one's borders. Schulhofer is correct that there are risks to transnationally negotiated privacy protections. But his argument overlooks a central, and in our view, decisive point: absent such negotiations, there are unlikely to be any meaningful protections vis-à-vis the actions of a foreign government outside of its own territory and affecting foreign nationals. It is that privacy issue to which our proposal is directed. We do not expect a uniform standard of privacy to be adopted by all countries, but believe that on the issue of cross-border spying, where the status quo imposes no limits, an agreement to impose some reciprocal limits would be an improvement for everyone. The question, therefore, is not *whether* we should pursue that route, but *how* we go about doing so.

Schulhofer is right to caution that transnational negotiations pose real risks. But those risks are (1) unavoidable; (2) not unique to the transnational sphere; and (3) not a good reason to oppose transnational negotiation, but a reason to engage in such processes with awareness of the potential downsides. At the end of the day, there really is no alternative—particularly in the context of EU-US relations.

Schulhofer offers three reasons to be sceptical about transnational negotiations: 'regression to the mean, institutional dynamics, and the merger of floor and

[11] Commission Communication, 'Transatlantic Data Flows: Restoring Trust through Strong Safeguards', 29 February 2016, COM(2016)117 final.
[12] See J Daskal, 'The Unterritoriality of Data' (2015) 125 *Yale Law Journal* 326.

ceiling'.[13] He predicts that any negotiation will lead to a level of protection that falls short of that provided by the most protective nations. This tendency will be exacerbated, he contends, by the fact that security service officials are likely to be the principal negotiators. And he warns that if transnational protections fall below any given nation's own domestic laws, the transnational norm may exert pressure to reduce domestic privacy protections in countries whose safeguards exceed whatever might be agreed upon in a transnational pact.

None of these concerns should be a deal-breaker.

First, transnational negotiations do not inevitably revert to the mean. The evolution of international human rights reflects, at least in part, a series of international treaties that pushed nearly all countries to improve their own laws with respect to human rights.[14] There is no inherent reason why a transatlantic compact on privacy would somehow gravitate toward the midpoint. In addition, as we have previously explained, the existing state of the law in Europe and the US provides virtually no protection for foreign nationals from foreign government surveillance outside the foreign government's borders.[15] The protections of the European Convention on Human Rights (ECHR) extend only so far as a state exercises authority and control over an individual,[16] and no cases have thus far treated the mere fact of surveillance as sufficient authority and control to extend ECHR protections. And the US Supreme Court has, with the exception of the unusual circumstances of the Guantanamo detainees,[17] not extended constitutional protections to foreign nationals beyond US borders.[18] The US courts routinely recognise the constitutional rights of foreign nationals residing in the US, and have also extended constitutional protections to US citizens living overseas, but foreign nationals abroad are, under existing jurisprudence, largely unprotected. Thus, when it comes to the particular area of concern to which our proposal is addressed—privacy rights for EU citizens against US government surveillance conducted in Europe, and, vice versa, privacy rights for US citizens against European governments surveillance conducted in the US—both sides of the Atlantic are starting with nothing. At least within that domain, the situation can't get any worse. There is nowhere to regress to.

Second, Schulhofer raises concerns about who will be at the negotiating table. We agree that the negotiators of any agreement affecting intelligence gathering and national security surveillance will include security officials, and that their interest will be in preserving their ability to conduct surveillance overseas. But that is true

---

[13] Schulhofer (n 5) 187.

[14] To name just three of countless examples, the International Covenant on Civil and Political Rights, the European Convention on Human Rights, and the Convention Against Torture have each caused many nations to reform their domestic laws and practices to meet treaty obligations. See P Alston and R Goodman, *International Human Rights Law* (Oxford, Oxford University Press, 2012).

[15] See Cole and Fabbrini (n 2) 222.

[16] See *Al-Jedda v United Kingdom* Application No 27021/08, ECtHR., judgment, 7 July 2011.

[17] See *Boumediene v Bush* 553 US 723 (2008).

[18] See *United States v Verdugo-Urquidez* 494 US 259 (1990).

with respect to domestic statutory negotiation as well.[19] So this concern is equally applicable at the domestic and international levels, and therefore does not necessarily provide a reason to prefer one over the other. The answer at either level lies in the necessity for civil society advocacy for privacy. Without popular demands for privacy protections, state officials are likely to prefer rules that make their jobs easier. But where the populace demands privacy, there will be countervailing pressures.[20] Thus, after Snowden disclosed the existence of the NSA's telephone metadata bulk collection program, in which the NSA collected metadata—who one calls, when, and for how long—on virtually every American's every phone call, popular outcry and civil society groups' advocacy led the executive and legislative branches in the US to adopt reforms that first curtailed and then ended the bulk collection programme.[21]

A similar phenomenon may operate in litigation. Courts are notoriously deferential to the judgments of security officials on matters implicating national security, but civil society demands may alter that custom in particular instances. Thus, while the ECJ has been building up a strong privacy case law over the years, it may not be a coincidence that the ECJ invalidated EU data retention legislation and the Safe Harbour agreement only after non-governmental organisations mobilised to challenge public invasions of privacy.[22] And it may also not be a coincidence that the US federal courts declared the NSA phone metadata program illegal only after Snowden's disclosures touched off public objections.[23] In the absence of public demands for privacy protection, courts too are likely to favour security concerns. The answer to Schulhofer's second worry is not abandonment of transatlantic negotiations, but an insistence on the importance of transnational advocacy to ensure that privacy concerns are taken seriously in the process.[24] It is true that transnational agreements often offer less opportunities for civil society organisations' input than domestic legislative, regulatory, or judicial processes, but they are by no means immune from such influence, and those who negotiate them must ultimately answer to their own domestic constituents.

Third, Schulhofer contends that if transatlantic agreements adopt a level of privacy protection that falls below that in any particular state subject to the agreement, it may lead such states to revise their own laws downward to match the transatlantic agreement. Here, too, while Schulhofer is certainly right to be

---

[19] See D Sklansky, 'Two More Ways Not to Think about Privacy and the Fourth Amendment' (2015) 82 *University of Chicago Law Review* 223 (detailing the prominent role that security officials have played in negotiating federal legislation regarding surveillance and privacy).

[20] See D Cole, 'Reining in the NSA', *New York Review of Books*, 2 June 2015.

[21] See USA Freedom Act of 2015, Pub L No 114–23, 129 Stat 268.

[22] See F Fabbrini, 'Human Rights in the Digital Age: The European Court of Justice Ruling the Data Retention Case and its Lessons for Privacy and Surveillance in the United States' (2015) 28 *Harvard Human Rights Journal* 65.

[23] See *Klayman v Obama* 957 F Supp 2d 1 (DDC 2013).

[24] See generally D Cole, *Engines of Liberty: The Power of Citizen Activists to Make Constitutional Law* (Basic Books, 2015) (detailing the critical role that civil society organizations play in the development and enforcement of constitutional rights).

concerned about this prospect, it is not a reason to abandon the project, but a reason to be aware of the risks. It is certainly not inevitable that domestic law will be defined down to meet international standards. US law, for example, is more protective of privacy from official state intrusion than many other nations, yet the adoption of the International Covenant on Civil and Political Rights (ICCPR) did not cause US privacy protections to regress to international minima.[25] Similarly, in both the US and the EU, states are bound to respect federal or supranational rights, but states can, and in many circumstances do, offer protections under their own constitutions or laws that go beyond the floor set by federal constitutional or supranational law.[26] Floors do not necessarily become ceilings. In this particular instance, moreover, the fact that neither EU nor US law offers any meaningful protection to foreign nationals from foreign government spying means that there is no lower that these domestic regimes can go in terms of the protection at issue. You can't give foreign nationals less than zero protection. As such, the risk that privacy guarantees in a transatlantic agreement will exert a downward pull on EU or US privacy protections for foreign nationals subject to extraterritorial foreign government surveillance is virtually nil.

Finally, Schulhofer contends that domestic law development may be a more promising route for the expansion of privacy rights, in part because market forces create incentives for countries to provide privacy protections so that the world's customers will have sufficient confidence to use their nation's services. He makes this case specifically with respect to the US. We do not discount these forces. But we are sceptical that nations will extend meaningful protections to foreign nationals beyond their borders absent something in exchange, namely, an assurance that their own citizens will receive reciprocal privacy protections from extra-territorial spying on them by other nations. In the absence of such a quid pro quo, there will be little domestic political pressure from the citizenry to extend protections to foreign nationals abroad. And while a nation's internet and cloud service providers might be inclined to advocate on behalf of would-be foreign customers in hopes of attracting their business, there is little evidence, at least as of yet, that this will be sufficient. In the wake of Snowden's disclosures, for example, American internet service providers became as vocal as they have ever been in criticising US surveillance tactics, as they saw a threat to their business if customers around the world felt that using their services would render them vulnerable to NSA spying.[27]

[25] See V Jackson, 'Translating Rights across Centuries: U.S. Constitutional Protection against Unreasonable Searches and Seizures in a Transnational Era', in F Fabbrini and V Jackson (eds), *Constitutionalism Across Borders in the Struggle Against Terrorism* (Elgar 2016) 101.
[26] Compare E Katz and A Tarr (eds), *Federalism and Rights* (Rowman and Littlefield 1996) (explaining how US federalism allows states on occasion to provide standards of human rights protection which are higher than that set in federal law) with F Fabbrini, *Fundamental Rights in Europe* (Oxford University Press 2014) ch 1 (explaining that the same is true in the European multilevel system for the protection of fundamental rights).
[27] See J Hafetz, ch 5 in this volume.

But even with a unified push from Silicon Valley, the US Congress repealed only the NSA's domestic bulk collection programme, an initiative that implicated US citizens' rights. Thus far, the US Congress has done nothing to limit the NSA's much more intrusive surveillance of foreign nationals abroad.[28] The key to extending rights over borders is the reciprocal benefit that one's own citizens would receive in return from foreign government's rights intrusions. Those reciprocal benefits are most likely to come through a transnational agreement. And if domestic US or EU courts or legislatures break from their historical patterns and begin unilaterally extending rights to foreign nationals from overseas surveillance, there is little reason to believe that a transatlantic agreement would make them less inclined to do so.

To be sure, Schulhofer identifies genuine areas of concern. If we were advocating a global agreement on privacy, applicable in every state and agreed on by all, there would be a real basis for concern that any agreement that resulted would not protect much. Security officials will have a central role in the negotiation of any privacy regime, simply because privacy protections interfere with their ability to do their jobs, and thus governments will want them at the table. Domestic law is not immune from the influence of international and transnational forces, so there is as a general matter a legitimate basis for concern that the adoption of lenient transnational standards may trickle down to the domestic level. But none of these conclusions is inevitable, and counterexamples abound. Perhaps most importantly, because existing domestic regimes provide no protection from cross-border spying by other governments, transnational engagement cannot make matters worse.

III. The Interaction of Domestic and Transatlantic Processes: The *Schrems* Decision and the EU-US Privacy Shield

Our exchange with Schulhofer has proceeded as if there are only two choices for protecting the cross-border privacy rights of foreign nationals: the development of domestic privacy law, or a transnational agreement. In fact however, these options are not mutually exclusive. It is possible, and indeed in the modern globalised world, increasingly likely, that law will develop through an interaction of domestic and transnational mechanisms. Transnational agreements might create obligations on the nations entering any such agreement to conform their domestic law to the promises made in the pact. But in addition, domestic legal decisions may serve as a catalyst for transnational negotiations. In this way, privacy can be

---

[28] See D Cole, 'Can the NSA Be Controlled?' *New York Review of Books*, 19 June 2014.

advanced (or, for that matter, diminished) through the interaction of domestic and transnational legal developments.

This point was brought home recently by the ECJ judgment in *Schrems*, and the transatlantic agreement, the EU-US Privacy Shield, that it sparked. In this instance, a pre-existing transatlantic agreement, the Safe Harbour agreement, was declared invalid by a domestic ECJ ruling. But that domestic ruling then prompted the negotiation of a new transatlantic agreement affording greater extraterritorial privacy protections. In some sense then, the story of *Schrems* and its aftermath suggests that Schulhofer and we are both right. On the one hand domestic mechanisms can provide a forum for the advancement of privacy protections, but on the other hand, achievement of such protections will require, ultimately, a transatlantic agreement.

The *Schrems* case concerned the legality of the EU-US Safe Harbour agreement. This was an accord reached between the EU and the US authorities on the privacy protections to be applied to personal data transferred from the EU to the US. Article 25 of the EU Data Protection Directive,[29] currently the principal EU data protection legislation,[30] permits private companies to transfer data collected in the EU to third countries only if the latter ensure 'an adequate level of protection'.[31] The directive empowers the European Commission to find that 'a third country ensures an adequate level of protection … by reasons of its domestic law or of the international commitments it has entered into … for the protection of the private lives and basic freedoms and rights of individuals'.[32] In 2000, the European Commission had determined, based assurances from US authorities, including the US Department of Commerce and the US Federal Trade Commissions, memorialised in a Safe Harbour agreement, that the US framework of data protection satisfied EU standards, and thereby permitted the commercial transfer of data from the EU to the US.[33] After Snowden's disclosures revealed the sweeping nature of NSA data collection, Max Schrems, an Austrian citizen who owned an account on Facebook (a company registered under Irish law), petitioned the Irish Data Protection Authority (DPA) for an order enjoining transfer of his Facebook data to the US, on the ground that Snowden's revelations established the inadequacy of US laws to protect the privacy of his data. When the Irish DPA denied the request, citing the previously approved Safe Harbour agreement, Schrems sought review in the High Court of Ireland. The High Court in turn referred the matter to the ECJ.

The ECJ agreed with Schrems, and ruled that in light of the Snowden disclosures, the Safe Harbour agreement was no longer adequate to meet the requirements of

---

[29] Directive 95/46/EC, [1995] OJ L281/31 (Data Protection Directive).

[30] But see now Regulation (EU) 2016/679, [2016] OJ L119/1 (new Data Protection Regulation, entering into force in 2018).

[31] Data Protection Directive, art 25(1).

[32] ibid, art 25(6).

[33] Commission Decision 2000/520/EC, [2000] OJ L215/7.

the EU Data Protection Directive.[34] The ECJ reasoned that the Directive 'must necessarily be interpreted in the light of the fundamental rights guaranteed by the Charter [of Fundamental Rights of the EU]',[35] in particular 'the fundamental right to respect for private life, guaranteed by Article 7 of the Charter, and the fundamental right to the protection of personal data, guaranteed by Article 8 thereof'.[36] The ECJ ruled that a '[European] Commission decision [deeming an agreement adequate under the Data Protection Directive] cannot prevent persons whose personal data has been or could be transferred to a third country from lodging with the national supervisory authorities a claim … concerning the protection of their rights and freedoms in regard to the processing of that data'.[37] In addition, it determined that national DPAs were authorised to engage in legal proceedings before national courts to challenge the legality of a Commission adequacy decision which they regarded as inconsistent with the principles of the Data Protection Directive.[38]

Turning to the merits of Schrems's claim, the ECJ explained that the requirement of 'adequate' protection in third countries does not require 'protection identical to that guaranteed in the EU legal order', but does require 'a level of protection … that is essentially equivalent to that guaranteed within the European Union by virtue [of the Data Protection Directive] read in the light of the Charter'.[39] Subjecting the Safe Harbour agreement to strict scrutiny, the ECJ identified a number of flaws. The Safe Harbour agreement did not contain rules limiting US authorities' access to transferred data for national security purposes.[40] The agreement applied only to private companies' interference with individuals' privacy, and not to intrusions 'that result from measures originating from the State'.[41] Moreover, the agreement did not include mechanisms of redress, whereby EU citizens could obtain the remedies in case of misuse of their data.[42] Relying on its prior decision in *Digital Rights Ireland*,[43] invalidating the EU Data Retention Directive,[44] the ECJ held that 'legislation permitting the public authorities to have access on a generalised basis to the content of electronic communications must be regarded as compromising the essence of the fundamental right to respect for private life, as guaranteed by Article 7 of the Charter'.[45] Similarly, 'legislation not providing for any possibility for an individual to pursue legal remedies in order to have access to personal data relating to him, or to obtain the rectification or

---

[34] *Schrems* (n 10).
[35] ibid §38.
[36] ibid §39.
[37] ibid §53.
[38] ibid §65.
[39] ibid §73.
[40] ibid §88.
[41] ibid §89.
[42] ibid §90.
[43] See Joined Cases C-293/12 and C-594/12, *Digital Rights Ireland* ECLI:EU:C:2014:238.
[44] See Directive 2006/24/EC, [2006] OJ L105/54.
[45] *Schrems* (n 10) §94.

erasure of such data, does not respect the essence of the fundamental right to effective judicial protection'.[46]

Thus, the ECJ ruled that the Safe Harbor agreement was invalid.[47] The ruling produced major uncertainties for transnational businesses, as it returned to national DPAs the power to decide whether companies could legally transfer data from Europe to the US.[48] With the aim to secure the free flow of data between the EU and the US, therefore, policymakers in Brussels and Washington DC rushed to develop a replacement for the Safe Harbour agreement.[49] A four month negotiation culminated in the approval in February 2016 of the EU-US Privacy Shield.[50] The agreement contains important improvements in privacy protection for transferred data. More could certainly be done, as pointed out by the Article 29 Working Party (A29WP)—the network of national DPAs—as well as by the European Parliament (EP) and the European Data Protection Supervisor (EDPS).[51] However, this merely suggests that the dialogue between domestic institutions (DPAs, the Commission, the EP and the ECJ) and transatlantic negotiators is likely to continue. The diplomatic process to renegotiate the transatlantic compact was led for the EU, by the Commissioner for Justice and Consumer Protection, and for the US, by the Secretary of Commerce. Because one of the core areas of concern was government access to transferred data for law enforcement and national security purposes, security and law enforcement officials were also involved in the process on the US side. Yet, in part because of close attention by civil society and in part because the negotiation was conducted in the shadow of the ECJ ruling, the involvement of security officials did not produce an agreement that abrogates privacy interests.[52]

The resulting agreement, the EU-US Privacy Shield, is designed to replace the invalid Safe Harbour agreement, and to provide protections adequate to meet the ECJ decision in *Schrems* and the Data Protection Directive.[53] On the basis of the agreement the Commission has issued a draft decision finding the protection of privacy in the US adequate under the Data Protection Directive.[54] As evidence of its assessment that the US system now 'ensures an adequate level of protection for personal data transferred from the Union to organizations in the United States',[55] the decision includes seven annexes. These are letters from the US Secretary of

---

[46] ibid §95.

[47] ibid.

[48] See K Kuner, 'Reality and Illusion in EU Data Transfer Regulation Post *Schrems*' (University of Cambridge Faculty of Law Research Paper No 14/2016).

[49] See M Scott, 'Europe Seeks to Reach Data Transfer Pact by Early 2016', *The New York Times*, 6 November 2015.

[50] Commission press release, 'EU Commission and United States Agree on New Framework for Transatlantic Data Flows: EU-US Privacy Shield', 2 February 2016, IP/16/216.

[51] See infra nn 70–77.

[52] See Z Sheftalovich, 'The Phone Call that Saved Safe Harbor', *Politico*, 5 February 2016.

[53] Commission press release, 'European Commission Presents EU-US Privacy Shield', 29 February 2016, IP/16/433.

[54] Draft Commission Decision of 29 February 2016.

[55] ibid, Art 1.

Commerce; the US Secretary of State; the head of the Federal Trade Commission; the US Secretary of Transportation; the General Counsel of the Office of the Director of National Intelligence; and the Deputy Assistant Attorney General of the US Department of Justice. These documents are diplomatic assurances by the competent US authorities to the EU institutions. The European Commission, however, has given emphasis to the fact that they will also be published in the US Federal Register.[56]

The Commission's draft adequacy decision lists a number of fundamental privacy principles which are to be applied to the transfer of data by private corporations from the EU to the US. Specifically, private enterprises transferring personal data from the EU to the US must abide by (1) the notice principle, informing data subjects of the transfer;[57] (2) the choice principle, allowing data subjects to opt out of the transfer if their personal data shall be disclosed to third parties;[58] (3) the security principle, which requires companies to take reasonable and appropriate measures to secure the transferred data;[59] (4) the data integrity and purpose limitation principle, which restricts processing to what is strictly necessary;[60] (5) the access principle, which requires that data subjects have access to their own personal data;[61] (6) the accountability for onward transfer principle, which subjects further transfer of data to third parties to the existence of equivalent levels of data protection;[62] and (7) the recourse, enforcement and liability principle, which opens the door for remedies against organisations that fail to comply with the previously mentioned principles.[63] Like the Safe Harbour Agreement, the EU-US Privacy Shield compels private enterprises transferring data from the EU to the US to comply with these principles and enlists the US Departments of Commerce and Transportation and the Federal Trade Commission in their enforcement.[64]

In addition, as required by *Schrems*, the EU-US Privacy Shield spells out the limits on US national security and law enforcement authorities' ability to access data transferred by private corporations from the EU to the US. The draft Commission decision cites recent US executive[65] and legislative[66] measures imposing new limits on surveillance as a sign that the US legal framework of privacy protection has been significantly strengthened since 2013. Moreover, the Commission attaches importance to the US government diplomatic assurances, which clarify the conditions and limitations on police and intelligence access to data transferred

---

[56] ibid, Recit 12.
[57] ibid, Recit 17.
[58] ibid, Recit 18.
[59] ibid, Recit 19.
[60] ibid, Recit 20.
[61] ibid, Recit 21.
[62] ibid, Recit 22.
[63] ibid, Recit 23.
[64] ibid, Recit 29.
[65] See Presidential Policy Directive 28 (PPD-28) on Signal Intelligence Activities, 17 January 2014.
[66] See Judicial Redress Act of 2015, Pub L No: 114–126.

from the EU to the US. In the Commission's view, US law now 'contains clear limitations on the access and use of personal data transferred under the EU-U.S. Privacy Shield for national security purposes as well as oversight and redress mechanisms that provide sufficient safeguards for those data to be effectively protected against unlawful interference and the risk of abuse'.[67]

Finally, as also required by *Schrems*, the new EU-US Privacy Shield also introduces a new mechanism of legal redress for data subjects who claim their data rights have been abused by US national security and law enforcement authorities. In particular, as explained by the European Commission 'the US Government has decided to create a new mechanism, the Privacy Shield Ombudsperson'.[68] The Ombudsperson will be established within the US Department of State, and will be independent of the US intelligence community.[69] The Ombudsperson will be empowered to hear complaints that US authorities have violated the EU-US Privacy Shield principles, and to investigate the facts. The Ombudsperson will provide an additional forum for oversight and individual redress, complementing existing legal mechanisms—such as the Foreign Intelligence Surveillance Act, or the Freedom of Information Act.

While the EU-US Privacy Shield represents a step forward in terms of privacy protection compared to the Safe Harbour agreement, the A29WP group of DPAs has identified a number of remaining problems.[70] In its April 2016 report, the A29WP expressed concern that the EU-US Privacy Shield lacks 'an explicit data retention principle',[71] which would limit the ability of private companies transferring data overseas to retain the data beyond that which is strictly necessary. Moreover, it also criticised the fact that 'massive and indiscriminate data collection is not fully excluded by the US authorities',[72] and expressed reservations 'as to whether the Ombudsperson has sufficient powers to function effectively',[73] and therefore to provide meaningful redress. Several concerns have also been raised by the EP in its May 2016 resolution:[74] The EP welcomed the efforts made by the Commission and the US administration to achieve substantial improvements in transatlantic privacy protections,[75] but called on the Commission to continue negotiations with the US—notably with a view to limiting potential future bulk collection of personal data by US intelligence agencies.[76] The EDPS also warned

---

[67] Draft Commission Decision (n 54) Recit 55.
[68] ibid, Recit 100.
[69] ibid, Recit 104.
[70] Article 29 Data Protection Working Party, Opinion 01/2016 on the EU-US Privacy Shield draft adequacy decision, 13 April 2016, WP 238.
[71] ibid, 33.
[72] ibid, 52.
[73] ibid, 57.
[74] European Parliament resolution of 26 May 2016 on transatlantic data flows, P8_TA(2016)0233.
[75] Ibid, §1.
[76] Ibid, §14.

in its May 2016 report that the Privacy Shield 'may not be robust enough to withstand future legal scrutiny before the [ECJ]'.[77]

Given the extensive powers of the DPAs and the EP—and the potential for a future judicial challenge—the Commission sought further reassurances from its US counterparts.[78] Based on additional representation by the US government, the Commission amended its draft February 2016 decision, and eventually published its final decision in July 2016.[79] As the Commission decision underlines, the US government agreed to limit bulk collection of personal data to exceptional situations when targeted collection is not possible,[80] and to strengthen the role of the Ombudsperson.[81] The Commission implementing decision therefore declares the adequacy of privacy protection by the US, and allows the resumption of transatlantic data flows between the EU and the US, pursuant to the new principles set out in the EU-US Privacy Shield.[82] However, the final decision clarifies that the Commission retains the power to suspend the validity of the decision 'where there are indications that the U.S. public authorities do not comply with the representations and commitments contained in the documents annexed to this Decision, including as regards the conditions and limitations for access by U.S. public authorities for law enforcement, national security and other public interest purposes to personal data transferred under the EU-U.S. Privacy Shield; of a systematic failure to effectively address complaints by EU data subjects; or of a systematic failure by the Privacy Shield Ombudsperson to provide timely and appropriate responses to requests from EU data subjects.'[83]

The story is not over—and new judicial and legislative developments will have to be followed closely.[84] Protecting privacy is by necessity a continuing obligation. Data privacy will remain an ongoing concern on both sides of the Atlantic, and, as technology and public awareness develop, further changes will be necessary.[85] Thus far, the process has involved and will no doubt continue to involve, both domestic and transatlantic processes. Indeed, given the subject matter—the protection of data transferred across state borders—it could not be any other way.

---

[77] European Data Protection Supervisor, Opinion 4/2016 on the EU-US Privacy Shield draft adequacy decision, 30 May 2016, EDPS/2016/11.

[78] Commission press release, 'European Commission Launches EU-US Privacy Shield: Stronger Protection for Transatlantic Data Flows', 12 July 2016, IP/16/2461.

[79] Commission implementing Decision of 12 July 2016, C(2016) 4176 final.

[80] Ibid, Recit. 76.

[81] Ibid, Recit. 117.

[82] Ibid, art. 1.

[83] Ibid, art. 4.

[84] See ceteris paribus Opinion 1/15, Request for an Opinion Submitted by the European Parliament, Opinion of AG Mengozzi delivered on 8 September 2016 (stating that the PNR agreement between the EU and Canada is incompatible with EU privacy rights).

[85] See P Hustinx, Ch 12 in this volume.

IV. Conclusion

Transatlantic negotiations are necessary to protect transatlantic rights. The concerns Schulhofer raises, while sound, are not a reason to reject such negotiations. Some of the concerns he has at the transatlantic level are equally present at the domestic level, and Schulhofer has not shown that the dynamics he predicts (a race to the bottom, or the watering down of domestic standards to meet transnational standards) are inevitable. Most importantly, because current domestic law in both the EU and the US provides no meaningful protection to foreign nationals from cross-border surveillance, and safeguards are unlikely to expand unilaterally on this front in the future, there is little or no downside, and considerable upside, to a transatlantic effort to address this concern.

However, the interaction between the *Schrems* decision and the Privacy Shield negotiation illustrates that the debate between domestic and transnational developments of privacy standards may be in an important sense artificial. Domestic and transnational avenues are not mutually exclusive routes to protect privacy. In the context of EU-US relations, powerful pressure at the domestic level catalysed by the *Schrems* ruling prompted negotiation of a new agreement—the Privacy Shield—which has improved the protection of privacy for data transferred between the EU and the US. The EU-US Privacy Shield is not perfect, as pointed out by DPAs and the EP. But it represents an improvement compared to the previous Safe Harbour agreement, invalidated by the ECJ. Thus, transatlantic cooperation is possible, and at least in this situation was necessary, to enhance privacy against surveillance across borders.

Moreover, it will not always be the case that domestic developments prompt transatlantic negotiations; it may sometimes be the other way around. In the case of transferred data, domestic courts wield a powerful stick as they can block the transfer of data if foreign nations do not promise adequate protections. Thus, in this instance, the *Schrems* judgment, a domestic European decision, had outsized influence. The negotiators had to satisfy the ECJ's principles, or their agreement would risk invalidation. In the case of extraterritorial spying by contrast, domestic actors are unlikely to wield the same sort of influence. No European institution authorises, and therefore has legal power to halt, US electronic surveillance in Europe. Thus, in this realm, it is more likely that transatlantic agreements will drive domestic law than vice versa.

The EU-US Privacy Shield addresses one particular manifestation of privacy protections across borders: namely, the safeguards that attach to data transferred from the EU to the US by private companies. It does not address the transfer of data between public authorities, or the problem of direct cross-border surveillance. Here lies, in our view, the main weakness of the EU-US Privacy Shield agreement. It is not enough to protect data that companies knowingly transfer across the Atlantic, if state intelligence agencies have carte blanche to directly surveil non-citizens overseas. Much like the protections that follow transferred data, the only way to achieve such protection will be through a transnational agreement that accords reciprocal protections to the citizens of each signatory party.

In fact, the EU and the US have also initialed a transatlantic Umbrella Agreement on the protection of personal data when transferred and processed for the purposes of preventing, investigating, detecting and prosecuting criminal offences in the framework of police and judicial co-operation in criminal matter.[86] This agreement, signed in June 2016 on the EU side by the Council, and now subject to the vote of consent of the EP, would complement and partially supersede existing accords in the field of law enforcement—such as the EU-US Public Name Record (PNR)[87] agreement and the Terrorist Finance Tracking program[88]—thus simplifying the field. However, the Umbrella Agreement covers only law enforcement operations, and not foreign intelligence or national security surveillance—a main point of contention both for the ECJ in *Schrems* and for the DPAs and the EP in their assessments of the EU-US Privacy Shield.

As we have previously argued, 'what is needed is a framework transatlantic compact that enshrines in legal language specific protections against unwarranted dragnet surveillance by the intelligence agencies of one state against the citizens of the other state'.[89] The EU-US Privacy Shield does not address that issue. Yet the aftermath of *Schrems* illustrates that transatlantic cooperation in the protection of privacy is feasible, where there is the will. The speed with which EU and US diplomats struck a new transatlantic agreement in the wake of *Schrems*, and revised it in light of EP pressures, shows a willingness to work jointly in this field, at least where prompted to do so by powerful forces. The substance of the EU-US Privacy Shield, which increases the protection of privacy for transferred data, demonstrates that transatlantic cooperation can lead to an improvement in privacy protections. In this instance, a domestic legal development (on the model advocated by Schulhofer) served as a catalyst for a new transatlantic data privacy pact (on the model we advocated). In the end, we suspect that this sort of dynamic is inevitable in an interlinked world where borders are increasingly irrelevant, especially when it comes to data and electronic surveillance.[90]

As US President Barack Obama acknowledges in the epigraph to this chapter, protecting the privacy of Americans and Europeans is a shared concern. The debate here suggests that, given the nature of transatlantic relations and our common concerns, one may not need to choose between Schulhofer's approach and ours. Both domestic and transnational routes are available and will be necessary if we are to preserve cross-border privacy in the digital era.

---

[86] See Council press release, 'Enhanced Data Protection Rights for EU Citizens in Law Enforcement Cooperation: EU and US Sign "Umbrella Agreement"', 2 June 2016, 305/16.

[87] See Council Decision 2007/551/CFSP/JHA, [2007] OJ L204/16.

[88] See Council Decision 2010/412/EU, [2010] OJ L195/3.

[89] Cole and Fabbrini (n 2) 237.

[90] See F Fabbrini and V Jackson (eds), *Constitutionalism Across Borders in the Struggle Against Terrorism* (Elgar 2016).

12

Concluding Remarks

PETER HUSTINX

I. Introduction

In March 2015, three keynote speakers addressed a record size audience of about 3,000 privacy professionals at the IAPP Global Privacy Summit, only a few blocks from the White House in Washington DC.[1] The first one was Glenn Greenwald, the Pulitzer Prize winning journalist who first interviewed Edward Snowden and played a key role in the subsequent news reports in the *Guardian* and the *Washington Post*.[2] He addressed two questions: (1) how was it to meet Edward Snowden, and (2) what has changed since? His answer to this second, more relevant question was, put very briefly: at first sight not a great deal, but at further analysis quite a lot. Two aspects of this deeper change are that issues relating to surveillance are now much more the subject of public debate, and the role of the privacy profession in addressing them has become much more obvious.[3] The second keynote speaker was Michael Sandel, a political philosopher from Harvard with a special reputation in ethical dilemmas.[4] He animated a fascinating Socratic debate with the vast audience on 'why privacy matters'. The third keynote speaker was an historian and curator, Sarah Lewis, who gave a clear answer

---

[1] The International Association of Privacy Professionals (IAPP) was established in 2003 and now has about 25,000 members of which 3,000 are in Europe. Membership worldwide grew in 2015 by 19% and in Europe by 30%. The Global Privacy Summit in Washington DC is the main annual event, with other events taking place at various locations in the world throughout the year. The author has been on the IAPP Board of Directors since early 2015.

[2] See also Glenn Greenwald, 'No place to Hide: Edward Snowden, the NSA and the US Surveillance State' (New York, 2014).

[3] The full text of Greenwald's keynote is still available at www.iapp.org/news/a/glenn-greenwald-the-full-keynote-address. See also Greenwald, 'Call to Privacy Pros: Subverting Injustice Rests on Your Shoulders' (2015) *The Privacy Advisor*.

[4] See eg, Michael J Sandel, Justice; 'What's the right thing to do?' (2009, New York) and Michael J Sandel, 'What Money Can't Buy; The Moral Limits of Markets' (2012, New York).

on this topic from her perspective: privacy is an essential ingredient of creativity and innovation and she mentioned a series of success stories that were born out of failure.[5]

II. Lessons Learned

There is no doubt that privacy has emerged as a hot subject in recent years. To a large extent this is due to the Snowden revelations. However, further developing a theme touched on by Greenwald, the question should be asked: what have we learned since? Here we can see a broad landscape with different layers. First, the breathtaking scale and far reaching impact of the Digital Society can no longer be ignored, but also the vulnerability of our digital environment has now become evident. Second, we have now seen many illustrations of the vast impact of unlimited mass surveillance. Third, the complicity of different well known internet giants—active or passive—in wide-ranging surveillance by the state has become abundantly clear. Fourth, we should finally also take a careful look at our internet infrastructure and admit that it was not only used to facilitate—lawful or unlawful—state surveillance. Most successful business cases on the internet—involving 'free services' in exchange for profitable advertising— are still largely based on virtually unlimited surveillance by private actors. This is why some experts argue that the internet itself has developed into an instrument of surveillance.[6]

This dubious mix of factors has contributed to an increase in political attention for privacy and data protection in many parts of the world and to their reaffirmation as corner stones of a democratic society based on the rule of law.[7] In Europe this has resulted in an approach at different levels and with different means, but with a strong emphasis on both public and private organisations that are involved in the processing of personal information, without necessarily being engaged in any kind of mass surveillance. Those that are involved in surveillance receive special attention under a different heading. Any connections between these different worlds also receive special attention. This makes great practical sense and has so far led to good results.

---

[5] See 'Privacy: An Essential Ingredient in Failure and Success' (2015) *The Privacy Advisor*, with examples ranging from Martin Luther King to Harry Potter author JK Rowling.

[6] Bruce Schneier, 'Data and Goliath; The Hidden Battles to Collect Your Data and Control Your World' (2015) New York, London.

[7] In the European Parliament, in spite of heavy lobbying by industry and vested interests, these factors have no doubt galvanised a large majority in support of the Data Protection Reform package (see nn 8 and 9 below).

III. EU Charter

The strongest reaffirmation of privacy and data protection in the EU took place at the end of 2009 when—due to the entering into force of the Lisbon Treaty—the EU Charter of Fundamental Rights became directly binding, not only for the EU institutions and bodies, but also for the Member States when acting within the scope of EU law.[8] Articles 7 and 8 of the Charter lay down separate rights to the respect for private and family life, and to the protection of personal data. A few years later, the European Court of Justice ruled that the Charter *always* applies when a Member State acts within the scope of EU law.[9] In addition, Article 16(2) of the Treaty on the Functioning of the European Union (TFEU) provides that the European legislature shall lay down rules on the protection of individuals with regard to the processing of personal data, thus providing a mandatory basis for a wide ranging review of the existing legal framework on data protection.[10]

The inclusion of privacy and data protection in two separate articles did not happen by accident. The distinction in the Charter between the right to the respect for private and family life in Article 7 and the right to the protection of personal data in Article 8 could build on a legal development of several decades. Although these provisions are closely related, they also have a different character that should not be overlooked. The first one deals with a classic fundamental right—providing legal protection against *interference*—while the second one has been conceived as a positive right to be protected according to certain conditions and standards.[11]

IV. Respect for Private Life

A rather weak version of the concept of a 'right to privacy' first emerged in international law in Article 12 of the Universal Declaration of Human Rights,[12] according to which no-one shall be subjected to *arbitrary* interference with his privacy, family, home or correspondence. A more substantive protection followed soon in

---

[8] The Treaty of Lisbon amending the Treaty on European Union and the Treaty establishing the European Community, signed at Lisbon, 13 December 2007, entered into force on 1 December 2009. Article 6(1) of the TEU now provides that the Union recognises the rights, freedoms and principles set out in the Charter of Fundamental Rights of the European Union of 7 December 2000, as adapted at Strasbourg, on 12 December 2007, 'which shall have the same legal value as the Treaties'.

[9] Case C-617/10 *Åkerberg Fransson* and Case C-399/11 *Melloni* both 26 February 2013.

[10] The entering into force of the Treaty coincided with the start of a new Commission mandate. Vice-President Viviane Reding made the Data Protection Reform one of her top priorities.

[11] See Peter Hustinx, 'EU Data Protection Law: The Review of Directive 95/46/EC and the Proposed General Data Protection Regulation' *Collected Courses of the European University Institute's Academy of European Law* (24th Session on European Union Law, 1–12 July 2013).

[12] UN General Assembly, Paris 1948.

Article 8 of the European Convention on Human Rights (ECHR),[13] according to which everyone has the right to *respect* for his private and family life, his home and his correspondence, and no interference by a public authority with the exercise of this right is allowed except in accordance with the law and where necessary in a democratic society for certain important and legitimate interests.

According to the case law of the European Court of Human Rights, the scope of Article 8 is not limited to 'intimate' situations, but also covers certain aspects of professional life and behaviour in public.[14] On the other hand, those cases often concern specific situations, which involve sensitive information (medical or social services), justified expectations of privacy (confidential use of telephone or email at work) or inquiries by police or secret services. The Court has so far never ruled that *any* processing of personal data—*regardless* of its nature or context—falls within the scope of Article 8. This provision now fully corresponds with Article 7 of the Charter.

V. Protection of Personal Data

The concept of 'data protection' has a different genesis. In the early 1970s the Council of Europe concluded that Article 8 ECHR had a number of shortcomings in the light of recent developments, particularly the use of information technology: the uncertain scope of 'private life' under Article 8 ECHR, the emphasis on protection against interference by 'public authorities', and the lack of a pro-active approach, also dealing with the possible misuse of personal information by companies or other relevant organisations in the private sector.[15]

This resulted in the adoption in 1981 of the Data Protection Convention, also known as Convention 108,[16] which has now been ratified by 47 countries, including all EU Member States, most Member States of the Council of Europe and one non-European State.[17] The purpose of the Convention is to secure in the territory of each Party for every individual, whatever his nationality or residence, respect for his rights and fundamental freedoms, and in particular his right to privacy, with regard to automatic processing of personal data relating

---

[13] Council of Europe, Rome 1950.

[14] 14. See, eg, *Klass v Germany* Series A no 28 (1978), application no 5029/71; *Malone v United Kingdom* Series A no 82 (1984), application no 8691/79; *Leander v Sweden* Series A no 116 (1987), application no 9248/81; *Gaskin v United Kingdom* Series A no 160 (1989), application no 10454/83; *Niemietz v Germany* Series A no 251-B (1992), application no 13710/88; *Halford v United Kingdom* Reports 1997-III, application no 20605/92; *Amann v Switzerland* Reports 2000-II, application no 27798/95, and *Rotaru v Romania* Reports 2000-V, application no 28341/95.

[15] Explanatory Report to Convention 108 (see n 16), para 4.

[16] Convention for the Protection of Individuals with regard to Automatic Processing of Personal Data, Strasbourg, 28 January 1981, ETS 108.

[17] Uruguay was the first non-European State to ratify the Convention in April 2013.

to him ('data protection').[18] The concept of 'personal data' has been defined as 'any information relating to an identified or identifiable individual ('data subject')'.[19]

The main EU instrument on the subject so far, Directive 95/46/EC,[20] took Convention 108 as a starting point and further developed and specified it in different ways. This basically amounted to a system of 'checks and balances' with substantive principles, rights for data subjects, obligations for responsible organisations and oversight by an independent authority.[21] These main elements of the protection of personal data are now also visible in Article 8(2) and (3) of the Charter.[22]

VI. National Security

The above provisions of EU law do not apply to the national security of EU Member States. According to Article 4(2) TEU, this is an 'essential function' of the Member States, which remains their 'sole responsibility'.[23] However, the national security of third countries is not covered by this exemption. Moreover, the exclusion of Member States' national security from the scope of EU law does not mean that this remains an unregulated area, in particular as regards the protection of fundamental rights: the Council of Europe instruments mentioned above and national laws are in most situations fully applicable to this field.

In particular, the ECHR and Convention 108 apply to many of the relevant processing operations by member states as the general application to most of their parties does not exclude national security as a whole.[24] These instruments also create a positive obligation for the parties to secure privacy and data protection

---

[18] Article 1.

[19] Article 2(a).

[20] Directive 95/46/EC of the European Parliament and of the Council of 24 October 1995 on the protection of individuals with regard to the processing of personal data and on the free movement of such data (OJ L281, 23.11.1995, p 31).

[21] See Hustinx (above n 11).

[22] Article 8(2): 'Such data must be processed fairly for specified purposes and on the basis of the consent of the person concerned or some other legitimate basis laid down by law. Everyone has the right of access to data which has been collected concerning him or her, and the right to have it rectified.' Article 8(3): 'Compliance with these rules shall be subject to control by an independent Authority.'

[23] Article 4(2): 'The Union shall respect the equality of Member States before the Treaties as well as their national identities, inherent in their fundamental structures, political and constitutional, inclusive of regional and local self-government. It shall respect their essential State functions, including ensuring the territorial integrity of the State, maintaining law and order and safeguarding national security. In particular, national security remains the sole responsibility of each Member State.'

[24] Only a minority of the parties to Convention 108 have deposited declarations in accordance with Article 3(2)(a) stating that the Convention will not apply to 'automated personal data files' relating to 'state security' or 'state secrets'.

rights to everyone within their jurisdiction and to adopt domestic law giving effect to data protection principles.[25]

Where the above-mentioned EU and Council of Europe instruments apply, the rights to privacy and data protection can be restricted if necessary to safeguard national security or state security, among other reasons.[26] However, such limitations have to be applied in a restrictive way, and any limitation to the rights granted can only be allowed if laid down by a foreseeable and accessible law and only if necessary in a democratic society.[27] The exceptions provided by these instruments for national security purposes cannot justify massive limitations, for purposes which go beyond what is strictly necessary to safeguard national security.

VII. Enforceability

National laws implementing Directive 95/46/EC are applicable to processing operations in the context of the activities of an establishment of controllers in the EU.[28] They are also applicable where a non-EU controller is established in a place where a Member State's national law applies by virtue of international law, or if the responsible controller is using equipment in the EU.[29] EU Data Protection Authorities have thus competence in these cases to directly enforce their national data protection laws against organisations that have provided access to or disclosed personal data to any government agency in breach of national data protection laws.

Articles 1 and 8 of the ECHR create—as just mentioned—a positive obligation for Parties to the Convention to protect privacy and data protection rights. In cases of unlawful or excessive surveillance, or complicity of private organisations in such activities, this obligation has not been fulfilled. Convention 108, which applies to processing operations in the States party to that Convention, both in the public and in the private sector, has in that situation not been respected either. EU Member States and any other Party to the ECHR can be brought in front of the European Court of Human Rights for not complying with their obligation to

---

[25] See Articles 1 and 8 of the ECHR and Article 4(1) of Convention 108. See also *von Hannover v Germany* Reports 2004-VI, application no 59320/00 and *KU v Finland* Reports 2008-V, application 2872/02, ECtHR 2008-V.

[26] See eg Article 8(2) of the ECHR, Article 9(2)(a) of Convention 108 and Articles 9(2)(a) and 13(1)(a) of Directive 95/46/EC.

[27] See, eg, ECtHR in *Klass v Germany* Series A no 28 (1978), application no 5029/71, and CJEU in Joined Cases C-293/12 and C-594/12 *Digital Rights Ireland and Seitlinger* 8 April 2014.

[28] See Article 4(1)(a) of Directive 95/46/EC.

[29] See Article 4(1)b) and (c) of Directive 95/46/EC.

'secure to everyone within their jurisdiction the rights and freedoms provided in the Convention'.[30]

VIII. Need for More Effectiveness

Although all these arrangements have now been in place for a while, there is still the need for greater effectiveness of applicable safeguards in practice. This is mostly for two reasons: first, the main legal instrument for data protection, Directive 95/46/EC, was adopted when the internet was still in its infancy and mobile applications were completely unknown. Second, current legal arrangements are too often only 'law on the books' and not enough 'law on the ground'.[31] Moreover, the implementation of Directive 95/46/EC in presently 28 national laws has resulted in too much legal diversity and complexity. This has also worked to erode the effectiveness of current data protection laws in a cross-border or EU-wide context.

This is why the EU data protection reform set in motion in 2009 was designed to ensure stronger and more effective protection of data subjects and more consistency across the European Union. In January 2012, the European Commission presented a package of proposals in order to update and modernise the present EU legal framework.[32] This package has since then been the subject of very intense discussions, both inside and outside the European Parliament and the Council, and resulted in a political agreement between the two legislative branches, which was confirmed and finalised by the spring of 2016.[33] Although these efforts did not address surveillance for national security purposes per se, they will undoubtedly have an indirect effect on it, since the new arrangements will apply, from spring 2018, to all companies active in the EU, regardless of the location from where they are operating.[34]

---

[30] See Article 1 of the ECHR.

[31] See Kenneth Bamberger and Deirdre Mulligan, 'Privacy on the Books and on the Ground', (2011) 63 (No 2) *Stanford Law Review* 247–316, and *Privacy on the Ground: Driving Corporate Behavior in the United States and Europe* (Cambridge, Mass, MIT Press, 2015).

[32] See Communication from the Commission to the European Parliament, the Council, the Economic and Social Committee and the Committee of the Regions: 'Safeguarding Privacy in a Connected World—A European Data Protection Framework for the 21st Century' COM (2012) 9 final.

[33] See Proposal for a Regulation of the European Parliament and of the Council on the protection of individuals with regard to the processing of personal data and on the free movement of such data (General Data Protection Regulation) and Proposal for a Directive of the European Parliament and of the Council on the protection of individuals with regard to the processing of personal data by competent authorities for the purposes of prevention, investigation, detection or prosecution of criminal offences or the execution of criminal penalties, and the free movement of such data (both published on 15 December 2015). See now also the final text of the Regulation and the Directive, as adopted on 27 April 2016 and published in OJ L 119 of 4 May 2016, p. 1 and 89.

[34] According to its Article 4(2), the new Regulation will also apply to companies which are not established in the EU, but offer goods or services to data subjects in the EU or monitor their behaviour in the EU.

IX. Rebuilding Trust in EU-US Data Flows

In November 2013, a few months after the first Snowden revelations, the Commission adopted two relevant communications: one focused on the functioning of the Safe Harbour arrangement for data flows between the EU and US, and another reflected more in general on the political situation.[35] The European Data Protection Supervisor (EDPS) issued a formal Opinion with comments on both communications, and more specifically on eight future steps to be taken.[36]

A. Data Protection Reform

The first point raised by the EDPS was the need for a swift adoption of the EU data protection reform.[37] In this context, this involved in particular the extension of the territorial scope of application of EU rules, the clarification of the conditions for transfers of personal data to third countries, the harmonisation and reinforcement of the enforcement powers of EU Data Protection Authorities, the inclusion of clear rules on the obligations and liabilities of controllers and processors, and the establishment of comprehensive rules for the protection of personal data in the law enforcement area.

The EDPS also emphasised the need for adequate protection of commercial data in the case of their further use for law enforcement purposes and clear rules on international conflicts of jurisdiction. The first issue may arise where personal data initially subject to the proposed Regulation—eg, at a bank or air carrier—are subsequently processed for purposes of law enforcement and by authorities subject to the proposed Directive. This issue has not been solved entirely, also due to the fact that national laws implementing the Directive may take different positions. The second issue has been addressed in a provision in the proposed Regulation on transfers or disclosures to third countries not authorised by EU law.[38]

---

[35] See Communication from the Commission to the European Parliament and the Council on 'Rebuilding Trust in EU-US Data Flows' COM(2013) 846 final, and Communication from the Commission to the European Parliament and the Council on 'the Functioning of the Safe Harbour from the Perspective of EU Citizens and Companies Established in the EU' COM(2013) 847 final.

[36] EDPS Opinion of 20 February 2014 on the Communication from the Commission to the European Parliament and the Council on 'Rebuilding Trust in EU-US Data Flows' and the Communication from the Commission to the European Parliament and the Council on 'the Functioning of the Safe Harbour from the Perspective of EU Citizens and Companies Established in the EU', available at www.edps.europa.eu.

[37] ibid at 40–44.

[38] Article 43a will now read: 'Any judgment of a court or tribunal and any decision of an administrative authority of a third country requiring a controller or processor to transfer or disclose personal data may only be recognised or enforceable in any manner if based on an international agreement,

B. Safe Harbour

The second point was the need to strengthen the Safe Harbour along the lines proposed at the time by the Commission.[39] The EDPS would have preferred the use of more affirmative language and stricter deadlines in addressing the deficiencies already previously identified in the scheme. On the basis of the outcome of a review, different scenarios could be envisaged, including suspension or revocation of the Safe Harbour arrangement, where necessary.

On 6 October 2015, the European Court of Justice invalidated the Commission's Decision 2000/520 finding that the Safe Harbour arrangement provided an adequate level of protection under Article 25 of Directive 95/46/EC.[40] Since then the Commission and the US Government have stepped up their efforts to conclude a new arrangement, without the deficiencies identified before. The most difficult issues seem to relate to the need for better assurances against excessive surveillance. We will return to this subject at the end.[41]

C. EU-US Law Enforcement Co-operation

The third point was the need to strengthen data protection safeguards in EU-US law enforcement co-operation.[42] Current negotiations on an 'umbrella agreement' should according to the EDPS not legitimise massive data transfers, but comply with the existing data protection framework and with the outcome of its current review process. In particular, effective redress mechanisms should be accessible to all data subjects, regardless of their nationality. This should in due course also apply to existing international agreements, where necessary on the basis of appropriate transition clauses.

In September 2015, the Commission announced that negotiations for an EU-US data protection 'umbrella agreement' for EU-US law enforcement co-operation were finalised and the agreement had been reached. However, the agreement would be signed and formally concluded only after the US Judicial Redress Bill, granting judicial redress rights to EU citizens, and presently still pending before the US Congress, had been adopted.[43]

---

such as a mutual legal assistance treaty, in force between the requesting third country and the Union or a Member State, without prejudice to other grounds for transfer pursuant to [Chapter V].' This may help to prevent unlawful disclosures and points the way to diplomatic solutions of any conflicts of jurisdiction.

[39] EDPS Opinion at 45–52.
[40] Case C-362/14 *Maximilian Schrems v Data Protection Commissioner*, 6 October 2015.
[41] See below at X.
[42] EDPS Opinion at 53–60.
[43] Questions and Answers on the EU-US data protection 'Umbrella Agreement' (MEMO/15/5612).

D. US Reform Process

The fourth point was the need to address European concerns in the ongoing US reform process.[44] According to the EDPS, the Commission should support efforts by the US Administration and US Congress to enact a general privacy act with strong safeguards and adequate oversight, in particular in areas where any substantial protection of privacy is currently lacking.

In February 2012, President Obama published a white paper with a blueprint for comprehensive privacy safeguards for consumers online.[45] In February 2015, this was followed by the presentation of a preliminary draft for a Consumer Privacy Bill of Rights Act.[46] Any further legislative efforts along these lines have so far failed. However, the Federal Trade Commission has gradually emerged as the leading privacy regulator in the US, mainly exercising its general authorities on the basis of the FTC Act of 1914 against unfair and deceptive trade practices.

E. Transatlantic Trade

The fifth point concerned the ongoing negotiations between the EU and the US on a Transatlantic Trade and Investment Partnership (TTIP).[47] These negotiations should according to the EDPS not have an adverse impact on the protection of personal data of citizens. At the same time, the Commission should consider setting a common goal of gradual development towards greater inter-operability of legal frameworks for privacy and data protection. At the time of writing, the negotiations are still ongoing.

F. International Privacy Standards

The sixth point raised in the EDPS Opinion was the need to promote privacy standards internationally.[48] In his view, this international promotion of privacy standards should include: promoting full consistency of any new international instruments with the EU data protection framework; promoting the adhesion of third countries and in particular the US, to Council of Europe Convention 108 and supporting the adoption of an international instrument—eg, at UN level on the basis of Article 17 of the International Covenant on Civil and Political Rights

---

[44] EDPS Opinion at 61–66.
[45] 'Consumer Data Privacy in a Networked World: A Framework for Protecting Privacy and Promoting Innovation in the Global Digital Economy', White House, February 2012.
[46] Administration Discussion Draft: Consumer Privacy Bill of Rights Act of 2015, February 2015.
[47] EDPS Opinion at 67–69.
[48] EDPS Opinion at 70–73.

(ICCPR)—requiring the respect of privacy and data protection standards by intelligence activities.[49]

G. Intelligence Activities

The seventh point was the need to subject intelligence activities to appropriate safeguards.[50] The EDPS argued that surveillance activities should at all times be obliged to respect the rule of law and the principles of necessity and proportionality in a democratic society. Legal frameworks at relevant levels should therefore be clarified and where necessary supplemented. These frameworks should include appropriate and sufficiently strong oversight mechanisms.

H. Effective IT Security

The eighth point was the need to ensure effective IT security.[51] The EDPS pointed out that EU institutions and all relevant entities in the Member States are, as controllers, also directly responsible for ensuring effective IT security. This involves carrying out a data security risk assessment at the appropriate level. It also requires encouraging research on encryption mechanisms and raising data controllers and citizens' awareness on privacy risks of the products sold or used, and requiring that developers use concrete design methods to avoid or at least reduce these risks.[52]

X. The CJEU decision in *Schrems*

The author concludes these remarks with a few observations on the CJEU's decision in *Schrems*.[53] The Safe Harbour arrangement has been controversial since its start in 2000. While the criticism focused initially on the substance of the arrangement and later on the way it was implemented in practice, since the Snowden

---

[49] Initiatives by Germany and France to find a bilateral arrangement with the US have not succeeded so far. Initiatives in the UN by Germany and Brazil and others have inter alia led to the appointment of a Special Rapporteur on the right to privacy (see:www.ohchr.org/EN/Issues/Privacy/SR/Pages/SRPrivacyIndex.aspx).

[50] EDPS Opinion at 74–76.

[51] EDPS Opinion at 77–78.

[52] The EDPS has also established an Internet Privacy Engineering Network (IPEN) with the purpose 'to bring together developers and data protection experts with a technical background from different areas in order to launch and support projects that build privacy into everyday tools and develop new tools which can effectively protect and enhance our privacy' (see: www.secure.edps.europa.eu/EDPSWEB/edps/EDPS/IPEN).

[53] See n 40. The first question in the case, ie, whether the Irish DPA had the power to investigate Mr Schrems' complaint, will remain untouched.

revelations Safe Harbour was more and more perceived as a facilitator of data transfers subject to US surveillance.[54] The Commission's strategy has been to strengthen the Safe Harbour on a number of points, including those defining the scope of possible exceptions for lawful access or onward transfers. The Court's invalidation of the Commission's initial decision on Safe Harbour allowed all different opponents to claim victory and to agree on the practical outcome of the case.

However, the subtlety of the Court's decision has not been noticed by everyone. For one thing, the Court has not directly evaluated US law—either in general or on surveillance in particular—and not even evaluated the general merits of the Safe Harbour arrangement.[55] Instead, it has almost entirely concentrated on the role of the Commission in finding adequacy—in terms of what it did or not do in 2000, and what it should have done and should do at any point in the future. Moreover, in that context, the Court was legally bound to respect the findings of the referring Irish Court.

As to the validity of Decision 2000/520, the Court basically found that the Commission had not respected the requirements stemming from Article 25(6) of Directive 95/46/EC, inter alia by only assessing the Safe Harbour arrangement itself and not whether US law in fact 'ensures' adequate protection, and by applying the wrong standard: according to the Court, the Commission should not only have checked the 'adequacy' but the 'essential equivalence' of the protection under US law.[56] The Court also emphasised that the Commission's discretion in this assessment is reduced, with the result that its review of those requirements, read in the light of the Charter, should be strict.[57] This is evidence of the Charter's impact on the Commission's role, since the entry into force of the Lisbon Treaty in 2009.

The Court only went into the substance of the Safe Harbour arrangement in order to raise questions about the scope and the limits of the protection afforded by it under US law. These questions were all the more relevant, as the Commission had seriously criticised US practice along similar lines in its own communications. At the same time, the Commission's decision did not contain any finding as to the existence in the US of effective protection against interference with fundamental rights.[58] The Court also added a few observations about what could be expected from such protection under EU law.[59] These observations are no doubt very useful,

---

[54] The word 'safe' in Safe Harbour—initially only used as a shelter against regulatory action—turned into a misleading term after revelations that some or even much personal data had not been so safe after all. This in spite of the fact that the purpose of the arrangement had been much wider and the problem of lawful or unlawful surveillance was a general issue, also arising under other instruments for transborder data flow (such as model contracts and binding corporate rules) and in fact also under the EU framework itself.

[55] See the CJEU in *Schrems* at 98: 'Consequently, without there being any need to examine the content of the safe harbour principles, it is to be concluded …'.

[56] See *Schrems* at 68–98.

[57] See *Schrems* at 78.

[58] See *Schrems* at 82–90.

[59] See *Schrems* at 91–95.

but do not contain any direct findings on the quality of US law. In other words, they should mostly be regarded as important guidelines for the Commission.

It is also striking to see that the Court at different points seems to accept and even to emphasise the diversity of legal systems in the world. This is first implicit in the term 'essential equivalence'. A third country cannot be required to ensure an 'identical' level of protection.[60] However, the Court adds two separate observations in order to further develop this idea. First, different means 'must [...] prove, in practice, effective in order to ensure protection essentially equivalent to that guaranteed within the EU'.[61] In other words: a functional requirement and an example of 'principled pragmatism'. Second, a system of self-certification—as in Safe Harbour—is not in itself unacceptable, but depends on the establishment of 'effective detection and supervision mechanisms enabling any infringements [...] to be identified and punished in practice'.[62] Again, this is a Court speaking indirectly and very well aware of the stakes, both in general and in this particular case.

As a result, the Commission—and everyone else interested—is now much better informed about the requirements for an adequacy finding, both under the current Directive and the new Regulation.[63] The Commission will have to make a duly motivated finding that the third country in question ensures a level of protection that is essentially equivalent to that guaranteed in the EU under the current Directive or the new Regulation, read in the light of the Charter. Its discretion in reaching that result will be limited.

Whether the Commission and the US Government will be able to arrive at a 'Safe Harbour 2.0' meeting that test, will mostly depend on the availability of effective assurances that any limitations or exceptions in such a scheme will not go beyond what is necessary in a democratic society for legitimate reasons, which must be subject to adequate legal safeguards and effective remedies in case of disputes. Other points on the EU list will be less controversial. However, it will also be important to see whether the US will ensure 'effective detection and supervision mechanisms enabling any infringements [...] to be identified and punished in practice'. Moreover, further to the Court's emphasis on effective remedies, it will also be important to ensure that data subjects can exercise their rights of access and correction or deletion, including the right to judicial redress, in case of disputes with private parties in the US.[64]

If a Safe Harbour 2.0 is produced and the requirement of 'essential equivalence' is met, that would not yet amount to a comprehensive Transatlantic Data

---

[60] See *Schrems* at 73.

[61] See *Schrems* at 74.

[62] See *Schrems* at 91.

[63] The Directive will continue to apply for two more years after the formal adoption of the new Regulation. The need for an 'adequate level of protection' is maintained in the Regulation, but explained in more detail, both in Article 41(2) and recital 81, in the latter case with implicit reference to the CJEU: '[...] The third country should offer guarantees that ensure an adequate level of protection essentially equivalent to that guaranteed within the Union, [...]'.

[64] It is likely that any 'Safe Harbour 2.0' will be scrutinised and challenged in court, in which case the CJEU would be able to take a second look at the subject. Meanwhile, the next stages of the *Schrems*

Peter Hustinx

Protection Framework for commercial data flows, as long as—what is likely—
companies would still have the option to join it or not. Nor would it amount to an
EU-US agreement on standards for 'legitimate surveillance' or something similar.
However, it would confirm once again that bridges can be built between the EU
and the US, and it would set a benchmark for international relations in a wider
context.[65]

case in Ireland and similar cases before DPAs elsewhere may give rise to further case law about the
same issues.

[65] The 'Umbrella Agreement' for EU-US law enforcement co-operation mentioned above at IX—if
finally concluded—might have a similar effect.

INDEX

www.ingramcontent.com/pod-product-compliance
Lightning Source LLC
Chambersburg PA
CBHW071420050326
40689CB00010B/1915